VIETNAM

MEDAL OF HONOR

HEROES

VIETNAM

MEDAL OF HONOR

HEROES

EDWARD F. MURPHY

BALLANTINE BOOKS · NEW YORK

Library of Congress Catalog Card Number: 86-91575

ISBN: 0-345-33890-1

Cover design by Richard Aquan
Photo by Don Banks
Book design by Alex Jay/Studio J
Manufactured in the United States of America
First Edition: July 1987
10 9 8 7 6 5 4 3 2 1

To Kay, who has made it all possible.

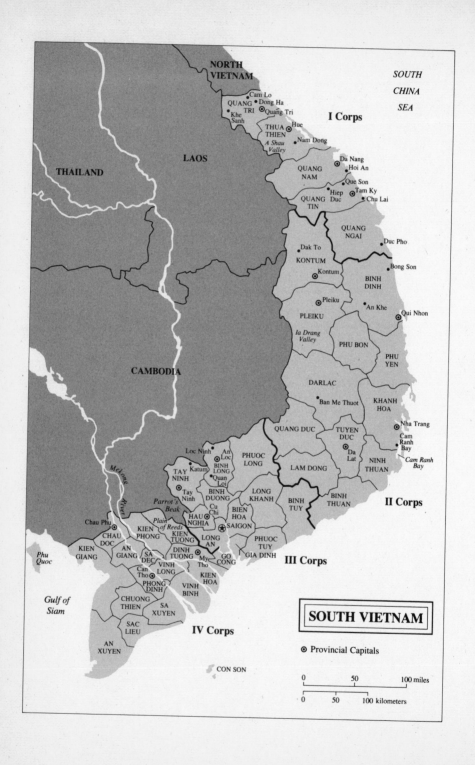

SOUTH VIETNAM

⊙ Provincial Capitals

CONTENTS

PREFACE

_____

America's military involvement in South Vietnam polarized this country as have few other events in our history. Despite the deep divisions, most of the young American men who were eligible to serve in the Armed Forces accepted their government's call to arms and acquitted themselves extremely well as soldiers.

While the United States may not have won the war in Vietnam, its soldiers never lost a battle. Individual soldiers demonstrated tremendous competence—even heroism—in pursuit of their country's uncertain military goals.

In brief but bitter firefights in isolated rice paddies, and in savage urban house–to–house fighting that rivaled the campaigns in France and Germany during World War II, American soldiers, marines, sailors, and airmen routinely proved that they could take the best that Viet Cong and North Vietnamese regulars could dish out and still emerge winners.

General William C. Westmoreland, commanding general of U.S. forces in Vietnam, called them "fighters" and "tough combatants."

Leading these youngsters was a solid cadre of senior enlisted men and officers; men who had devoted their lives to the defense of their country. Recipients of the finest military training in the world, these dedicated career men provided leadership and inspiration unprecedented in the history of warfare.

Two hundred and thirty-eight of these soldiers fought so bravely that their grateful nation awarded them the Medal of Honor. One hundred and fifty died performing the act which earned them the Medal. Others received permanently crippling injuries; several have never fully recovered from the mental anguish caused by the war.

PREFACE

America's youth fought the enemy in Vietnam as well as, if not better than, their fathers fought World War II, or their grandfathers fought World War I.

Unlike heroes from earlier wars, though, the returning Vietnam heroes received scant public attention.

When Audie Murphy received the Medal of Honor for his World War II exploits, his picture appeared on the cover of *Life* magazine—but no Vietnam Medal of Honor hero was accorded the same recognition.

During World War II, newspapers, magazines, and newsreels were full of stories about how our soldiers had killed so many enemy troops, or shot down scores of enemy pilots. World War II heroes sold war bonds, toured manufacturing plants, kissed movie stars, received job offers, had their pictures taken with civic leaders. An admiring public made them objects of adulation.

The heroes of earlier wars received tremendous publicity. Men like Alvin York, Eddie Rickenbacker, Jimmy Doolittle, Joe Foss, and "Commando" Kelly were as familiar to some people as their own families.

They were treated like heroes.

The heroes of the Vietnam War weren't so lucky.

Being a hero in such an unpopular war was often a heavy burden. Friends and even families felt uncomfortable in their presence. Strangers wanted to know how many Vietnamese babies they had killed, or women they had raped, to earn the Medal. "Hey," someone asked one Medal of Honor recipient, "If you're so brave, why didn't we win over there?"

No one wanted to hear about the heroism of the soldiers from America's longest and most frustrating war.

Most of the surviving recipients of the Vietnam War Medals of Honor quickly settled into a lifestyle of obscurity. Few sought public recognition. A surprisingly large number of the eighty-eight survivors—fifty-six—decided to return to, or remain in, the military. A military career offered them an anonymity—and acceptance from their peers—not found on the "outside."

PREFACE

By the time Saigon fell in 1975, almost all of Vietnam's heroes had retreated into the security of building careers, raising families, and paying mortgages. Few were active in community affairs. Few led parades. The graves of posthumous Medal recipients went unacknowledged, except by relatives.

American society had said, in effect, "The war is over. We lost it. Let's forget it—and forget the men who fought there. If we ignore them, maybe the painful memories will go away."

"Time heals all wounds" is a well-worn cliché, but is a strikingly appropriate description of America's reaction to the Vietnam War. As the years have passed, the agony of the war—and the disputes and recriminations that followed—has faded from most people's minds.

Today there are millions of Americans who had not even been born while the war was raging—and millions more are too young to remember it. It is becoming distant history.

With enough distance from the war, people have begun to respect Vietnam veterans for the sacrifices they made. The vets themselves have begun to play a more visible role in society.

The dedication of the Vietnam Veteran's Memorial in Washington, DC, on November 11, 1982, catalyzed national recognition of the Vietnam veteran. It had taken the American public nearly twenty years to realize that it was all right to hate the war, but not to hate their warriors.

From this beginning, the true story of the Vietnam combat soldier began to be told. History books and memoirs have appeared that reveal the unbelieveable hardships that American troops experienced during the war—and the uncommon valor and heroism with which they responded.

Only now can the most neglected group of warriors in our history receive the public praise they deserve. The stories of the incredible heroism they displayed in fighting an unpopular war can finally be told.

Their deeds of valor equal, and sometimes surpass, the heroics of soldiers from earlier wars. Their achievements deserve an equally respected place in American history.

PREFACE

A NOTE ON SOURCES: As founder of the Medal of Honor Historical Society, I began gathering information on Vietnam War Medal of Honor recipients nearly twenty years ago. In addition to studying the contemporary literature, including books, government documents, newspaper accounts, and magazine articles, I've interviewed dozens of Medal recipients, their families, and the men who fought with them for this book.

Since war is by nature a confusing event, few combatants are able to recall exactly what happened, what was said, by whom, or why. The actual words spoken by an individual are often lost forever in the heat of combat.

Therefore, rather than simply reproduce the official Medal of Honor citations—which are terse and often dry—I have reconstructed battle scenes based on the available information, adding dialogue where necessary for dramatic purposes. Whenever possible, events are depicted as the participants recall them.

Edward F. Murphy
Mesa, Arizona

VIETNAM
MEDAL OF HONOR
HEROES

CHAPTER
ONE

A History of
the Medal of Honor

W hen President Lyndon B. Johnson placed the blue ribbon of the Medal of Honor around Captain Roger H. C. Donlon's neck on December 5, 1964, the Army Special Forces officer became only the 3,154th person so honored, and the first who had earned his medal for service in Vietnam.

Since its birth during the Civil War, many men have coveted the medal; only a few have earned it. President Harry S. Truman told one recipient, "I'd rather have this medal than be president." General George S. Patton once remarked, "I'd give my immortal soul for that medal."

Since the beginning, 3,394 men have received 3,412 medals. Eighteen Americans have received the august decoration twice.

The Medal of Honor can only be earned by a member of the Armed Forces through a display of the most conspicuous gallantry and intrepidness above and beyond the call of duty—in the presence of an armed enemy. There must be a clear risk of life. Also, two eyewitnesses must attest to the deed. These strict guidelines reserve the Medal of Honor for the "bravest of the brave."

But it wasn't always that way.

Civil War Navy Secretary Gideon Welles was looking for a way to motivate his more reluctant sailors when he hit upon the idea of an honor medal. By rewarding those who exhibited courage in front of the enemy, maybe he could inspire others to new heights of daring. At Welles's urging, Iowa Senator James W. Grimes proposed a Congressional bill "to promote the efficiency of the Navy." One clause of the bill authorized the creation of a "medal of honor" for sailors and marines who distinguished themselves through gallantry in action. The bill—and the Medal of Honor—was signed into law on December 21, 1861.

Not to be outdone, the Army convinced Massachusetts Senator Henry Wilson to introduce a similar proposal in February of 1862. That law was signed into effect on July 12, 1862.

Both medals were originally reserved for enlisted men and limited to the "present insurrection." Additional legislation the following year extended the life of the medal beyond the Civil War. Also, Army officers were made eligible; Naval officers remained ineligible until 1915. The Army limited its award to heroism in combat, while the Navy permitted theirs to be awarded for heroism in "the line of one's profession."

The original medal was designed by a Philadelphia silversmith firm, Wm. Wilson & Son. The piece was described as:

A five-pointed star, one point down. On the obverse the foul spirit of Secession and Rebellion is represented by a male figure in crouching attitude holding in his hands serpents, which, with forked tongues, are striking at a large female figure (portrayed by Minerva, the Roman Goddess of wisdom) representing the Union or Genius of our country, who holds in her right hand a shield, and in her left, the fasces. Around these figures are thirty-four stars, indicating the number of states in the Union.*

Both medals would be suspended from identical ribbons: a blue horizontal top bar above alternating vertical stripes of red and white, with only the suspension devices differing. The Navy's medal connected to the ribbon with a rope-foiled anchor; the Army's via an eagle, wings spread, astride crossed cannon and cannonball stacks.

The first Medals of Honor were awarded to six soldiers from Ohio who survived the legendary "Great Locomotive Chase." This ill-fated mission to disrupt Confederate rail lines in Georgia in April 1862 ranks as one of the most daring of the Civil War. When six of the survivors were paroled from a Confederate prison in March of 1863 they were taken to an audience with Secretary of War Edwin M. Stanton in Washington, DC, on March 25th.

After listening to the group's hair-raising tales, Stanton

---

*Medal of Honor Recipients 1863–1978. Washington, D.C.: U.S. Government Printing Office, 1979.

praised their courage and devotion to duty. He then said, "Congress has recently created a special medal to honor the brave defenders of the Union. None have yet been awarded. I have the honor of presenting you the first." He pinned the first medal to the tunic of the group's youngest member, nineteen-year-old Jacob Parrott. The others, in turn, were William Bensinger, Robert Buffum, Elihu Mason, William Pittinger, and William H. Reddick.

A few days later the Navy awarded its first medals. There was no formal ceremony for these heroes, though. Instead, their medals were forwarded to their respective commanding officers, who handled the presentations on an individual basis.

After the Civil War, medals continued to be awarded to soldiers who fought Indians in America's West and to sailors and marines who were exploring the far reaches of the globe. Medals went to the brave men who stormed San Juan Hill; who battled the Chinese at Tientsin; and who fought the insurrectionists in the Philippines.

Just after the turn of the century, living recipients of the Medal of Honor—who had formed a Medal of Honor Legion in 1890—became concerned about the growing number of imitation Medals of Honor being issued as membership badges by various veterans groups. At the Legion's urging, Brigadier General Horace Porter, ambassador to France and a Civil War Medal of Honor recipient, had the Parisian jewelry firm of Messrs. Arthur, Bertrand, and Berenger prepare several proposals for a new medal. One was approved by both the members of the Legion and Secretary of War Elihu Root. On November 22, 1904, a patent was issued to protect the medal.

The new design retained the chief feature of the old medal, the five-pointed star. At its center appears the head of Minerva, surrounded by the words, "United States of America." An open wreath, enameled in green, encircles the star. Green oak leaves fill the prongs of the star. Above the star is a bar bearing the word VALOR. Atop the bar sits an eagle, wings spread.

The medal's new ribbon was a light blue watered silk material spangled with thirteen white stars, representing the original colonies. At first the medal was pinned to the recipient's left breast. Later a neck ribbon was added.

The Navy elected to retain its original design. They did change the suspension ribbon to the light blue of the Army in 1913, and adopted the neck ribbon in 1917. In 1919, the Navy adopted a gold cross pattee (the cross's arms are narrow at the center and expand towards the end) design for its Medal of Honor, using it to reward combat heroism. The original five-pointed star was retained for non-combat deeds. The two medal system proved too confusing, however, and the practice was dropped in 1942. The Navy went back to the original design, and has used it ever since.

In 1916 the Army convened a special board to review all of its Medal of Honor awards.

Out of all the medals awarded up to that time, the Civil War alone accounted for 1,519 medals—nearly half of those awarded—under rules that were much less strict. Many of the medals awarded for Civil War service were based on sketchy information—often submitted by the intended recipient himself. A large number of Civil War medals were awarded for deeds that would not be considered worthy today. However, the Army had no other medals that could be used to recognize heroism, regardless of its degree. It was the Medal of Honor or nothing. Too often, it was the Medal of Honor.

Following the board's recommendations, the Army rescinded 911 awards as not meriting the decoration. The board further recommended the creation of additional medals to properly reward heroism in its varying degrees. Not all displays of bravery warranted a Medal of Honor—it should be reserved for only the most outstanding displays of bravery. New eligibility rules would clearly spell out the criteria for each award.

During World War I, the Army created several new decorations. The Distinguished Service Cross now ranked immediately below the Medal of Honor, honoring heroic deeds of a lesser degree. Below the DSC was the Silver Star. The Navy created a Navy Cross—on par with the DSC—and also used the Silver

Star. These new decorations assured that only the top heroes of the American Expeditionary Force (AEF) would receive the Medal of Honor.

As a result of the board's insight, the Medal of Honor was elevated to the pinnacle of a so-called "Pyramid of Honor." Since then the Medal of Honor has become the most prestigious of all decorations. A strict review process ensures the medal will not be conferred upon unworthy candidates. The standards are so high that over fifty-five percent of the medals awarded since World War I have been posthumous. During the Korean and Vietnam Wars nearly seventy percent of the awards were posthumous. Those who wear the Medal of Honor are a special breed.

Only 123 Medals of Honor were awarded for World War I: 95 in the Army; 21 in the Navy; and 7 to marines. (Five of these marines also received the Army medal for the same deed. These men are also counted in the Army's total.) For the first time, posthumous awards accounted for a large percentage of the total. Thirty-one recipients died performing the act which earned them the medal.

It was during World War II that the Medal of Honor truly came into its own, achieving the prominence it holds today. To ensure only the most deserving acts of heroism received the top medal, the different service branches created internal decorations boards to review award recommendations. Each recommendation had to pass several levels of review. The higher the proposed award, the longer the review process. Recommendations for both Army and Navy Medals of Honor went all the way to Washington, DC, where senior, combat-tested officers reviewed the required documentation. They, or any intermediate board, could downgrade a recommendation for the Medal of Honor to a lesser award.

The review became a lengthy, time-consuming process. So exacting were the standards that only 433 medals were awarded for World War II (294 Army; 57 Navy; 81 marines, and 1 lone Coast Guardsman). For the first time, posthumous awards outnumbered living awards—only 190 of the 433 men survived to have their medals placed around their necks.

Unlike World War I, when most Medal of Honor presentation ceremonies were held at General John J. Pershing's headquarters at Chaumont, France, during World War II every effort was made to bring the heroes who survived to Washington for the presentation. President Franklin D. Roosevelt delighted in presenting the medals. He often delayed more pressing matters in order to attend the ceremony and chat with the recipients afterwards. President Truman's World War I combat experience gave him a deep appreciation for Medal of Honor heroes. As a combat veteran, he understood how most men's accomplishments paled in comparison to their heroic acts, and he viewed his participation in presentation ceremonies as a humbling experience. Subsequent presidents have continued the practice of presenting the Medal of Honor to living recipients, or to the survivors of deceased heroes.

Although World War II was thought to be the war to end all wars, reality soon proved different. Five short years later America found itself embroiled in its first limited commitment war—in Korea. Although the military strategy in Korea was one of holding actions rather than the mass movements of earlier wars, the opportunity for heroic action did not disappear. The valor displayed by American fighting men in Korea was incredible. One hundred and thirty-one of them earned Medals of Honor during the three years of the Korean War (seventy-eight Army; seven Navy, forty-two marines; and four members of the newly-created U.S. Air Force). Over seventy percent of the awards were posthumous—only thirty-seven survived their deeds.

In the years after the Korean War the U.S. military recognized changes in the style of warfare it was likely to face. The global political situation decreased the likelihood of the United States again participating in great land battles as seen in the two World Wars. Instead, it would probably continue to become involved in limited warfare, as allies to governments threatened by uprisings or insurgencies. Soldiers would be fighting alongside troops of other nations or serving in advisory roles. It was a very different kind of war, to be sure, but fighting it could be just as deadly.

To properly recognize the bravery of its troops in these new situations, the military revised the conditions under which the Medal of Honor could be granted. On July 25, 1963, Congress amended the U.S. Code to permit awarding the Medal of Honor for distinguished service:

(1) while engaged in an action against an enemy of the United States;
(2) while engaged in military operations involving conflict with an opposing foreign force; or,
(3) while serving with friendly forces engaged in an armed conflict against an opposing armed force in which the United States is not a belligerent party.*

With these new provisions, which also applied to other combat decorations, the United States was well prepared to honor distinguished gallantry on the part of its troops wherever they might be sent.

Since its designation as a separate branch of the Armed Forces in 1947, the Air Force had used the Army's Medal of Honor. In 1965 it announced its own design. The five-pointed star was retained, as was the green-enameled wreath and the oak leaf-filled prongs. The main change was the replacing of Minerva with the head of the Statue of Liberty, looking now to the viewer's left instead of right, as had Minerva. The eagle was gone, too. In its place a bar bearing the word VALOR was placed above an adaptation of the thunderbolt sprays from the Air Force's coat of arms. The medal is about fifty percent larger than its Army and Navy counterparts, giving it a somewhat heavy appearance.

The 238 Medals of Honor awarded for Vietnam service went to 155 soldiers; 14 sailors; 57 marines, and 12 airmen. Like their comrades from earlier wars, these men were characterized by their willingness to sacrifice themselves so that others might live, to fulfill their mission, and to defeat the enemy.

---

*Medal of Honor Recipients 1863–1978.

CHAPTER
TWO

The First Hero

ROGER H. C. DONLON

T he attack was coming to-_____ night. Captain *Roger H. C. Donlon* could smell it in the air. All of his finely tuned senses told him that tonight would be the night the Viet Cong tried to overrun his Special Forces camp at Nam Dong. The attack had been imminent for the past week. Intelligence reports from headquarters at Da Nang had reported the presence of an unusual number of VC in the nearby mountains. Reports from local sources told Donlon that the VC commander felt he needed to test the Americans' resolve.

Two days earlier, July 3, 1964, one of Donlon's patrols had radioed back from a village far up the valley from the camp: "The villagers are scared, but they won't tell us why." Sgt. Terry Terrin had returned from a three-day patrol that morning to report he had found the corpses of two village chiefs who had been friendly to the Americans. That afternoon several fist-fights broke out between the camp's contingent of South Vietnamese soldiers and the Nungs (ethnic Chinese who functioned as mercenaries for the American Green Berets). Donlon was sure dissension was being sown by enemy agents.

As the sun moved lower on the horizon that Sunday night, Donlon cautioned his team sergeant, Master Sgt. Gabriel R. "Pop" Alamo, "Get everyone buttoned-up tight tonight, Pop. The VC are coming. I can feel it. I want everyone ready."

For the better part of the past ten years Donlon had been preparing for this moment. He was determined that he and his men would survive and prevail over the enemy.

Donlon was born January 30, 1934, in Saugerties, New York, just up the Hudson River from the U.S. Military Academy at West Point. One of eight children born to Paul A. and Marion Donlon, he attended the local parochial school before graduating from Saugerties High School with the class of 1952.

As far back as he could remember, Donlon had wanted to be a soldier. This goal had its roots in his involvement with the Boy Scouts. He joined the local troop as soon as he was eligible. He excelled at Scouting, earning every merit badge he could and holding every position of leadership in his troop. He loved the challenge of being a Scout. A military career seemed like a logical choice.

His mother, unfortunately, had other plans. She wanted her son to continue his education. At her urging, he enrolled at the New York State College of Forestry, at Syracuse University. He stayed a year, but was never happy, and he decided not to return for his sophomore year. On December 18, 1953, with his mother's blessing, he enlisted in the U.S. Air Force.

Donlon liked the Air Force, but quickly realized the only way to make the most of a military career was as an officer. On July 4, 1955, he entered West Point as a cadet. He attended until April 1957 when personal reasons forced his resignation.

Donlon's exposure to the Air Force and the harsh regime at West Point did not dampen his enthusiasm for a military career. He enlisted in the Army on February 5, 1958, and a year later was selected to attend the Infantry Officers Candidate School at Fort Benning, Georgia. He received his commission as a second lieutenant on June 24, 1959.

Four years later he started training with the Army's new elite troops, the Special Forces. When Donlon graduated from the Special Warfare School at Fort Bragg, North Carolina, in September 1963, he was entitled to don the distinctive headgear of these counterinsurgency experts, the green beret.

Donlon was given command of Special Forces Team A-726, with orders to prepare it for deployment to the Republic of Vietnam. They were ready in May 1964.

At that time, the American involvement in Vietnam was technically limited to an advisory role. Special Forces teams worked with Army of Vietnam commanders to provide a level of training unavailable to ARVN officers. They could not lead men into combat. They could not give orders to their ARVN counterparts. All they could do was "strongly suggest" a course of action. Americans were only allowed to fire their weapons when directly fired upon.

In reality, the Americans were even then carrying the brunt of the fighting. Incompetence, and pure cowardice, on the part of some ARVN officers forced Americans to assume leadership. Many ARVN officers and enlisted men lacked an aggressive fighting spirit. Their senior officers could not motivate them. Some field commanders were known to be on the payrolls of both the South Vietnamese government and the Viet Cong. Their lack of enthusiasm for battle made winning the war a difficult task.

Upon arrival in Vietnam, Donlon and his eleven-man team were assigned to relieve another A-team at Camp Nam Dong. Thirty miles northwest of Da Nang and near Khe Sanh, Nam Dong was in the high plateau country close to the borders of Laos and North Vietnam. It was actually two camps in one. The inner camp was manned by the Americans and their Nungs. The outer camp, surrounded by a double barbed-wire fence, was the responsibility of the South Vietnamese. Much of the surrounding country was heavily wooded and sparsely populated, making it ideal for guerilla operations.

The camp's ARVN commander had 311 soldiers organized into three companies. The Special Forces has about sixty Nungs on their payroll. Many of the Vietnamese had their families with them. The contingent was completed by two other westerners: Australian Army Warrant Officer Kevin Conway, who represented his country at this lonely outpost, and Dr. Gerald C. Hickey, an American anthropologist studying the Vietnamese mountain tribes.

Just before two o'clock in the early morning hours of July 6, 1964, Captain Donlon relieved Conway from guard duty. As was his custom, Donlon made a circuit of the oval-shaped inner perimeter. It took him about twenty-five minutes to make a complete round of the football-field-sized area, checking the sandbagged mortar positions and the fighting holes manned by the Nungs. He moved slowly, assuring himself all was in readiness for the attack he was sure was coming. Donlon finished his rounds by inspecting the four 81mm mortar positions spaced evenly around the inner perimeter. All stood ready. His team members and the Nungs were awake and alert. As he headed for the mess hall to check the guard roster, Donlon thought that it might be a quiet night after all.

Donlon's watch read 2:26 A.M. when he stepped through the mess hall's screen door. At that moment, the building erupted in a brilliant white flash. The concussion blew Donlon back through the door.

Instantly realizing that an enemy mortar round had exploded on the mess hall roof, Donlon scrambled into his command post next door. There he found two team members already fighting back.

A curtain of mortar rounds crashed down on the camp, spewing out death and destruction. The lesser explosions of hand grenades added to the din. Tracers from automatic weapons criss-crossed the night sky. A fire blazed in the mess hall, spreading quickly to the adjoining command post. Donlon routed some Vietnamese soldiers huddled in a corner of the command post. "Put the fire out," he shouted. "Put the fire out in the mess hall."

With Pop Alamo helping, Donlon started battling the flames threatening to consume the command post. Unmindful of the shrapnel flying through the air, the two men began dragging weapons and ammo out of the burning structure. Donlon didn't worry about his men; he assumed they would take up their battle stations without orders from him. He was right. The other Green Berets manned mortars, threw grenades, or fired their automatic weapons at the fleeting shadows of the VC.

Sgt. Michael Disser fired off an illuminating round from his mortar, then peeked over the rim of his pit. The light from the flare revealed hundreds of men moving on the camp. He later called it, "The most frightening sight of my life." What he witnessed was the main assault force of two reinforced battalions—eight hundred to nine hundred men—ringing Nam Dong.

Once he had salvaged all possible equipment and supplies, Donlon hurried to help his men throw back the VC. Racing across the open ground, acutely aware of the exploding grenades and mortars, he headed for the mortar pit of Staff Sgt. Mervin Woods. Suddenly, a VC mortar round went off at his feet, hurtling him through the air like a rag doll. Dizzy from the concussion, and minus a boot, Donlon stumbled into Woody's fighting hole. He hardly had time to gather his thoughts when Sgt. John Houston called from a nearby position, "They're over here! By the ammo bunker." Houston turned back and fired a burst from his light machine gun into the bunker enclosure.

Donlon started over to help him. A third mortar round picked the young captain up and slammed him down. He lost his pistol belt, his other boot, and all his equipment except his AR-15 rifle and two clips of ammo.

Bleeding from wounds in his left forearm and stomach, Donlon diverted to Disser's mortar pit where he picked up several more magazines of ammo.

"Conway's dead and Alamo's hit. Hit bad." Disser reported.

God, thought Donlon, it had only been a few minutes since he'd left Pop.

He started to say something to Disser when movement by the main gate, only twenty yards away, caught his eye.

"Illuminate the main gate, Mike!" Donlon yelled.

Disser fired an illumination round. In its light Donlon saw three VC scurrying alongside a fallen log. They were already inside the inner perimeter. Donlon swore, then fired. Two VC dropped. The third crawled into the grass. Donlon threw a grenade. The VC stopped crawling.

Donlon looked back to where he had left Houston. Two VC had snuck up and killed him. Their continued heavy fire pinned Donlon down. While he watched, two Nungs dispatched the VC. Donlon could now move to the rear of the camp to check on his men manning positions there.

Once on the other side Donlon called for his medic. Sgt. Thomas L. Gregg answered from his position in Sgt. First Class Thurman R. Brown's mortar pit. Ducking and dodging, Donlon made his way to them.

"How're you doing?" he shouted above the noise.

"Okay, so far," they responded.

17

Donlon ordered Gregg to check on the wounded. Gregg first wanted to treat the captain's wounds, but Donlon refused. "Tend to the others first," he said, and Gregg took off.

A second later the team's communications man, Staff Sgt. Keith Daniels, stumbled into the hole.

"Did you call Da Nang, Dan?" Donlon asked him.

Daniels said he had. Donlon couldn't understand where the reaction force was. The battle had been raging for over an hour. He questioned Daniels again. The commo (communications) sergeant assured his captain the message had gone out. Donlon did not know the commo bunker had been destroyed in the opening minutes of the battle, cutting off further communications and delaying the needed air support. Daniels didn't tell him, either. He thought Donlon had seen the wrecked building burning in the night.

"I'm going over to Beeson's pit to see how he's doing," Donlon announced. He left Brown's position and tried to cover the forty yards towards Sgt. First Class Vernon Beeson's bunker. Mortar shells crashed around him. Automatic-weapons fire drove him twice to the ground. On his third try, pain stabbed his foot. He looked down to see a nail protruding from the top of his foot and a piece of plywood nailed to its bottom. He had stepped on the board and moved several yards before the pain registered. In disgust he tore it off and made his way back to Brown's mortar pit.

A few minutes later medic Gregg bounced back into the position. "Captain, you're badly wounded. Let me fix you up," he said.

"I'm all right," Donlon replied. "Take care of the others."

Gregg left again. Donlon, assured Brown was handling his mortar well, headed back to Disser's position to see how the situation was at the front gate. Just as he passed the supply room, fire reached the ammunition stored there, exploding it with a tremendous roar. For the fourth time that night Donlon was slammed to the ground. This time, shrapnel painfully ripped through his left leg. Bleeding profusely and wracked with pain, Donlon continued to Disser's position.

It was a mess.

The VC had overrun the ARVN troops manning the outer perimeter in front of Disser's mortar pit. They formed just outside the inner barbed wire. Only heavy small arms fire from the Nungs prevented them from attacking. They still threw grenades, though. Six or seven at a time exploded around Disser's pit.

Disser fired his mortar as fast as he could drop shells down the glowing barrel. He didn't take time to aim, he just knew the shells were landing among the enemy. Alamo fired an AR-15 from the front rim of the pit, a ragged hole in his shoulder streaming blood. Lieutenant Jay Olejniczak stood next to him firing an M-79 grenade launcher into the enemy.

As Donlon watched, an enemy soldier jumped on the parapet, set to fire his machine gun into the pit. Donlon fired first, and the VC fell backwards. A split second later a fragmentation grenade landed with a thud. It went off at Olejniczak's feet.

Fortunately, VC grenades didn't pack the punch of American grenades. The blast broke the lieutenant's foot, but didn't stop him. He kept on firing his M-79.

So many grenades landed in the next five minutes that the defenders could do nothing but ignore them. But each explosion cut a little more flesh. Alamo fell, fresh wounds sending new rivulets of blood coursing down his body. Olejniczak was a mass of wounds. Disser watched in amazement as a grenade peppered his left leg and foot with shrapnel.

Fighting off fatigue—caused by loss of blood from his old wounds and the shock of the new ones—Donlon fired his AR-15 at the wire, trying to disrupt any attempt by the VC to exploit their grenade barrage.

In spite of his efforts, grenades continued to rain into the hole. In desperation Donlon picked up the grenades and threw them back at the enemy. The others joined him. But the grenades were too plentiful. They reached the same conclusion at the same time.

"Let's get out of here," Donlon yelled.

"Right," the others responded.

19

At that instant, a concussion grenade exploded between Donlon and Disser, knocking them both down. Donlon staggered to his feet, helped Disser up, and passed him along to the others. As they raced to safety Donlon covered their withdrawal with quick bursts from his rifle.

Pop Alamo was crouched in the corner of the pit, blood running from his face, shoulder, and stomach. Donlon went to him, got one of the sergeant's arms around his neck, and stood up. He was about halfway up when a tremendous blast went off in his face. A mortar shell had exploded on top of the sand bags in front of him. He felt himself falling backwards. "You're dead," Donlon told himself.

Disser, too, thought Donlon was dead. He didn't see how anyone could survive that blast.

Miraculously, Donlon was still alive, but badly damaged.

Fresh wounds poured forth blood from his arm and face. His stomach wound was bleeding again. But he was still full of fight; he wasn't about to give up.

A quick glance told him that Alamo had not survived the blast. Stopping only to grab a 60mm mortar, Donlon evacuated the position. Thirty yards away he stumbled on four wounded Nungs lying beside a brick wall. In pidgin English he urged them to return the enemy's fire but they were too shocked to continue fighting. Using bits of his own clothing, Donlon bound their wounds. He pushed a left-over piece into the hole in his stomach.

"Come on, you'll be all right," Donlon told the Nungs. "Get your weapons and fight."

He propped them up, put weapons in their hands, and then went back to Disser's pit for mortar ammo. The intense pain from his multiple wounds forced him to walk in a crouch. Donlon returned to the Nungs with the ammo, got the mortar back in action, then made three more trips to the mortar pit, stripping it of anything that could be of value to the enemy should they overrun the position. On his last trip, shrapnel from an exploding grenade tore yet another hole in his leg.

Satisfied that the Nungs were responding well, Donlon once again made his way through the carnage to Woods's 81mm mortar pit. He spent time there helping the sergeant drop deadly rounds on the enemy. Assured that Woods was holding his own, he returned to where he had left Disser and the others. Another mortar blast knocked him down.

The effects of his multiple wounds and the repeated concussions started to tell on Donlon. He had been fighting nonstop for more than two hours. He moved more slowly. He thought less clearly. He kept asking himself, "Did I do this? Did I say that?" He shook his head, groggy and tired, but remained determined to stay in command and beat off the VC.

Donlon scurried through the explosions to where Gregg had set up an aid station in an area protected from gunfire by the terrain. The medic had done a good job of patching up the many wounded. When he saw his CO he insisted on checking him over.

"I'm all right," Donlon said. "I'll be okay, just a little tired is all. I want you to make sure the others are taken care of."

"You're all shot up," Gregg said. "I'll fix you up."

"No," Donlon said. "I haven't got time."

Before Gregg could say more Donlon was on his way back to the front gate. He thought the VC would be making a determined assault there and wanted to direct the effort to drive them away. Donlon was also wondering again where the air support requested by Daniels was. It shouldn't have taken them two hours to get there.

As he reached Disser's position the drone of an airplane could be heard above the battle. At last, a flare ship. Suddenly, the sky lit up. It was just after 4:30 A.M.

The arrival of the flare ship brought a momentary lull to the battle as the VC sought cover. They knew, too, the arrival of the plane signalled the beginning of the end.

In the eerie light of the flares, a loudspeaker suddenly boomed forth with a chatter of Vietnamese. Donlon grabbed one of his interpreters. "What's he saying?" he demanded.

The shaking ARVN soldier responded, "He say put down weapons. VC going take camp and we all be killed."

Those around Donlon resolved to go down fighting. As they

lay there in the silence waiting for the expected attack, the loud-speaker cracked again, this time in English.

"Can you pick up the direction of the loudspeaker?" Donlon asked Disser.

"Yes, sir."

"Drop a volley of rounds that way and let's see if we can't knock the damn thing out."

With Donlon directing his fire, Disser managed to place a round on the loudspeaker, destroying it. The field of battle was silent for a few seconds. Then one of the Nungs shot at a shadow, signalling the renewal of the battle. Almost instantly, the air was filled again with the crack of bullets, the sharp explosion of grenades, and the deep thump of mortars.

For the remaining two hours of the battle, Donlon continued making his rounds, checking on his men. He was everywhere, doing everything. He threw grenades, shot at VC running through the night, and helped man mortars. He brought up ammo. He continued to offer encouragement to his troops. Seemingly invincible to the shrapnel slashing through the air, Donlon walked as upright as he could, a tower of strength to those who witnessed his inexhaustible courage.

As the sun broke across the morning sky, Donlon was manning a mortar with Woods. In the growing light he spotted four or five VC hiding in some tree stumps about fifty yards away throwing grenades everywhere.

"Think we can drop a round on them that close?" Donlon asked.

"I don't know, sir, but we can try," Woods replied.

Manhandling the heavy steel tube to a nearly vertical position, the two dropped a round down the barrel. It landed right, but was a dud.

Cursing, Donlon fed the weapon another round. The stumps blew sky-high, taking the enemy with them. Except for occasional small-arms fire that continued for several more hours, the battle for Nam Dong was over. It was almost 7:30 A.M.

One hundred fifty-four Viet Cong died during the fight. Over fifty ARVN and Nungs were killed. Two Americans died; seven were wounded. Donlon refused evacuation until his wounded men received care. Only when convinced they had received the necessary treatment would he allow his wounds to be treated. Later that day he, too, was evacuated. He spent over a month in a hospital in Saigon where his visitors included General Westmoreland and Ambassador Maxwell Taylor. In his first battle Donlon had led a magnificent fight and word of his exploits quickly spread.

When he recovered from his wounds, Donlon rejoined the surviving members of his team. They completed their six-month tour in Vietnam in November 1964 and flew home together.

The nine survivors gathered with Donlon at the White House on December 5, 1964, where President Johnson presented Captain Donlon with the Medal of Honor for his "conspicuous gallantry and intrepid leadership" in defending Nam Dong.

Donlon was justifiably proud of his team members. "The medal belongs to them, too," he told the president.

Donlon remained in the Army, served another tour in Vietnam, and today is a full colonel, close to retirement.

CHAPTER THREE

America Goes To War

O ne month after the attack on Donlon's encampment, on August 2, 1964, the U.S. Navy destroyer *Maddox* was patrolling off the coast of North Vietnam on an electronic surveillance assignment. Unknown to the *Maddox*'s crew other elements of the Navy were supporting ARVN commando raids on two nearby North Vietnamese islands, Hon Me and Hon Ngu. Although the *Maddox* had no part in the raids, the electronic eavesdroppers aboard the vessel recorded increasingly frequent references to their vessel among the North Vietnamese radio traffic. Commander Herbert L. Ogier, Captain of the *Maddox,* was sufficiently alarmed to request clarifying instructions from his CO. The reply was terse: "Resume itinerary."

Just after two o'clock that afternoon the *Maddox*'s radiomen intercepted a North Vietnamese message: Three PT boats were ordered out from Hon Me island to attack the *Maddox*. The North Vietnamese had assumed the *Maddox* was in control of the covert operations. The enemy PT boats raced toward the lone destroyer at a speed of fifty knots. Commander Ogier sounded battle stations. "This is not a drill," he announced.

At 3:08 P.M. two of the destroyer's six five-inch guns fired. The PT boats remained on course. Three minutes later the *Maddox* opened up with all six guns. The exploding shells raised huge plumes of ocean water around the enemy craft. The PT boats spread out, loosing torpedoes at the *Maddox*. The destroyer managed to evade the deadly missiles.

The *Maddox* gunners continued firing. One round connected with a PT boat, which stopped dead in the water. A second PT boat slowed, damaged by a near hit.

At that moment four F-8 Crusaders from the carrier USS *Ticonderoga* appeared overhead in response to Ogier's earlier request for help. With their 20mm cannons blazing away, the jets drove off the PT boats. The entire engagement lasted but eight minutes.

The consideration of a proper response included top government officials—all the way up to President Johnson. It was decided to continue the patrols. The American government took the position that their ships were in international waters and that they had every right to cruise the Gulf of Tonkin free from harassment. To emphasize that position a second destroyer, the *Turner Joy,* was added to the patrol. Also, constant air cover would protect the vessels. The gauntlet had been thrown down to the North Vietnamese.

On the night of August 4, a pitch-black stormy night, the *Maddox*'s radar picked up unidentified surface blips approaching the two destroyers. The blips appeared and disappeared, possibly due to the effects of the adverse weather. At 9:30 P.M. the blips seemed to gather speed as they bore down on the *Maddox*. The *Turner Joy* also reported picking up the blips.

When the blips approached the four-thousand-yard range, the two destroyers opened fire. The inky blackness prevented the sailors from seeing either the enemy vessels or the explosions of their own shells. There were those aboard the two destroyers who doubted whether the enemy vessels really existed. They thought the blips were due to the effect of the nearby storms on their radar, a not uncommon event. Yet some crewmen aboard the *Turner Joy* reported seeing a torpedo pass within one hundred feet of the ship.

Eight jets from the *Ticonderoga* appeared overhead but could find no evidence of enemy craft. The *Maddox* and *Turner Joy* continued firing at the blips while taking evasive action against reported enemy torpedoes, but still had no visual contact with the enemy. Within thirty minutes the "attack" was over. The two destroyers broke off the "engagement" and resumed patrolling. The presence of the enemy vessels was never confirmed.

On the basis of this second attack, President Johnson ordered retaliatory air strikes against North Vietnamese torpedo boat bases. He also told his key advisors to draft a Congressional resolution endorsing his action and allowing him wide latitude in responding to further hostilities in Vietnam. On August 7, Congress approved these measures with the "Gulf of Tonkin Resolution."

The first major step toward committing the U.S. to the war in Vietnam had been taken.

The second major step came six months later, after the Viet Cong attacked a U.S. Army installation near Pleiku in the Central Highlands. On February 7, 1965, four hundred soldiers of the 52nd Combat Aviation Battalion were retired for the night when enemy 81mm mortar rounds crashed down on their barracks. VC sappers raced through the night, blowing up helicopters and planes with satchel charges and firing automatic weapons at the Americans.

The GIs reacted instantly. They manned defensive positions. Firemen doused fires on the aircraft. Uninjured soldiers carried their wounded comrades to safety.

In fifteen minutes the attack was over. It had cost the Americans seven dead and more than one hundred wounded.

The next morning presidential assistant McGeorge Bundy, in South Vietnam on a fact-finding mission for President Johnson, visited the scene of the attack with General Westmoreland. In Westmoreland's words, once Bundy, "smelled a little gunpowder he developed a field marshal psychosis." The former Army captain telephoned the president with one suggestion: strike back.

Twelve hours after the attack on Pleiku, forty-nine Navy bombers attacked Dong Hoi, a guerilla training camp forty miles north of the 17th parallel—in North Vietnam.

On February 10, 1965, near Qui Nhon, the Viet Cong blew up a barracks housing members of the U.S. Army's 140th Maintenance Detachment. Twenty-three Americans died and twenty-two were wounded in the attack.

The next day, 160 U.S. and South Vietnamese planes streaked northward to retaliate again against VC staging points in North Vietnam. Further, President Johnson agreed on February 13 to execute a program of "measured air action" against North Vietnamese targets. Under the code name "Rolling Thunder," twice-weekly air raids would strike selected targets in North Vietnam.

Because the Air Force base at Da Nang provided most of the support for Rolling Thunder, General Westmoreland became concerned about the base's security. He had no faith in the South Vietnamese troops guarding the base. Westmoreland cabled the

Pentagon asking for two battalions of U.S. Marines to guard the complex. Four days later the approval was granted. The final step toward major U.S. involvement in Vietnam had been taken.

At 9:18 A.M. on March 8, 1965, the 3rd Battalion, 9th Marines, 9th Marine Expeditionary Brigade, began landing at Red Beach Two, just north of Da Nang. Two hours later the 1st Battalion, 3rd Marines arrived by airlift from Okinawa. The marines deployed to defensive positions around Da Nang.

Reinforcement for Johnson's actions came on March 29, 1965, when a car bomb exploded outside the U.S. embassy in Saigon, killing and wounding dozens of embassy employees. Two more Marine infantry battalions and one Marine air squadron were deployed to South Vietnam. By April 6, twenty-seven thousand American fighting men were in Vietnam. The United States was in South Vietnam for keeps.

During their first few weeks in the country the newly-arrived forces were generally limited to purely defensive roles. The bulk of the actual fighting was still the exclusive work of isolated Special Forces detachments.

CHARLES Q. WILLIAMS AND MARVIN G. SHIELDS

In the Viet Cong attack on the outpost at Dong Xoai, 55 miles north of Saigon, on June 10–13, 1965, 1st Lieutenant *Charles Q. Williams* earned the war's second Medal of Honor.

During the fourteen-hour assault on the camp, the thirty-one-year-old South Carolinian assumed command of the unit after his CO was seriously wounded in the early minutes of the battle. Williams organized the camp's personnel for a valiant defense. He repeatedly dashed through heavy gunfire to rally the outnumbered defenders. He received five wounds during the battle.

At one point the American forces were pinned down by a VC machine gun. Williams grabbed a 3.5-inch rocket launcher and asked for a volunteer to help him go after the gun. *Marvin G. Shields,* a twenty-six-year-old member of the camp's Navy construction battalion who had already been wounded three times, stepped forward.

Completely ignoring the extremely heavy enemy fire, the two crept toward the machine gun. In full view of the VC, they knelt together, Shields loading, Williams firing. With one well-placed shot they destroyed the enemy gun, breaking the back of the attack. On the way back to safety, Shields was mortally wounded.

In the words of his citation, Williams "continued to rally his men, to protect the wounded, and to hold off the enemy until help arrived."

When President Johnson presented the medal to Williams on June 23, 1966, the gallant father of three said, "I had a mission to perform and I did it. The thought that I was a hero didn't occur to me. I just wanted to protect my men."

Joan Elaine Shields accepted her husband's posthumous Medal of Honor from President Johnson on September 13, 1966. The president called Shields "a new kind of fighting man, forged and tempered in a new kind of war, who gave his life for his country, his comrades, and a good cause." Shields is the only Seabee to have earned his country's highest award.

The U.S. Marine Corps had never trained for a defensive mission. It seemed unlikely that their assigned role as security guards around the air base at Da Nang would last too long. The young, aggressive marines were not content to sit idle while waiting for the Viet Cong to attack them. Within weeks of their landing the marines were on the offensive, patrolling several miles from Da Nang on the look-out for any guerillas intent on attacking their base. It wasn't long before the two forces clashed.

FRANK S. REASONER

On the afternoon of July 12, First Lieutenant *Frank S. Reasoner* led Company A, 3rd Reconnaissance Battalion, on a recon mission south of Da Nang. The area was a flat, dangerous land, spotted with tree lines and hedgerows. It was perfect country for an ambush.

At twenty-nine, Reasoner was old for a lieutenant, but he'd already been in the Marine Corps for twelve years. Born in Spokane, Washington on September 16, 1937, Reasoner moved with his family to Kellogg, Idaho, when he was ten. Just after graduation from high school in 1955 he enlisted in the Marines.

He served three years before receiving a special Congressional appointment to the U.S. Military Academy. At West Point Reasoner excelled in baseball, wrestling, and boxing. In 1962 he was designated the Academy's outstanding boxer, winning an unprecedented four straight Brigade Championships in four different weight classes.

When he graduated in June 1962 Reasoner was appointed a Marine Corps second lieutenant. His first and only assignment was with the 3rd Reconnaissance Battalion. He joined them in Hawaii in January 1963, moving to Da Nang in April 1965.

A short, stocky man, Reasoner often spoke of his wife, Sally, and their young son, Mike, back in Idaho. After a difficult day's work, he liked to retire to his tent to spend several hours writing to his wife about the war. A common topic was the young men of his company. As a former enlisted man, Reasoner exhibited a tremendous concern for his marines. He went out of the way to see to their welfare. He would not rest until his company had settled in. He refused to eat until his men had had their chow and saw to it that his officers had no "creature comforts" not shared by the enlisted men.

Reasoner was well-respected and loved by his marines. He, in turn, loved and respected them. It pained him deeply when one was hurt. One of his most difficult tasks was writing to the relatives of dead and wounded men from his company. He tried to write as comforting a letter as he could, hoping to ease some of the pain.

The patrol that July afternoon was to be a routine sweep of a suspected VC area. The marines' purpose was to deter any VC activity aimed at the airbase at Da Nang.

Helicopters inserted the company into the landing zone

(LZ). No enemy activity was reported. Reasoner detailed his platoons into combat formation and began the sweep.

The marines had barely begun when they were viciously attacked by an estimated fifty to one hundred Viet Cong. Reasoner and the five-man point team he was accompanying were cut off from the main body of the company.

Instantly realizing his company could not advance through the slashing fury of the enemy fire, Reasoner organized the few men near him to provide a base of fire for an assault on the enemy positions.

"Come on, marines," he shouted. "Give 'em hell! Pick your targets. Don't waste any ammo."

Inspired by Reasoner's courage, the isolated marines began returning the fire. Repeatedly exposing himself to enemy fire, Reasoner seemed to be everywhere. He killed two VC and single-handedly destroyed an enemy machine gun that was preventing the evacuation of a wounded marine. He calmly and professionally directed the marines in their valiant efforts to prevent the VC from overrunning their position. He pointed out targets to the marines, directing their fire and encouraging them through words and actions.

When his radio operator was wounded, Reasoner unhesitatingly moved to the youngster's side. He couldn't stand to see one of his men hurt.

"Take it easy, son," he spoke softly, "We'll get you out of here."

With cool determination Reasoner applied a battle dressing to the wound. When finished he gave the youngster a reassuring pat. "You're going to make it, corporal," he said.

He moved away from the marine, still shouting encouragement to his remaining troops. As Reasoner moved among his embattled troops the wounded radio operator began crawling to a position of safety. The VC concentrated their fire on the man, wounding him again.

Ignoring the wall of enemy fire, Reasoner ran to his radio operator's assistance. His only thought was to get the marine to safety. He had almost reached the casualty when a burst of enemy machine gun fire ripped into his belly, killing him instantly.

The firefight raged for another half an hour before the VC were beaten off. Reasoner's executive officer pursued the VC but was unable to reengage them. He called in choppers to take the company back to Da Nang.

Less than three hours after Reasoner had left camp a helicopter returned his body. A young corporal sobbed uncontrollably as he jumped from the chopper, "My skipper's dead. He should be covered up. Will someone get a blanket?"

When Navy Secretary Paul H. Nitze presented the Medal of Honor to Reasoner's widow and son in ceremonies at the Pentagon on January 31, 1967, he spoke of Reasoner's willingness to die for his men.

"Lieutenant Reasoner's complete disregard for his own welfare will long serve as an inspiring example to others."

ROBERT E. O'MALLEY

Five weeks after Lieutenant Reasoner died, twenty-two-year-old Corporal *Robert E. O'Malley* became the first marine to survive earning the Medal of Honor in Vietnam.

In early August 1965 Marine intelligence received word that the VC intended to attack the isolated base at Chu Lai, down the coast from Da Nang. The marine operations officer recommended a spoiling attack to prevent the VC attack. The offensive operation was dubbed "Operation Starlight." It would be the first major engagement between U.S. and Viet Cong forces.

In the early morning hours of August 18, O'Malley's unit, Company I, 3rd Battalion, 3rd Marines, made an amphibious landing near the village of An Cuong-1. Their mission was to push north, clearing the VC from the area south of Chu Lai. The operation proceeded smoothly until the company tried to clear the hamlet of An Cuong-2 enemy snipers. Suddenly, heavy enemy fire threw two platoons back. In trying to reorganize his command, Captain Bruce D. Webb was killed. His executive officer, Lieutenant Richard M. Purnell, assumed command of the company.

While Purnell prepared the company for a counterassault, O'Malley spotted a trench concealing an enemy squad. With complete disregard for his own safety O'Malley raced across an open rice paddy to the trench. Jumping in, he used his rifle and hand grenades to kill eight VC. He then returned to his squad and led them to the relief of another platoon.

"It was like watching the U.S. Cavalry come over the hill," Purnell recalled. "Under Corporal O'Malley's expert leadership the threatened marines were able to beat off a fanatical enemy attack."

Disregarding three wounds received in this action, O'Malley personally assisted several wounded marines to an evacuation point. He then regrouped his squad and led it to the area of heaviest fighting. There, he helped repel another VC assault.

Ordered by Purnell to secure a landing zone for an evacuation helicopter, O'Malley led his besieged and badly wounded squad to the LZ. Although himself eligible for evacuation due to his painful wounds, O'Malley refused to climb aboard the chopper. Instead, he moved to an exposed position and delivered telling suppressive fire against the enemy until the wounded were removed. Only then did he allow his injuries to be treated. Fortunately, his wounds were not serious enough to incapacitate him.

O'Malley, a native of Woodside, Queens, New York, received his medal from President Johnson in an impressive ceremony held at the Texas White House on December 6, 1966.

The first major Army combat unit to arrive in Vietnam was the elite 173rd Airborne Brigade. Formed on Okinawa in May of 1963, the 173rd began training immediately for the type of fighting it would encounter in Vietnam. As the U.S. Army's only ready-action unit in the Pacific, it was inevitable the 173rd would be tapped for duty in Vietnam.

On May 7, 1965, the 173rd landed at Vung Tau, at the mouth

of the Saigon River. They established their headquarters at Bien Hoa, twelve miles north of Saigon, guarding the U.S. Air Force base there. Like the marines before them, it was only a matter of time before the "Sky Soldiers" of the 173rd went over to the offensive.

Their first significant contact with the Viet Cong came on June 10, 1965, when one battalion was sent to the aid of an ARVN unit trying to secure the area around the district headquarters at Dong Xoai. On June 28–30, the paratroopers from the 173rd conducted the first officially announced search-and-destroy mission of the Vietnam War. Held within the notorious War Zone D, twenty miles northwest of Saigon, the initial effort was inconclusive. The sixty-square-mile area, also known as the Iron Triangle, would be visited often by the troopers of the 173rd in their remaining six years in Vietnam.

MILTON LEE OLIVE III

He was an unlikely looking hero. A kind, delicate face was *Milton Lee Olive*'s chief feature. He was a soft-spoken, gentle youth who grew up in a middle-income black neighborhood on Chicago's south side. Olive's mother died when he was a youngster, leaving a void quickly filled by his stepmother, Antoinette, a Chicago public school teacher. His father and Antoinette raised Milton as their own natural son.

A desire for adventure caught young Olive between his junior and senior years at Saints Junior College High School. He had had his fill of school. There was a whole world beyond Chicago's south side he wanted to see. Father and son sat down one evening and talked. Although he wanted his son to finish high school, Milton Olive II understood the need to fulfill one's dreams. In addition, blacks were beginning to reap the benefits of President Johnson's Great Society. A three-year tour in the Army might do young Olive more good than another year of high school. The senior Olive consented to his son's enlistment.

Olive entered the U.S. Army on August 17, 1964, three

months short of his eighteenth birthday. Basic training followed at Fort Knox, Kentucky. After basic, Olive was assigned to advanced training at the Artillery School at Fort Sill, Oklahoma. The lure of fifty dollars a month extra pay, however, drew Olive to the airborne infantry. In April 1965 he reported to the Airborne School at Fort Benning, Georgia. Upon graduation he was assigned to the 173rd's 2nd Battalion, 503rd Infantry, which was already deployed in Vietnam.

By the time the summer of 1965 was over Private First Class Olive was a hardened combat veteran. Though not yet nineteen years old, he had participated in the heavy fighting in War Zone D, as well as in numerous firefights with the VC. He had witnessed more death in those four months than most adults see in a lifetime. He understood what fear was, and had learned how to overcome it. He was well-respected by both the officers and enlisted men of his unit, Company B. In spite of the numerous hardships encountered by the Sky Soldiers, Olive maintained a positive sense of humor that inspired the members of his platoon. No task was too hard for him. He did what needed to be done without complaint. He was a good soldier.

On October 22, 1965, Olive's company was on a routine patrol near Phu Cuong, about thirty-five miles northwest of Saigon, on the southern fringes of the Iron Triangle. As the unit moved through the thick jungle it was subjected to varying degrees of enemy fire. Several times the company was pinned down temporarily. Each time the men rallied to drive off the VC.

PFC Olive was in the forefront of most of these counterattacks. Without hesitation, he repeatedly exposed himself to hostile fire to repulse the enemy.

Late in the afternoon Olive and four other soldiers, including his platoon commander First Lieutenant James Sanford, moved through dense jungle foliage in pursuit of one band of VC. As the GIs moved stealthily through the jungle, a VC threw a hand grenade into their midst.

Knowing full well the risk, Olive dashed forward, scooped up the deadly missile, and moved away from the others.

"I've got it," he yelled, tucking the grenade into his middle

37

and falling on it to absorb the full, deadly blast with his own body.

"It was the most incredible display of selfless bravery I ever witnessed," Lt. Sanford later said.

Eighteen-year-old Milton Lee Olive's willingness to sacrifice his own life had saved the lives of four other soldiers.

Six months later, when he was notified of the Medal of Honor awarded to his only son, Mr. Olive penned a letter to President Johnson. In it he said:

> It is our dream and prayer that some day the Asiatics, the Europeans, the Israelites, the Africans, the Australians, the Latins, and the Americans can all live in One-World. It is our hope that in our country the Klansmen, the Negroes, the Hebrews, and the Catholics will sit down together in the common purpose of goodwill and dedication; that the moral and creative intelligence of our united people will pick up the chalice of wisdom and place it upon the mountaintop of human integrity; that all mankind, from all the earth, shall resolve "to study war no more."

The city of Chicago honored its deceased warrior hero by naming in his memory a junior college, a lakefront park, and a portion of the McCormick Place convention center.

LAWRENCE JOEL

Two weeks later after Olive died, a twenty-year Army veteran became the first living black to earn the Medal of Honor since the Spanish-American War (two blacks had died earning their medals during the Korean War).

Specialist Five *Lawrence Joel* was serving as a medic with the 1st Battalion, 503rd Airborne Infantry, 173rd Airborne Brigade, when that unit was attacked in the Iron Triangle by a numerically superior and well concealed enemy force on November 8th.

In spite of a severe leg wound suffered in the early stages of the battle, Joel kept moving from man to man, administering first aid. He was wounded a second time, the bullet lodging deep in his thigh, but continued treating his wounded comrades, completely oblivious to the battle raging around him. At one point the thirty-eight-year-old father of two saved a man's life by placing a discarded plastic bag over the casualty's sucking chest wound.

Even after the twenty-four-hour battle had subsided and the VC dead numbered 410, Joel never lost sight of his mission and continued to comfort and treat the wounded until his own evacuation was ordered.

On March 9, 1967, President Johnson presented the Medal of Honor to Joel in ceremonies held on the South Lawn of the White House. A good deal of room was needed to accommodate Joel's family, his parents, his nine brothers and sisters, his foster parents, and five foster brothers and sisters.

By the end of the summer of 1965 the U.S. was fully committed to the ever expanding war in Vietnam. General Westmoreland had received permission to use U.S. troops "in any situation." With that dictum his next request was predictable: Send more troops.

There were no more maneuver battalions available in the Pacific. It was time for deployment of an entire division directly from the States. Just the unit Westmoreland needed was waiting at Fort Benning, Georgia.

Organized in July 1963 as a test division, by June 1965 the 1st Cavalry Division was fully trained in helicopter and "airmobile" tactics. The unit was eager to prove itself under fire.

Relocated to Vietnam in September 1965, the 1st Cavalry Division set up headquarters at An Khe in Binh Dinh Province, a part of the II Corps Tactical Zone. They barely became acclimated to Vietnam when one of its battalions was sent to the aid of an ARVN unit under attack near Pleiku. Once the siege at the isolated camp at Plei Me had been broken, division commander

Major General Harry W. B. Kinnard received permission from General Westmoreland to "find, fix, and defeat the enemy forces that had threatened Plei Me." The cavalrymen would meet the enemy in a one thousand-square-mile area southwest of Pleiku known as the Ia Drang Valley. It would be the first major battle between the Americans and North Vietnamese regulars.

WALTER J. MARM, JR.

As part of the U.S. offensive action Lieutenant Colonel Harold G. Moore's 1st Battalion, 7th Cavalry, 1st Cavalry Division aggressively swept its assigned sector—only to find it empty of the enemy. Determined to close with the NVA, Moore requested and received permission to move his battalion further west, near the Chu Pong Hills. By noon on November 14, 1965, most of his men had choppered into LZ X-Ray. The companies fanned out in search of the enemy.

Moore was spoiling for a fight. His men had been in the Ia Drang Valley for five days and had only had sporadic contact with the foe. Moore wanted more.

Company B had advanced only a few kilometers northwest of LZ X-Ray when it came under fire from troops of the NVA 33rd and 66th regiments. Within minutes the unit was pinned down. Moore ordered Company A to relieve the isolated troops.

Leading one of the platoons in Company A was Second Lieutenant *Walter J. Marm, Jr.* A twenty-three-year old native of Washington, Pennsylvania, the handsome officer had enlisted in the Army the previous June after receiving a degree in business from Duquesne University in Pittsburgh. He joined the 7th Cavalry upon completing officer training, and arrived in Vietnam in September.

As Marm's platoon moved through the thick scrub toward Company B it was subjected to increasingly heavy enemy fire. He quickly realized this was no ordinary fight. The NVA were well-organized. Their fire was deliberate and well-controlled rather than the sporadic volleys seen in the past. They were determined to keep the relieving unit from reaching its objective. Marm's platoon ground to a halt under withering enemy fire.

As he directed his squads into a tight defensive perimeter Marm detected four NVA moving to flanking positions. Shouting, "I'll take 'em," Marm moved forward under heavy fire and killed all four.

He next saw his men were receiving heavy fire from an enemy machine gun. Unable to pinpoint its exact location, Marm deliberately exposed himself to draw the enemy's fire so that his men could spot the gun. Once the gun's location was known, Marm tried to destroy it with an anti-tank weapon. His fire caused casualties among the enemy, but didn't silence the well-concealed automatic weapon.

Frustrated by his ineffectiveness but still determined to destroy the gun, Marm moved across thirty meters of open ground to a better position. Subjected to a strong barrage of enemy small-arms fire, Marm moved to within a few meters of the enemy bunker. Completely in the open, he hurled grenades into the emplacement, killing some of the eight NVA manning it.

As he prepared to move forward to finish off the position, an enemy round severely wounded him, driving the intrepid officer to the ground. Only momentarily slowed by the pain, Marm crawled forward, determined to relieve the pressure on his platoon. Armed only with an M-14 rifle, Marm picked off the remaining gun crew one by one. Only when assured his platoon was safe did Marm consent to have his wounds treated. His selfless actions had reduced the fire on his platoon, broken the enemy assault, and allowed his company to continue on its mission.

When the fight was over and Company B relieved, Marm and the other casualties were medevaced (evacuated by helicopter) to the base hospital. It would be four months before he recovered from his wounds.

Marm received his medal on December 19, 1966. He elected to make the Army his career.

HARVEY C. BARNUM

The last Medal of Honor earned in 1965 went to twenty-five-year-old marine 1st Lieutenant *Harvey C. Barnum*. On temporary duty from his billet at the U.S. Naval Base, Pearl Harbor, Hawaii, Barnum was serving as an artillery forward observer with Company H, 2nd Battalion, 9th Marines, 3rd Marine Division. Barnum had been in Vietnam less than two weeks when, on December 18, his company was suddenly pinned down by a hail of extremely accurate enemy fire during a battalion-sized sweep of suspected enemy territory near Ky Phu in Quang Tin province.

While marines dropped around him, Barnum moved over the battlefield seeking targets for his artillery. Finding the company commander mortally wounded and the radio operator dead, Barnum removed the radio from the operator's body, strapped it to himself, and assumed command of the badly decimated unit.

Under Barnum's skilled command the panicked marines began to rally against the VC. Whenever a squad leader went down Barnum replaced him with an unwounded marine, regardless of rank. Privates with less than a month in-country led rifle squads; a corporal took over a shattered platoon. Barnum didn't care about rank, he just wanted men who could shoulder responsibility.

When he had the marines settled down and reorganized, Barnum led them forward in an attack on the entrenched enemy. More than once Barnum stood completely exposed to the enemy's fire to point out targets to his men. His shouted words of encouragement steaded the inexperienced marines so their return fire became more accurate, and more deadly to the VC.

Under Barnum's guidance two armed helicopters strafed the enemy's bunkers, while he moved fearlessly through the enemy's fire to direct one of his platoons in an assault on the bunkers. When he had cleared a small area he called in two medevac helicopters to take out the dead and wounded. Once assured of their safety, Barnum spearheaded a final assault that threw the VC off the battlefield.

After receiving his Medal of Honor in February, 1967, Barnum, held a variety of stateside assignments. He returned to Vietnam in October 1968, to command an artillery battery in the 12th Marines. During this one-year tour he added two Bronze Stars and a Purple Heart to his collection of medals. Barnum continued his career in the Marine Corps, eventually reaching the rank of colonel.

By the end of 1965 one hundred eighty-four thousand American military personnel were in Vietnam. Their presence indicated the U.S. government's strong commitment to assisting the South Vietnamese in their struggle against aggression. It would be the courage of the individual fighting man, though, that would have to enforce that commitment.

CHAPTER
FOUR

Search and Destroy Operations

A fter testing each other's re-_____ solve in the latter part of 1965, both North Vietnamese and U.S. forces spent the next few months consolidating their positions and building up their forces. Military Assistance Command, Vietnam (MACV) started 1966 with three divisions—the 3rd Marine, 1st Infantry, and 1st Cavalry—and two separate brigades—the 1st Brigade of the 101st Airborne and the 173rd Airborne Brigade. Over the next twelve months four full divisions—the 1st Marine, 4th Infantry, 9th Infantry, and 25th Infantry—and three more combat brigades—the 11th Armored Cavalry Regiment, and the 196th and 199th Infantry Brigades—poured into Vietnam.

These new units, composed of mostly green, conscripted troops, arrived in Vietnam anxious for combat with the NVA. Filled with visions of the large scale attacks of World War II and Korea, they quickly found the traditional military strategy of seizing and holding terrain objectives ineffective in Vietnam. War in Vietnam necessitated a completely new strategy.

Shortly after taking command of MACV, General Westmoreland defined the American military's overall strategy as one whereby units would "find, fix in place, fight, and destroy," enemy forces and their base areas. It was, in essence, a war of attrition. If enough enemy troops could be killed, the enemy would lose its resolve to fight. To an army—and a nation—accustomed to liberating towns to the riotous cheers of once-captive people, this slow, costly program of "search and destroy" would prove to be a frustrating strategy.

The main American campaign effort for 1966 was to secure base areas for the incoming units, open and secure lines of communications, and acclimate the arriving units to the area warfare practiced in Vietnam. To search out and destroy the enemy new units went on "reconnaissance-in-force" missions. A small force, occasionally as large as a battalion, would conduct patrols in hopes of clashing with the enemy. If a firefight developed the superior American firepower would be brought to bear and the enemy destroyed.

It was a tough way to fight a war. And it produced numerous instances of unusual bravery.

JAMES A. GARDNER

On February 7, 1966, the 1st Battalion, 327th Infantry, 101st Airborne Division was conducting a routine reconnaissance-in-force mission near the village of My Canh in Pleiku Province when superior enemy forces in well-fortified positions pinned down one of its companies. The company commander tried to move his platoons forward, but to no avail. Attempts to outflank the village also failed due to heavy fire from enemy automatic weapons and mortars. He called for airstrikes and artillery but their combined effort still failed to dislodge the enemy.

Battalion headquarters dispatched several other companies to attack the village from another direction, but unless they moved quickly the pinned-down company would be destroyed.

Leading one of the relief platoons from the Battalion's Headquarters and Headquarters Company was 1st Lieutenant *James A. Gardner*. A native of Dyersburg, Tennessee, Gardner briefly attended West Point in 1961, then spent a year at the University of Tennessee before enlisting in the Army. Following basic training at Fort Polk, Louisiana, Gardner went to officer candidate school at Fort Benning, Georgia. Assigned to the 101st Airborne Division at Fort Campbell, Kentucky, he went overseas with their 1st Brigade in July 1965.

Lieutenant Gardner was ordered to take his platoon around behind My Canh and destroy the enemy from the rear. No sooner had he started his men forward than they were pinned down by heavy rifle fire from a series of supportive bunkers. Gardner pressed his men hard and they advanced a few meters, but intense enemy fire stymied his mission.

"Stay here and give me covering fire," Gardner told his platoon sergeant.

He took off running through the withering fire, splashing across a rice paddy, until he reached the first bunker. With a quick flick of the wrist he tossed in a grenade.

Even before the smoke cleared Gardner ran to the second bunker. Another grenade tossed, a second bunker destroyed.

Gardner low-crawled to the third bunker, using the raised dike of the rice paddy as protection from enfilading fire. Just as he prepared to pull the pin from a grenade, the enemy gunner burst forth from the hole. The gunner fired pointblank at the lieutenant and missed. Gardner didn't. From a distance of six feet he shot and killed the VC.

Gardner's brave action allowed the main body of troops to move forward and neutralize the center of the enemy's fortifications. Gardner gathered up the surviving members of his platoon to continue the attack. Once again automatic fire from a bunker pinned them down.

Calling for the grenades remaining among his men, Gardner repeated his earlier single-handed assault. He dropped a grenade into the bunker and vaulted over it. As the grenade exploded Gardner came under fire from a previously unseen position. He rolled into a drainage ditch for cover, and then crawled toward the source of the fire.

A few meters from his objective Gardner leaped from the ditch, grenade held in one hand, firing his rifle with the other. Just as he reached the bunker a burst of enemy fire slammed into him. With his last dying effort Gardner tossed the grenade into the bunker, destroying it. It was his twenty-third birthday.

Gardner's display of extraordinary courage so inspired his men they resumed the attack and completely routed the enemy.

His posthumous Medal of Honor was presented to his parents on October 19, 1967.

DANIEL FERNANDEZ

The 2nd Brigade of the 25th Infantry Division arrived in Vietnam on January 19, 1966, from its base at Schofield Barracks, Hawaii. The unit took up positions west of Saigon to guard Tay Ninh and Hau Nghia Provinces from Viet Cong forces located across the border in Cambodia. One of their top priorities was securing the area around Cu Chi in Hau Nghai Province.

During a routine patrol outside Cu Chi on February 18, 1966, Specialist Four *Daniel Fernandez,* Company C, 1st Battalion, 5th Infantry, of Albuquerque, New Mexico, earned the 25th's first Medal of Honor in Vietnam. Twenty-one-year-old Fernandez, a sergeant, and two others fought through heavy enemy fire to locate a wounded comrade isolated by a VC ambush.

As they administered first aid to the man an enemy hand grenade landed in their midst. Fernandez realized that not all of the men had seen the deadly missile. He vaulted over the sergeant and threw himself on the grenade just as it exploded.

ROBERT J. HIBBS

On March 5, 1966, 2nd Lieutenant *Robert J. Hibbs*'s Company B, 2nd Battalion, 28th Infantry, 1st Infantry Division set up a fifteen-man night ambush outside of Don Dien Lo Ke in War Zone D. Shortly after his men were in place an outpost reported a company of VC advancing toward Hibbs. The Cedar Falls, Iowa native quickly set up two Claymore mines in the enemy's path. When they entered the killing zone Hibbs detonated the mines, destroying half the force. He then provided a base of covering fire while the patrol withdrew back to the battalion perimeter.

Halfway back to friendly lines, the small force ran smack into another VC company intent on attacking the battalion. Without hesitation Hibbs led his men into the VC, disrupting the enemy and stalling their attack.

Just minutes from safety, Hibbs and a sergeant went back through the scattered VC to find a patrol member wandering dazed in the underbrush. Hibbs located the stricken soldier, turned him over to the sergeant, then advanced on two VC machine guns that were preventing the sergeant from reaching the safety of the perimeter. Alone, Hibbs attacked the positions. He died wiping out the bunkers, but managed to destroy his secret "Starlight" rifle scope before he succumbed to his fatal wounds.

The U.S. Air Force played a myriad of different roles in the Vietnam War. From B-52 bombers dropping high explosives high above North Vietnam to helicopters ferrying supplies and evacuating the wounded, the Air Force contributed significantly to the war effort.

One vital role was providing close air support to ground troops. When friendly forces were in close contact with the enemy it took pinpoint accuracy to spray machine gun fire effectively from a fast-flying airplane. The daring of Air Force pilots saved many American lives, sometimes in unexpected ways.

BERNARD F. FISHER

Early on the morning of March 10, Major *Bernard F. Fisher* and his wingman, Captain Francisco Vazquez, lifted off from the runway at Pleiku Air Base. Their mission lay one hundred fifty miles north at an isolated Special Forces camp in the A Shau Valley, near the Cambodian border. The four hundred defenders, including twenty Green Berets, were under siege by more than two thousand NVA. On this, the second day of the siege, the Allied defenders had been driven into a single bunker on the camp's northern perimeter. Without American air support the NVA would quickly overrun the beleaguered defenders.

To the Air Force pilots the mile-wide, six-mile-long valley was "The Tube." They were forced to fly their prop-driven World War II vintage A-1E Skyraiders straight down the valley, deliver their ordinance while in a left turn, continue the turn into a tight 180° maneuver, and race back up the valley to start all over again. To further complicate matters the NVA had placed twenty anti-aircraft guns and hundreds of automatic weapons on the surrounding hills. One Skyraider pilot said it was like "flying inside Yankee Stadium with the people in the stands firing at you with machine guns."

That morning Fisher and Vazquez rendezvoused with four other Skyraiders over the camp. They let down through an eight thousand-foot deck of clouds and broke out eight hundred feet above the floor of the valley.

The six flew straight up the valley, strafed, and continued around to the starting point. On the second run Lieutenant Colonel Dafford W. "Jump" Myers felt his plane shudder. He was hit. Flames streamed back from the engine compartment. Too low to bail out, Myers put the plane down on the outpost's littered runway, then ran into the underbrush to escape the NVA.

Fisher called for a rescue helicopter while the other four Skyraiders strafed the area around Myers' hiding place. Ten minutes later Fisher learned the chopper was still at least twenty minutes away. He made the decision to land himself and rescue Myers. "I knew it wasn't wise. It wasn't a very good thing to do," he said later, "but it was one of those situations you get into. You don't want to do it, but you've got to, because he's part of the family; one of our people. You know you have to get him out of there."

Debris littered the twenty-five hundred foot runway. Tin roofs from nearby buildings, buckets, fifty-five-gallon drums, unexploded rocket pods, and other material all made a landing very hazardous. In addition, the strip's steel planking had been ripped up, exposing jagged edges of metal. If Fisher hit these he'd rip up his tires and be unable to take off.

Fisher headed down, his wingman strafing the enemy positions. He touched down on the runway but was going too fast. He maneuvered his plane around the debris, hit full throttle, and took off.

He climbed rapidly, chopped the throttle back, kicked in full left rudder, and made a sharp 180° turn back to the runway he had just left. Fisher touched down right at the beginning of the strip but still took the entire twenty-five hundred feet to stop. He then turned the Skyraider around to taxi back along the runway while looking for Myers. Fisher saw him waving his arms from a clump of bushes. He hit the brakes but still rolled one hundred feet past Myers.

"I waited for just a moment, expecting him to be right there with me; you know, right on the side. But he wasn't.

"I figured he must be hurt more than I thought—maybe he couldn't move or something—so I set the brakes on the bird and climbed over the right seat to get on the side he was on. I looked through the mirror and saw two little red, beady eyes trying to crawl up the back of the wing."

Fisher reached out, grabbed Myers by the seat of the pants and pulled him headfirst into the cockpit. "It was hard on his head but he didn't complain," Fisher said.

A few minutes later Fisher and Myers were airborne, on their way back to Pleiku. The ground crew later counted nineteen bullet holes in Fisher's plane.

Born in San Bernardino, California, on January 11, 1927, Fisher grew up in Utah. He served in the Navy in 1945 and 1946, then moved to Kuna, Idaho, where his parents resided. He attended college in both Idaho and Utah, took his Air Force commission through ROTC, then learned to fly in 1953. His Medal of Honor, the first with the Air Force's new design, was presented to him by President Johnson on January 19, 1967.

Fisher retired from the Air Force as a full colonel and now makes his living as a farmer in Idaho.

Only limited anti-war sentiment existed in 1966. To be sure, there were demonstrations, protests, and disturbances, but these were limited to hardcore anti-war activists at the more radical college campuses. A majority of Americans supported the war. Those college students who marched against American involvement were considered "Communist-inspired."

Even members of the establishment who questioned Lyndon Johnson's war policy were decidedly in the minority. Arkansas Democratic Senator J. William Fullbright presented a resolution in Congress on January 29, 1966, calling for a "full and complete investigation of all aspects," of U.S. Vietnam policy. The subsequent hearings were well publicized but had little effect on Johnson's aggressive war policy.

Many who did protest the war were serious, idealistic young men willing to go to great lengths to get their message across. On April 11, 1966, anti-war protesters marched down New York's Fifth Avenue chanting slogans and carrying signs. That same afternoon, twenty-year-old Boston University student Arthur H. Zinner doused himself with gasoline in front of the White House. White House police wrestled him to the ground before he could immolate himself.

At the same time, half-way around the world, other young men of principle demonstrated *their* convictions.

JAMES W. ROBINSON

Twenty-five-year-old *James W. Robinson* didn't have to be in Vietnam. He was there by choice. He had already served a four-year hitch in the Marine Corps, enlisting after leaving high school in Cicero, Illinois, in 1959. The ruggedly handsome young man was a fiercely patriotic individual—his heroes were MacArthur and Churchill and he read all he could on military strategy and military history—who saw the war in Vietnam in black-and-white terms, a struggle between the forces of good and evil. Sacrifices needed to be made in order to ensure the victory of good. Robinson was willing to make them.

On December 9, 1963, he enlisted in the Army, hoping to be sent to Vietnam as an advisor. Instead the Army sent him to Panama as an MP. Disappointed, Robinson began a year-long letter-writing campaign for a transfer. In August of 1965 he joined the famed "Big Red One," the 1st Infantry Division in Vietnam.

During his tour in Vietnam Robinson remained completely dedicated to U.S. goals in Southeast Asia. In one letter home Robinson said, "Any American who doesn't believe in total victory in this conflict is a traitor." In another he declared, "There's a world on fire and we should do something about it." Just days before he died Robinson wrote his father: "The price we pay for freedom is never cheap."

On April 11, 1966, Staff Sgt. Robinson led a squad of C Company, 2nd Battalion, 16th Infantry on a sweep of coastal Phuoc Tuy Province east of Saigon. A part of Operation Abilene, the company was hacking its way through deep jungle when a friendly artillery shell fell short and burst in the tree-tops, showering the Americans below with red-hot shrapnel. Two died and twelve were wounded. The survivors started cutting an LZ for medevac choppers in the jungle, unaware they worked just yards away from the command post of the D800 VC Battalion.

Suddenly automatic rifle and grenade fire swept the perimeter. Mortars crashed through the trees. Snipers exacted a deadly toll on the GIs.

Robinson worked with his platoon leader, Lieutenant Kenneth Alderson, to place their men in advantageous positions. As he moved about under heavy fire, Robinson offered encouragement to the men. His willingness to expose himself to the enemy inspired the infantrymen.

Robinson located the most persistent sniper and killed him with a well-placed round from a grenade launcher. He then saw a medic take a round while treating a casualty. Unwilling to leave the two men at the mercy of the enemy, he dashed into the open and pulled them to safety, where he gave them first aid.

The fight raged on into the afternoon. The VC were so close that some Americans actually wrestled with their foes. Casualties mounted. Wounded, dead and dying littered the tight perimeter. One GI later said, "I've never heard such screaming in my life. Many of the wounded were calling for their mothers. I remember one guy yelling for Gloria."

Robinson continued to set an example for those around him. He crawled to the casualties, collected their weapons and ammo and redistributed them to the able-bodied soldiers.

When he saw a buddy of his cut down, Robinson sprang into action. "Hang on," he yelled, "I'm coming for ya!" He openly defied the enemy by racing to his friend. His luck was running out, though. Two VC bullets struck him, one in the leg, another in the shoulder. He ignored the pain, dragged his buddy to safety, and administered life-saving first aid.

While he was propped behind a tree patching his own wounds the gutsy NCO happened to spot the enemy machine gun causing the most casualties. Knowing full well his chances of survival were practically nil, but aware something had to be done to save the company from annihilation, Robinson grabbed two grenades and charged straight at the automatic weapon.

Hit in the leg by a tracer round that set his pant leg afire, Robinson stopped only long enough to rip the burning cloth from his body, then continued forward. As Alderson watched, the indomitable sergeant took two more rounds in the chest. Pulling himself to his full six-foot-three-inch height, he summoned his last bit of strength and threw the two grenades into the position, destroying it as he fell dead.

The battle continued into the night, but never reached its previous ferocity. By the time reinforcements reached the site the next morning more than a third of Company C had been killed or wounded. That there were not more was due to Staff Sgt. Robinson's willingness to pay the high price of victory.

JIMMY G. STEWART

The 1st Cavalry Division kept tangling with the VC in the untamed provinces of the II Corps in northern South Vietnam. On May 18, twenty-three-year-old Staff Sgt. *Jimmy G. Stewart*, who had already served six years in the Army, defended five wounded men of Company B, 2nd Battalion, 12th Cavalry against the onslaught of a VC company near An Khe in Binh Dinh province. For over four hours this father of two small boys fought off the enemy. When a reinforcing company finally drove off the VC, they found Stewart's body at the bottom of his foxhole, surrounded by eight enemy dead and signs that fifteen more had been dragged away.

In early June of 1966 intelligence reports reached Marine headquarters at Da Nang that a mixed force of VC and NVA were gathering in large numbers in the mountains west of Chu Lai in Quang Tin Province. To frustrate the enemy's plans the marines initiated Operation Kansas. Small teams of eight to twenty marines would scout the mountains looking for signs of the enemy. When they spotted the enemy the recon marines would call in air and artillery strikes. By staying hidden, the marines hoped to harass the VC for days before their presence was suspected. If the marines were discovered, choppers would pull them out.

JIMMIE E. HOWARD

When dusk fell on the night of June 13, a flight of helicopters deposited eighteen marines from the 1st Reconnaissance Battalion, 1st Marine Division on the top of Hill 488, twenty-five miles west of Chu Lai. At a height of one thousand five hundred feet the hill dominated the terrain for miles. It provided an ideal vantage point for the spotting team.

The leader of the patrol, Staff Sgt. *Jimmie E. Howard,* set his men as best he could among the rocks on the barren hilltop. The marines settled in, some taking refuge in old VC foxholes scattered throughout the site.

For the next two days Howard called in artillery on groups of the enemy he or his men spotted. And there were plenty of sightings. Hardly an hour went by that Howard didn't call in a fire-mission. In order to protect the isolated men not all requests for fire were honored. Howard's CO, Captain Timothy Geraghty, was concerned the enemy would become suspicious of all the artillery activity and go after Howard. In fact, at the end of the second day Geraghty wanted to pull Howard out. But the sergeant protested. There had been no trouble so far and he was hurting the enemy. Geraghty reluctantly agreed to give Howard one more day.

Geraghty couldn't have put a better man in charge. An epitome of the recruiting-poster marine, the cigar-chomping Howard enlisted in the Marines in 1950 after he left high school in Burlington, Iowa. As a young marine corporal with the 1st Marine Division in Korea, Howard picked up two Purple Hearts and a Silver Star. He later served as a drill instructor at the recruit depot in San Diego and was a star football player on the base's team.

While Howard checked his men's positions on the evening of June 15, a full NVA battalion began silently swarming up the hill toward him and his handful of young marines. Just past 10:00 P.M., Lance Corporal Richard Binns fired a rifle shot at a bush moving in on his position. The bush screamed, then pitched down the hill. Other marines tossed grenades down the hill. More screams filled the night.

Reacting instantly, Howard pulled his men into a tight circular perimeter, not more than twenty meters across, and personally placed each one in a firing position.

The marines were completely surrounded. Grenades flew through the black sky, exploding among Howard's men. Four enemy .50-caliber machine guns spat tracer rounds up the hill. Lighter machine guns pounded away at the defenders. Mortar shells rained down on the men, adding rock splinters to the deadly shrapnel already filling the air.

The NVA followed up the barrage with a full-blown human wave assault.

Under Howard's resolute leadership the young, mostly untried marines fought back savagely. Howard moved among his charges, pointing out targets and offering words of encouragement. His calmness steadied the men. They forced the Vietnamese back down the hill.

During the temporary lull Howard grabbed his radio. "You gotta get us out of here," Howard told Geraghty. "There are too many for my people."

Geraghty arranged for a reaction force, but it was inexplicably delayed. Just after midnight, the NVA came again.

Howard rallied his men. They fired back, tossed grenades, and yelled curses at their foe. Howard fired his M-16 on semiautomatic, conserving ammo but still hurting the enemy. He seemed to be everywhere. Whenever the NVA were about to overrun a section of his perimeter, Howard moved there, giving strength to the position.

By the time the enemy retreated again several marines lay dead and all but Howard were wounded. The marines had thrown the last of their grenades and ammo was low. But there was no evacuation. Geraghty told Howard they had to stay put.

"You know that movie, *The Longest Day?*" Howard later said. "Well, compared to our night on that hill, *The Longest Day* was just a twinkle in the eye."

Jets and choppers showed up a short time later. Howard directed the planes in strafing attacks against the enemy, bringing them to within thirty feet of his own position. Under his excellent direction the jets dropped napalm on the NVA, scattering them back down the slope. Howard brought the Huey choppers down to altitudes of twenty feet, where they fired their machine guns in long sweeping bursts down the hillside.

Isolated bands of Vietnamese still attacked the perimeter, throwing grenades and firing their rifles. The marines were reduced to throwing rocks at the enemy to confuse them. More often than not it worked.

Just after 3:00 A.M. fragments of shrapnel ripped into Howard's back. His legs were immobilized. Fearful of the drowsing effect morphine could have, Howard refused the painkilling injection. He pulled himself from position to position, gathering ammo from the dead, and giving it to those still fighting.

He kept telling the survivors they only had to hold out till morning. "If we can hold to dawn," he told them, "we'll be O.K."

At 5:25 A.M. he shouted, "O.K., you people, reveille in thirty-five minutes." At precisely 6:00 A.M. his voice boomed out across the perimeter, "Reveille, Reveille!" They had made it through the brutal night.

The enemy fire slackened off with daylight, but did not completely abate. Two of the .50-caliber machine guns still fired. A pair of helicopters were shot down. The NVA seemed determined to annihilate the defenders.

But then reinforcements arrived. Choppers dropped them off on the protected side of the hill. They fought their way to Howard's position, stepping over enemy bodies all the way. The fight wasn't over, though. It was noon before the NVA finally retreated.

Of the eighteen marines who had landed on Hill 488 three days earlier, six were dead; the surviving twelve were all wounded. Howard recommended fifteen of his men for the Silver Star and two for the Navy Cross. He received the Medal of Honor from President Johnson on August 21, 1967.

DONALD A. LONG

On June 30, 1966, Sergeant *Donald A. Long,* a twenty-six-year-old from Blackfork, Ohio, was with a reaction force of Troop C, 1st Squadron, 4th Cavalry going to the rescue of another 1st Infantry Division unit ambushed along Route 13 near Loc Ninh in Binh Long Province, adjacent to the Cambodian border. Elements of the 271st VC Regiment had isolated four tanks from Troop B with recoilless rifle and machine gun fire from well-entrenched positions immediately alongside the jungle road.

Under direct enemy fire, Long moved several wounded cavalrymen to positions of safety. He then stood completely exposed atop his armored personnel carrier to fight off VC attempting to climb aboard. When the VC overran another APC he braved the enemy fire to run to its assistance. While reorganizing the wounded an enemy grenade landed at Long's feet. He shouted a warning, pushed aside a wounded man who had not heard him, and dove upon the deadly missile, absorbing its full blast with his own body. His deliberate self-sacrifice saved eight men.

Up in Quang Tri Province south of the Demilitarized Zone (DMZ) weeks of heavy scouting by recon marines confirmed the presence of large NVA formations infiltrating across the DMZ. To counter the enemy advances, the marines set up a large base at Dong Ha astride Route 9—38 miles north of Hue—then helicoptered units into nearby Cam Lo. Six marine and five ARVN battalions combined in a sweep of the area in Operation Hastings. Two career marines from the same company earned Medals of Honor during the first three days of the operation.

ROBERT J. MODRZEJEWSKI
AND JOHN J. MCGINTY III

On the morning of July 15, 1966, CH-47 helicopters carrying the entire 3rd Battalion, 4th Marines, 3rd Marine Division settled into a landing zone in Song Ngan Valley, within rifle range of the DMZ. The first wave landed and took off without incident. Sniper fire harassed the second wave. Five helicopters downed in the third wave earned the LZ the sobriquet "Helicopter Valley."

The 3rd Battalion swept eastward while its sister battalion, the 2nd, moved west. The pincers movement would clear the area of NVA. Rugged terrain, though, combined with thick vegetation and high heat restricted their progress. By late afternoon the two forces had advanced only two miles toward each other. The units set up defensive positions for the night, sure that the NVA would attack. At eight o'clock that night they did, with the main assault coming against Captain *Robert J. Modrzejewski*'s K Company.

Born in Milwaukee on July 3, 1934, Modrzejewski earned a B.S. from the University of Wisconsin in 1957. While in college he was a member of the Marine Corps Platoon Leader Class, and received a second lieutenant's commission upon graduation. Modrzejewski arrived in Vietnam in March 1966.

Soon after landing at Song Ngan, Modrzejewski encountered a reinforced NVA platoon manning well-organized defensive positions. Under his skilled leadership K Company destroyed the entire platoon.

That night the NVA launched a series of massive frontal assaults.

Modrzejewski said, "It was so dark we couldn't see our hands in front of our faces." He had his marines send up flares so they could see the enemy. The captain raced from hot spot to hot spot, encouraging his young charges. The company managed to fight off the NVA after a wild three-hour fight. The next morning Modrzejewski counted twenty-eight NVA dead and saw evidence that thirty more had been dragged away.

That first day set the pattern for the next three. During the day snipers harassed the marines; at night the enemy attacked the marines' positions.

Throughout each attack Modrzejewski always showed up at the site of the heaviest fighting. On the second night he was wounded, but still managed to crawl two hundred meters to provide critically needed ammo to a threatened sector of his perimeter. Several times he was forced to call in supporting artillery strikes to within a few meters of his own position. It took nerves of steel and incredible self-confidence to do it, but it had to be done.

On the 18th both the 2nd and 3rd Battalions were ordered to pull out. Although it had been hit hard the previous two days, K Company stayed behind to destroy the choppers downed at the LZ. At about 2:30 P.M. the dense jungle erupted with automatic weapons-, mortar-, and small arms-fire. Over one thousand NVA, blowing whistles and bugles, bore down on the isolated company. The 1st Platoon, led by Sgt. John J. McGinty III, was cut off.

John J. McGinty III was born in Boston on January 21, 1940, but was raised in Louisville, Kentucky. He enlisted in the Marines just three months past his seventeenth birthday. His nine years of service included duty as a drill instructor and a brig warden. He volunteered for duty in Vietnam because he "thought it would be over before I got there. I didn't want to be earning my pay guarding a bunch of AWOL sailors."

He more than earned his pay on July 18.

In the opening minutes of the attack, McGinty's radio operator and three men standing nearby were hit. McGinty and the others dropped down. There was little cover. The NVA seemed everywhere. For the next four hours McGinty and the remainder of his thirty-two-man platoon fought off wave after wave of NVA attackers.

During one savage attack the enemy managed to cut off two squads. Unmindful of the shower of lead filling the air, McGinty charged forward to their position. He found twenty men wounded and the corpsman dead. He quickly reloaded rifle magazines and weapons and pressed them into the hands of the wounded. "You gotta fight back," he urged them.

A few minutes later an exploding grenade drove shrapnel into McGinty's leg, back, and left eye. Despite intense pain, McGinty continued encouraging the men and directing their resistance until the NVA retreated. When the enemy later tried to work their way behind him, McGinty killed five at point-blank range with his pistol.

In the meantime, Modrzejewski called in air strikes to fend off the NVA attacking the rest of his company. The bombs and napalm came in so close that one marine had to plunge into a nearby stream to avoid being roasted to death.

In the bloodiest fighting of Operation Hastings, K Company suffered over fifty casualties. The NVA left nearly five hundred dead on the battlefield.

Modrzejewski and McGinty received their Medals of Honor together from President Johnson on March 12, 1968. Both men remained in the Marine Corps, Modrzejewski attaining the rank of colonel. McGinty was commissioned in August 1967. He rose to the rank of captain before being medically discharged in 1976. Doctors had to remove the eye that never fully recovered from the 1966 injury.

In 1983, as a born-again Christian, McGinty gave away his medals. He considered the Medal of Honor's depiction of Minerva, the Roman goddess of wisdom and war, as blasphemous. "The medal is a form of idolatry because it has a false god on it," he told a reporter at the time. "I could never stand before God as a Christian with that thing around my neck."

BILLY L. LAUFFER

A 1st Cavalry Division trooper, PFC *Billy L. Lauffer* of Tucson, Arizona, died when he made a one-man assault on an enemy bunker position near Bong Son in Binh Dinh Province on September 21, 1966. Several of Lauffer's buddies in Company C, 2nd Battalion, 5th Cavalry, had been badly wounded by enemy machine gun fire while on patrol on Operation Thayer I, a 1st Cavalry Division offensive airmobile operation in Binh Dinh Province. Realizing the medics could not reach the casualties under the intense fire from the enemy, Lauffer rose to his feet and attacked the VC bunker. Lauffer, in Vietnam less than one week, was killed—but the wounded were saved.

The U.S. Navy played a key role in Vietnam. Ships anchored off the coast provided gunfire in support of land-based troops. Navy fighter pilots flew bombing missions over North Vietnam as well as close air support missions for Marine and Army infantry. Naval doctors manned evacuation hospitals where they provided first-class medical treatment to the wounded, while Navy corpsmen operated with marine combat units as front line medical aidmen. The elite Sea, Air, and Land (SEAL) commandos conducted a wide variety of behind-enemy-lines operations. And to restrict VC use and control of the Mekong River and its dozens of tributaries, the Navy operated a fleet of river patrol boats.

Reminiscent of the glamorous PT boats of World War II fame, the river patrol boats, or PBRs, were charged with monitoring the heavy junk traffic on Vietnam's waterways. The VC used junks to smuggle men and supplies under the eyes of American and South Vietnamese troops. PBR crews had to develop a sixth sense about which junks to search and which to let go. Since the waterways were the lifeline of Vietnam, it was essential the VC be kept from controlling them. The men who manned the PBRs were a unique breed who experienced none of the glamour of World War II PT boats, but all of the danger.

JAMES E. WILLIAMS

In March 1966 Boatswains Mate 1st Class *James E. Williams* had an ideal life. After more than eighteen years of naval service he was less than two years from retirement. His career had consisted of one routine assignment after another. Now he was stationed within three hundred miles of his hometown of Charleston, South Carolina. His wife of seventeen years and their five children were all eager for him to complete his twenty years so he could retire to their new home in Darlington, South Carolina. In just eleven months he could hang up his whites.

Only one thing bothered him—the growing war in Vietnam. Although he had spent nearly twenty years in uniform, he felt he hadn't actually served his country. He requested a transfer to the war zone, and he arrived in Vietnam in June 1966. During the next eight months Williams would earn every combat decoration available, some more than once, to become one of the most decorated servicemen of all time.

Williams served as a boat commander for River Squadron 5, based at My Tho, south of Saigon. He earned his first medal, a Bronze Star, on July 1, when he captured important documents from an enemy sampan he destroyed after a brisk fight three miles south of My Tho.

Williams picked up a second Bronze Star three weeks later as the result of the capture of a sampan manned by nine VC. Williams's superior handling of his boat and aggressive leadership of the other three PBRs in his squadron were cited in the award.

At dusk on August 22, Williams was in charge of a routine two-boat patrol moving down the Mekong. Concealed on both sides of the river, one hundred enemy gun emplacements opened fire as the two PBRs cruised between them. At the height of the battle, and after knocking out a number of the enemy emplacements, Williams noticed a motorized sampan fleeing the area. Suspecting the vessel held highranking VC, Williams ignored the barrage of enemy fire to take up the pursuit. Although wounded in the subsequent firefight, Williams managed to de-

65

stroy the boat's occupants and capture over one hundred important enemy documents. He earned his first Purple Heart and a Silver Star in this fight.

On October 31 Williams was in charge of PBR 105, leading a two-boat patrol down the Mekong. Without warning, enemy fire erupted from two nearby sampans. Williams instantly ordered return fire, which killed the crew of one sampan and drove the other off. Williams chased it into a nearby inlet. AK-47 fire crackled from the shore. Maneuvering through the fire on the twisting waterway, Williams's patrol was suddenly confronted by two junks and two sampans. The VC had laid a neat trap.

In the savage fighting that followed, Williams, with utter disregard for his own well-being, directed the counterfire of the two PBRs against the enemy. As the battle raged, Williams recognized his small force was overwhelmingly outnumbered. He called for helicopters to aid him then pulled back.

Minutes later he stumbled into an even larger concentration of enemy vessels blocking his route. Unwilling to wait for the choppers, Williams led his boats boldly into the foray. He plowed his way through the enemy boats, twin .50s smoking out rounds. Seven junks and fifty sampans were destroyed in the hail of fire. A few minutes later the gunships arrived overhead. Williams directed their attack by radio.

Not content to let the choppers finish off the enemy, Williams ordered his boats' searchlights turned on. The double rays cut through the night's blackness. Although now a better target, Williams continued to press the attack.

Together, the choppers and Williams's two outnumbered boats completely routed the enemy, killing and wounding scores and destroying dozens more sampans. For his incredible display of courage during this hours-long fight, Williams would receive the Medal of Honor on May 14, 1968.

After such an experience, most men would have requested a transfer back to the States for early retirement. But not Williams. He never relented.

On January 9, 1967, he saved the lives of eight civilians from the dredge *Jamaica Bay,* destroyed by a VC mine on the Mekong

River. Williams earned the Navy and Marine Corps Medal, the highest Navy non-combat award, for repeatedly diving into the water to rescue the victims.

Six days later, Williams took his patrol of three boats to a suspected VC passage across the Nam Thon branch of the Mekong. Intense fire from fortified enemy positions drove off the PBRs. Williams called in an airstrike.

At its conclusion Williams took his boats back into the hostile area. The aerial attack hadn't killed all the VC. Williams manned the .50s, knocking out several automatic weapons with accurate fire. When he sent one of the other boats off to investigate several nearby sampans, the enemy took advantage of the moment to renew their fire on Williams's boat. Williams was hit in the shoulder and left arm.

According to the Navy Cross citation, "Williams led his patrol back through the heavy enemy fire, despite his painful injuries. His decisive leadership and courage succeeded in halting the crossing of four hundred enemy soldiers." He also earned his second Purple Heart.

Altogether, Williams's eight months of combat duty had earned him two-dozen medals. He had served his country exceptionally well.

Williams returned to his family in March 1967. He finished his remaining year in the Navy, then began a new career as a U.S. marshal.

ROBERT F. FOLEY
AND JOHN F. BAKER, JR.

Two members of Company A, 2nd Battalion, 27th Infantry, 25th Infantry Division earned the Medal of Honor while going to the rescue of another company pinned down by elements of the 9th VC Division in Tay Ninh Province on November 5, 1966. West Point graduate Captain *Robert F. Foley,* in spite of several wounds, destroyed three enemy machine gun bunkers, helped several wounded members of his company to safety, and continued to lead his men in the fight. At one point Foley picked up an M-60 machine gun and, firing from the hip, advanced directly into enemy fire so that wounded GIs could be rescued.

PFC *John F. Baker, Jr.,* a twenty-one-year-old native of Moline, Illinois, destroyed several enemy bunkers, killed at least six snipers, and rescued no less than seven wounded comrades from under hostile fire. Like his CO, Captain Foley, Baker had been wounded by an enemy grenade.

At the presentation ceremony in the East Room of the White House on May 1, 1968, President Johnson couldn't help commenting on the differences in the two warriors. Foley stood six-feet seven-inches tall, Baker five-feet two-inches tall. Both men remained in the Army.

TED BELCHER

Sgt. *Ted Belcher* fought as an infantryman in Germany during World War II. He returned home to raise a family but the military impulse stayed in his blood. In 1960 he enlisted in the Maryland National Guard. Three years later he requested a transfer to active duty. In October 1966 he went to Vietnam, where he joined Company C, 1st Battalion, 14th Infantry, 25th Infantry Division.

At forty-two Belcher was old for a grunt, but he kept up with his squad members, most of whom were the age of his daughter back in Zanesville, Ohio. On November 16, 1966, while leading his squad to the rescue of a friendly unit pinned down near Plei Djerang in Pleiku Province, Belcher died when he jumped on an enemy grenade to save the lives of his squad members.

In mid-September of 1966 the 1st Cavalry Division returned to the coastal Binh Dinh Province after helping the 4th Division in the Central Highlands of Pleiku Province. With the assistance of Republic of Korea Marine Corps units the "First Team" launched Operation Irving to keep the heat on the 5th NVA Division, which roamed Binh Dinh Province at will. Heavy combat erupted throughout the coastal province during the fall of 1966. Some of the bitterest fighting occurred in areas south of the provincial capital of Bong Son.

LEWIS ALBANESE

Lewis Albanese hated the Army. He frequently said he wasn't fit for soldiering. To emphasize his point he made a habit of avoiding any duty that required manual labor. The first sergeant of Albanese's unit, Company B, 5th Battalion, 7th Cavalry, Dayton L. Hare, called Albanese a "goof-off." He was correct, in a sense. Others, however, viewed the Albanese as young, full of life, and a bit mischievous.

Born in Venice, Italy, on April 27, 1946, Albanese emigrated to Seattle, Washington as a youth. He graduated from Seattle's Franklin High School in 1964, then was drafted in October 1965. He was originally assigned to the 5th Infantry Division at Fort Carson, Colorado, but, as the war heated up, was transferred to the 7th Cavalry Regiment as it organized for deployment to Vietnam. He arrived there in August 1966.

Albanese saw action all over Binh Dinh Province in Operation Thayer I and II and in Operation Irving. Binh Dinh was both a beautiful and dangerous place. Steep mountains covered by thick green foliage provided a striking background to the picturesque villages of thatched huts. Binh Dinh served as the home base of the NVA 18th Regiment and the VC 2nd Regiment. In the nine years of the Vietnam War, Binh Dinh would never be under American control.

On December 1, 1966, Albanese's platoon, led by Lieutenant William E. Kail, went to the aid of a 9th Cavalry company pinned down in the hamlet of Phu Huu, twenty kilometers south of Bong Son. As the platoon entered a graveyard at the edge of the village, enemy rifle fire pinned it down. A sergeant killed the gunner, allowing the platoon to move forward.

Staff Sgt. George Porod had the left flank squad, Albanese's squad. A huge man, who sported a flaming red handlebar mustache, Porod maneuvered his men through the scattered huts and foliage. As he brought his squad into an open area, Porod noticed a drainage ditch to his left. Suddenly automatic-weapons fire erupted from the ditch. Porod realized he had walked into an ambush. He and his men faced certain death.

Porod's squad dashed for cover to the right. All except Albanese. As the left flank man in the squad he dropped to the ground to give covering fire to his buddies while they scurried for cover. Then he crawled into the ditch.

According to Porod and Kail, even though the slightly built grunt was out of sight in the ditch, his progress could be followed by the sound of firing and exploding grenades. No one witnessed Albanese's single-handed attack but it was easy to reconstruct his movements.

With fixed bayonet Albanese dropped into the ditch. He found it was actually a one hundred-meter-long trench connecting a series of bunkers and fighting positions. "Goof-off" Albanese moved down the trench assaulting each of the VC positions. He'd take the enemy under fire, then toss a grenade. Six VC died under Albanese's assault.

It didn't take long, less than fifteen minutes. Albanese broke the enemy's resistance, allowing Kail to overrun the VC main line of resistance and rescue the trapped company. Sixty-seven enemy bodies were counted and four prisoners were taken. Then Kail and Porod went back for Albanese.

They found him at the end of the ditch. He was out of ammo, out of grenades. Blood stained his bayonet. Two VC lay in front of him, dead of bayonet wounds. Albanese was dead, too.

Albanese's Medal of Honor citation, presented to his parents on February 16, 1968, called the immigrant's heroism and devotion to his buddies "a tribute to himself, his unit, and the U.S. Army."

CHAPTER
FIVE

Westmoreland Takes
the Offensive

W hen General Westmoreland
_____ looked back on 1966 he
gave high marks to the major operations conducted against main
force enemy units. Not only had the enemy been forced to op-
erate within easy retreating distance of his sanctuary across
the Laotian and Cambodian borders, but U.S. units had developed the battlefield tactics necessary to conduct this new type
of warfare.

Lessons had been learned the hard way. Almost all of the
combat in 1966 had been initiated by the VC or NVA. Besides
having the upper hand in engaging American units in battle, the
enemy also had the power to break contact at their discretion.
As soon as the Americans seemed to be on the verge of victory,
whether through superior infantry tactics or superior fire power,
the enemy would fade back into the jungle.

In 1967 Westmoreland began going after the enemy. He
would strike the enemy's base camps in border provinces and
below the DMZ. Under his plan American forces would conduct
the offensive operations. ARVN units would come in behind
them to secure and pacify the area. His first big offensive campaign, the largest of the war to date, was Operation Cedar Falls,
followed by Operation Junction City.

Operation Cedar Falls (named for the hometown of Lieutenant Robert J. Hibbs) thrust sixteen thousand U.S. and fourteen
thousand ARVN troops into the Iron Triangle area northwest of
Saigon. Starting on January 8, 1967, two infantry divisions (the
1st and 25th) and three full brigades (196th, 173rd, and 11th
ACR) invaded the VC bastion from opposite directions in a clas-
sic hammer and anvil movement. Unfortunately, the VC simply
pulled out rather than let themselves be hammered. Infantrymen
did discover, however, a massive tunnel complex in the Iron Triangle, apparently used for guerilla raids and terrorist attacks on
Saigon.

Operation Junction City was to have been an immediate
follow-up to Operation Cedar Falls against VC and NVA in War

73

Zone C in upper Tay Ninh Province, but it was delayed for a month.

It wasn't until the morning of February 22, 1967, that paratroopers from the 2nd Battalion, 503rd Airborne Infantry, 173rd Airborne Brigade bailed out of aircraft above Katum, only seven miles south of the Cambodian border. The troopers parachuted to safety in what would be the only airborne operation of the Vietnam War. It was a glorious beginning to an inglorious campaign. As in Operation Cedar Falls, the enemy eluded the American forces, moving their supply depots and base camps into Cambodia.

Engagement rules prohibited U.S. forces from pursuing the enemy across the border. Officially their hands were tied as soon as the enemy crossed the border. In reality, U.S. forces crossed the border in direct violation of policy.

The first U.S.-led cross-border operation occurred in October 1965, when a small team penetrated the Laotian border near the Special Forces camp at Kham Duc in Quang Tin Province. Their mission: find the Ho Chi Minh Trail. They found it and confirmed its existence but at the cost of five men and two helicopters.

Under the title Operation Shining Brass, this small incursion came under the operational control of MACV's Studies and Observation Group (SOG). SOG was a joint service high command unconventional warfare task force engaged in highly classified operations throughout Southeast Asia. Composed of nearly two thousand Americans, mainly Army Special Forces and Navy SEALS, and eight thousand indigenous troops, SOG had five main responsibilities: (1) cross-border operations, (2) keeping track of American POWs, (3) organizing resistance movements in North Vietnam, (4) psychological warfare in North and South Vietnam, and (5) kidnapping and assassination teams.

While much of SOG's activities still remains classified, it is known that no less than nine of its members earned Medals of Honor. Because of the clandestine nature of their missions in Laos and Cambodia, the official citations for the awards state that the action occurred "deep within enemy-dominated territory," or simply, "in the Republic of Vietnam." No specific locations were given. Only in recent years have the details become available.

GEORGE K. SISLER

First Lieutenant *George Sisler* was no stranger to military secrets. He had served in Air Force Intelligence for four years before enlisting in the U.S. Army in August 1964. In November 1965 he graduated from the Army's Intelligence School at Fort Holabird, Maryland.

Although he had a wife and two sons back in his hometown of Dexter, Missouri, Sisler volunteered for Special Forces training. His knowledge of covert operations could be put to good use in Vietnam.

Sisler arrived in Vietnam in June 1966. His mail went to Headquarters Company, 5th Special Forces Group, but he was actually assigned to Command and Control-North, SOG. George Sisler began making cross-border intelligence missions into Laos.

Through stealth and cunning, Sisler managed to avoid direct enemy contact until February 7, 1967. On that date, while on patrol in Laos, a company of VC hit his unit on three sides.

Sisler immediately directed the team into defensive positions, then called for air strikes and an extraction chopper. While he pointed out targets to his men, Sisler discovered that two of the team had been wounded and were outside the perimeter. Concerned with keeping them out of enemy hands, Sisler raced through intense fire to their assistance.

He was carrying one of the Vietnamese into the perimeter when an enemy machine gun opened up. Laying down the wounded man, Sisler went after the gun with a hand grenade. He destroyed it and killed three enemy soldiers sneaking up on him.

Sisler had moved the second man into the enclave when a

small but determined enemy force burst out of the jungle, intent on overrunning the team.

Without regard for his own safety, Sisler picked up some grenades and charged into the midst of the enemy.

With rifle blazing—and throwing grenades as fast as he could pull the pins—Sisler single-handedly broke up the enemy attack. The VC faded back into the jungle.

A few minutes later U.S. gunships arrived on the scene. Sisler was directing their fire onto the fleeing enemy when a sniper shot him down. The rest of the team was rescued a short time later.

The Medal of Honor citation presented to Sisler's widow and sons on June 27, 1968, said the action happened in South Vietnam, not Laos.

Upon its arrival in Vietnam in September 1966, the 4th "Ivy" Infantry Division had been sent straight to the VC-dominated Central Highlands region. In keeping with General Westmoreland's plan for aggressive offensive operations the 4th's commanding general, William R. Peers, turned his men loose in the western halves of Pleiku and Kontum Provinces in January 1967.

The first month of Operation Sam Houston was relatively easy. After February 1, though, the action heated up.

Peers sent his 2nd Brigade into the heavy rain forest west of the Nam Sathay River in Kontum. Some of the world's most hostile jungle terrain could be found there. Huge trees reaching over two hundred feet into the sky combined with dense undergrowth made movement through the ruggedly mountainous ground extremely difficult. Visibility was restricted to a few meters at best. It was perfect country for ambushes.

LOUIS E. WILLETT

On February 15, Company C, 1st Battalion, 12th Infantry moved cautiously into the jungle from their LZ. They had not proceeded very far when heavy automatic weapons fire ripped into their ranks. The grunts hit the dirt. One squad was caught in a ravine, unable to move its wounded to safety. Suddenly PFC *Louis E. Willett,* a twenty-two-year-old from Brooklyn, New York, rose to his feet firing bursts from an M-60 machine gun. Under his covering fire the squad began withdrawing. Urged by his buddies to pull back with them, Willett ignored their pleadings and instead moved forward. He was hit several times but never gave up. He continued to take the enemy under fire, allowing his squad to rejoin the company. Willett was moving to a more advantageous position when he was cut down.

ELMILINDO R. SMITH

The next day, a few kilometers away, a platoon of Company C, 2nd Battalion, 8th Infantry was ambushed shortly after noon. Initially, the platoon thought only a few NVA were involved. When they moved forward, however, the enemy fire intensified. The platoon faced annihilation. They called for supporting artillery fire but the tightly-woven jungle canopy made it difficult to place the rounds accurately. The soldiers engaged the NVA in hand-to-hand combat. When finally rescued late that night, the survivors agreed that the actions of their platoon sergeant, *Elmilindo R. Smith,* saved their lives.

A native of Honolulu, Hawaii, the thirty-one-year-old Smith already had fourteen years of active duty behind him. He came to Vietnam with the 4th Infantry Division from Fort Lewis, Washington, where he left a wife and two children. Now, although hit three times, he inspired his frightened men through his deliberate disregard of the enemy fire, moving among the Ivy-men, directing their fire, repositioning them, and distributing badly needed ammunition.

He was moving forward to engage the enemy when a rocket exploded underneath him. Grievously wounded, Smith deliberately crawled into the jungle between the two forces so he could warn his platoon of the advancing enemy. The relieving company found his body there the next day.

JAMES ANDERSON, JR.

In northern Quang Tri Province on February 28, the first black marine to earn a Medal of Honor died when he covered an exploding hand grenade with his own body. PFC *James Anderson, Jr.,* a twenty-year-old from Compton, California, had been moving with Company F, 2nd Battalion, 3rd Marines, to the relief of a heavily engaged unit northwest of Cam Lo. The battalion commander, LTC Victor Ohanesian, and the sergeant major died when the VC showered the advancing column with grenades. Anderson dove for cover with other members of his squad. As they lay together a grenade rolled into their position. Anderson pulled it underneath him seconds before it detonated.

HILLIARD A. WILBANKS

One of the most dangerous jobs in the Air Force belonged to the Forward Air Controller. The FAC flew low and slow over a battleground, spotting targets for Army ground troops or Air Force attack planes. Flying in unarmed, light, single-engine aircraft, the FACs were particularly vulnerable to ground fire. In spite of this inherent danger, FACs knew they were often the only contact between ground forces and their desperately needed support—so they stayed above the battlefield, relaying vital information long after it was unsafe.

The aircraft most frequently flown by FACs was the Cessna-built O-1E Bird Dog. Closely resembling the popular Piper Cub, the O-1E offered no armor protection. The only weapons the pilot carried were an M-16 rifle and a .45-caliber pistol. They were supposed to be defensive weapons in case the plane went down. They were definitely not designed for offensive operations.

Hilliard Wilbanks earned his wings in 1954 after four years as an Air Force security guard. He served a year as an instructor before joining a squadron of F-86 Sabre Jets. In 1965 Wilbanks was tapped for training as a FAC. He trained at Hurlburt Field, Florida, then went to the 21st Tactical Air Support Squadron, operating out of the Vietnam coastal city of Nha Trang.

In February 1967 Captain Wilbanks had completed the tenth month of his tour. Most of it had been spent in the area of Dalat, fifty miles west of Cam Ranh Bay, flying missions for an assortment of ARVN units. Late on the afternoon of February 24, Wilbanks took off on his 488th mission.

Earlier that day the VC had attacked three ARVN companies from well-constructed positions hidden on two hills overlooking a tea plantation. From their advantageous positions the VC had let the friendly forces walk deep into a trap before springing an ambush. The loss of vital radio gear kept the approaching relief column from the 23rd Vietnamese Rangers from being warned of the deadly trap awaiting them.

Wilbanks was in contact with the Rangers' U.S. advisor, Captain R. J. Wooten, and two nearby helicopter gunships. The Rangers had entered the tea plantation when Wilbanks spotted the camouflaged positions. He grabbed his microphone to warn Wooten.

Realizing their ambush had been discovered, the VC immediately opened up on the Rangers, dropping them easily in a barrage of fire.

Overhead, Wilbanks brought his Bird Dog directly over the enemy's position. He marked their location with a smoke rocket, then called for the gunships. They roared in, guns blazing. Return fire hit one; the other chopper escorted it to safety. In the lull that followed the VC spilled out of their foxholes. With knives and bayonets bared they moved down the hill toward the badly disorganized and outnumbered Rangers.

Suddenly a smoke rocket exploded among the VC, diverting their attention. Wilbanks had brought his little Bird Dog down in an attack. When he came roaring in for another pass the VC let loose at him with .30- and .50-caliber machine gun fire. It

79

didn't stop Wilbanks. He fired off another smoke rocket, then came back again and let go his fourth, and last, rocket.

Captain Wooten said, "On each pass he was so close we could hear his plane being hit."

This would have been a good time for Wilbanks to retreat from the fight and let jet aircraft strafe the VC, helping the Rangers escape the trap. Wilbanks didn't think so—he still had one weapon at his disposal.

He poked his M-16 out the window of the Bird Dog and blazed away at the startled enemy. His audacious attack confused the VC. Some broke and ran, others ducked for cover. Wilbanks made three low passes over the enemy. Another advisor, Captain Gary Vote, recalled that, "He was no more than one hundred feet off the ground."

On the last pass disaster struck. Vote watched in stunned silence as VC rifle fire brought the little plane down between the opposing forces. Vote gathered up a handful of Rangers to go to Wilbanks's aid. They protected the unconscious pilot until a helicopter arrived. It took two attempts—under heavy fire—before the chopper set down. They got Wilbanks aboard but it was too late. He died on the chopper.

For his unsurpassed courage in disrupting the VC attack Wilbanks was posthumously awarded the Medal of Honor on January 24, 1968.

DAVID G. OUELETT

The quick action of a young sailor saved five lives on March 6, 1967. Seaman *David G. Ouelett* served as a gunner on Patrol Boat 124. While cruising slowly on the Cua Dai tributary of the Mekong River eighteen miles south of My Tho, the twenty-two-year-old from Wellesley, Massachusetts, saw a grenade tossed from shore. He pulled himself from his protected gun position and ran aft down the narrow gunwale, shouting, "Duck!"

He bounded onto the engine compartment cover, pushing the boat's commander, Seaman James W. VanZandt, to safety. A split second later the grenade landed. Ouelett threw himself between it and the rest of the crew, absorbing the lethal fragments with his own body.

Ouelett was evacuated to a hospital in Saigon, but died despite frantic efforts to save him.

STEPHEN E. KAROPCZYC

In the Central Highlands the 4th Infantry Division, with its attached 25th Infantry Division brigade, kept after the VC and NVA along the Cambodian border. On March 12, 1967, the entire 2nd Battalion of the 35th Infantry was attacked in Kontum Province. In the opening minutes of the fight 1st Lieutenant *Stephen E. Karopczyc,* a platoon leader in Company A, took a round in his chest just above the heart. Rather than accept medical evacuation he plugged the bleeding hole with his finger. For over two hours the twenty-three-year-old from Bethpage, New York, led his platoon in a spirited defense of their isolated position. When a grenade landed by him and two wounded soldiers, Karopczyc attempted to cover the deadly missile with a steel helmet. The explosion drove more shrapnel into his body. Two hours later, still at the head of his men, the gallant officer died from loss of blood.

Meanwhile, in Hau Nghia and Tay Ninh Provinces, west of Saigon, the GIs of Operation Junction City continued to push their offensive against the wily foe.

RUPPERT L. SARGENT

During a sweep of a hamlet in Hau Nghia Province on March 15, 1967, a former VC led 1st Lieutenant *Ruppert L. Sargent* and three members of his platoon to a Viet Cong meeting house and weapons cache. Sargent, twenty-nine years old, saw the tunnel entrance was booby-trapped. He called for a demolition man to place a charge. The resulting explosion didn't destroy the booby-trap but it did flush a VC from hiding. One of Sargent's men cut the man down.

Sargent and two of his men stepped toward the tunnel entrance. Suddenly another VC broke from cover, tossed two grenades at the Americans, then fled. Sargent fired three shots at the man then turned and threw himself over the grenades.

Sargent was killed in the explosion, but his gallant efforts saved the lives of his two comrades.

In July 1968 the recommendation for Sargent's posthumous Medal of Honor was approved, making him the first black officer so recognized. Pentagon officials who contacted Sargent's widow to arrange for the presentation ceremony were stunned when she refused to accept the award. Her position stemmed from her strong religious beliefs. A Jehovah's Witness, she professed allegiance to God alone and not to any organized government. Sargent's mother, also a Jehovah's Witness, supported her daughter-in-law. She had, in fact, opposed her son's entrance into the Army.

Born January 9, 1938, in Hampton, Virginia, Sargent enlisted in the Army in January 1959 after finishing two years of college. Although he was raised as a Jehovah's Witness, the attraction of the military overcame his religious training. After six years as an enlisted man Sargent was accepted for officer's training. He received his gold bars on October 15, 1965. He went to Company B, 4th Battalion, 9th Infantry, 25th Infantry Division in September 1966. Six months later he was killed in action.

For several months after Mrs. Sargent's refusal, Army officers continued their efforts to persuade her to accept the award. She continued to decline. At last, when the Army agreed to make the presentation in private, with no publicity, she consented.

On March 10, 1969, Brigadier General Donley P. Bolton drove from Washington to Hampton. In the presence of Sargent's two children, Bolton solemnly handed the widow the posthumous medal and citation.

One Pentagon official, after reading the citation, said he felt sure Mrs. Sargent had no right to keep her husband's award a secret. "He belongs to the country now," he said.

CHARLES E. HOSKING

The average Viet Cong soldier was a tenacious fighter whose willingness to die for his cause was reminiscent of the Japanese soldiers of World War II. He often went to great lengths to kill his enemy. Forty-two-year-old Special Forces Master Sergeant *Charles E. Hosking* was escorting a VC suspect back to his base camp in Phuoc Long Province on March 12, 1967, when the VC suddenly grabbed a grenade off of Hosking's belt and ran toward a group of four Americans standing nearby. Hosking took off after him. When he reached the VC he leaped on the man's back, forced him to the ground, and held him there in a bear hug. Hosking, an original member of the Special Forces who had been wounded during World War II's Battle of the Bulge, died in the explosion that followed, but saved his command group from certain death.

DAVID H. MCNERNEY

David H. McNerney typified what many of the young soldiers and marines serving in Vietnam derisively referred to as a "lifer." Born July 2, 1931, in Lowell, Massachusetts, McNerney grew up in Houston, Texas. McNerney's father, Edward, instilled a great sense of patriotism and responsibility in all his children. As a genuine World War I hero, he knew what he was talking about.

Serving as first sergeant of Company K, 104th Infantry Regiment, 26th Infantry Division, Edward McNerney earned a Distinguished Service Cross on July 22, 1918, for rescuing a wounded man under heavy enemy machine gun fire near Epieds, France. In addition, he came home from World War I with a Silver Star, two Purple Hearts, and the French Croix de Guerre.

Because of their father the McNerney children understood that life in a free country often carried a hefty price tag. Two McNerney children served in World War II. Another flew combat missions in Vietnam as a Navy pilot.

David McNerney served a four-year hitch in the Navy, then enlisted in the Army in 1954. When he arrived in Vietnam in September 1966 he had already served two one-year tours as an advisor to South Vietnamese Army units. Now, like his father before him, McNerney would serve as the first sergeant of a rifle company.

In the final days of the 4th Infantry Division's Operation Sam Houston, radio contact with a recon platoon operating near Polei Doc in Kontum Province was lost. McNerney's Company A, 1st Battalion, 8th Infantry, went in after the platoon.

At 7:30 A.M. on March 22, enemy machine gun fire hit Company A hard. McNerney assisted his CO in establishing a perimeter and a strong base of fire. He was moving a squad into position when he noticed several NVA moving through the thick jungle. He killed them all, but was blown off his feet by an enemy grenade. Badly injured in the right side of his chest but ignoring the pain, McNerney assaulted an enemy machine gun bunker and destroyed it. A few minutes later McNerney learned that his CO and the artillery forward observer had been blown to bits by a direct hit from an enemy B-40 rocket. The company panicked. Men threw away equipment and fought without coordination.

McNerney did what any good "first shirt" would do under similar circumstances: he took charge.

Running among his men, McNerney yelled, cursed, and cajoled the grunts into maintaining discipline under fire. "Pick your targets," he yelled. He had a radio operator bring him the FO's radio then called in artillery fire to within twenty meters of his company's position.

The rounds crashed into the ground, weakening the NVA grip on the unit. Soon, however, the company ran out of the colored smoke grenades used to mark their position for friendly aircraft. Without them friendly fire could strike the company.

McNerney solved the problem by dashing into a nearby clearing. Holding aloft an identification panel, he remained in the open, oblivious to enemy fire, until he was sure that the aircraft had spotted him. Then he climbed a tree and tied the panel in its highest branches.

Because of his actions aircraft fire was able to reduce the enemy's fire. In order to clear an LZ so that the dead and dying could be removed, McNerney crawled outside the company's perimeter to recover explosive charges from abandoned rucksacks.

Although his injuries would have allowed him a place on a medevac chopper, McNerney refused to go. The company needed him. He stayed with it until a new CO flew out the next day.

President Johnson presented McNerney with the Medal of Honor at the White House on September 19, 1968. McNerney finished twenty years service to his country in 1969, retired, and took a job as a customs inspector in Texas.

JOHN P. BOBO

Up in Quang Tri Province Company I, 3rd Battalion, 9th Marines, 3rd Marine Division spent March 30, 1967, in routine patrolling around Con Thien, south of the DMZ. As they were settling in for the night, an extremely vulnerable time, the NVA suddenly hit them with a murderous volume of fire.

Second Lieutenant *John P. Bobo,* a twenty-four-year-old from Niagara Falls, New York, helped organize a defense. He moved from position to position, encouraging his outnumbered marines. After he recovered a rocket launcher from a disabled marine and getting it back in action, a mortar exploded at Bobo's feet, blowing off his right leg below the knee.

The intrepid officer refused evacuation. Instead, he wrapped a belt around his leg then, with his bloody stump jammed into the dirt, he stayed on the firing line, covering the withdrawal of the command group to safety.

"I saw him kill at least five North Vietnamese soldiers although he had been seriously wounded," said the company's first sergeant, Raymond G. Rogers. "He killed the NVA who had wounded me in the leg and who was standing over me."

Bobo's heavy firing made him a target for the NVA. He was still kneeling there, rifle blazing, when he was cut down.

MICHAEL J. ESTOCIN

On April 20, 1967, Navy Lieutenant Commander *Michael J. Estocin* led three jet fighters from the carrier *Ticonderoga* in a raid on surface-to-air missile (SAM) sites located near Haiphong. Although his plane was struck early in the assault, Estocin pressed home his attack and destroyed three SAM sites. His plane was leaking fuel so badly it was necessary for him to fly the last one hundred miles back to the carrier sucking fuel from an airborne tanker. He coaxed his plane down to a perfect landing.

Six days later, and one day before his thirty-sixth birthday, Estocin was again over Haiphong. A SAM scored a direct hit on his aircraft, severely damaging it. Rather than depart the area and head to sea and safety, Estocin regained control of his plane, launched his missiles, and only then headed back to the *Ticonderoga*.

He never made it. The Navy searched for him but no trace was ever found. Hoping he might be a POW, his family declined to accept his well-deserved Medal of Honor. After the Navy officially declared him dead Estocin's widow accepted the decoration on February 27, 1978.

KENNETH E. STUMPF

When three men from Company C, 1st Battalion, 35th Infantry, 25th Infantry Division were critically wounded by an enemy machine gun near the hamlet of Duc Pho (on the coast in southern Quang Ngai Province) on April 25, 1967, Specialist Four *Ken-*

neth E. Stumpf made three trips through a barrage of mortar rounds to carry the casualties to safety. He then armed himself with grenades which he used to wipe out three enemy bunkers.

Discharged after his two years of active duty ended in September 1967, Stumpf returned to his home in Menasha, Wisconsin. After he received his medal on September 19, 1968, the twenty-three-year-old reenlisted, making the Army his career.

On April 28, 1967, General William C. Westmoreland made an unprecedented appearance before a joint session of Congress. Never before had a military commander addressed Congress while directing an ongoing war. He came at the express invitation of President Johnson, who sought a way to silence the increasingly vocal opponents of his war policy.

Westmoreland told the assemblage that no previous military man "could have more pride than is mine in representing the gallant men fighting in Vietnam today." But Westmoreland was not very optimistic. "In the months ahead," he said, U.S. soldiers would see "some of the bitterest fighting of the war, with no end in sight."

The general's concerns over the progress of the war were reflected in his new demands for additional troops. He submitted two plans: one he dubbed a "minimum essential" force of eighty thousand five hundred more troops for a total of five hundred fifty thousand five hundred. His optimum plan, though, called for two hundred thousand more men, raising the total to six hundred seventy thousand.

Under questioning by President Johnson and his advisors, Westmoreland exhibited the frustration being experienced by a growing number of Americans. Pressed for an answer on when the war might end, Westmoreland could only say "three or more years" with the minimum number of troops, perhaps "two years" with the higher level.

In a war where progress was based on specificity of numbers and systems analysis, it was not a very good estimate.

The 9th Infantry Division was the first unit specifically organized for deployment to Vietnam. Earmarked for the swamps and rice paddies of the Mekong Delta south of Saigon, the deployment of the division had to be speeded up by chopping three months off its training cycle. When it arrived in-country in December 1966, its mission was to clear the Viet Cong from Long An and Dinh Tuong Provinces south of Saigon. Long accustomed to operating unmolested in this area, the VC fought hard. Even after months of tough combat, the VC still controlled the countryside.

LEONARD B. KELLER
AND RAYMOND R. WRIGHT

For most of the morning of May 2, 1967, Company A, 3rd Battalion, 60th Infantry, 9th Division had slogged through the rice paddies around Ap Bac in Long An Province. Throughout the hot, sticky day intermittent sniper fire harassed the men. Captain Joseph Mazuta sent out small patrols to locate and destroy the snipers but had no luck. Now, as his company approached a tree line at the end of a rice paddy, he planned to break for lunch, then head back to his base camp.

Mazuta had finished giving instructions to his first sergeant, Hank Davis, when enemy automatic-weapons fire erupted from the treeline, dropping a dozen grunts. The rest of the company scattered to cover. Mortar rounds crashed into the paddy, spewing water and spreading death.

In response to Mazuta's call for help, three Air Force jets strafed the treeline. When they finished the captain prepared two platoons for an attack. But as the man arose a new burst of heavy fire drove them down. The VC were so well-entrenched that the strafing attack had caused little damage.

Mazuta was ready to take his company in after the enemy when movement at the end of the line caught his eye. Two of his GIs were going into the tree line alone.

Two draftees, twenty-year-old Sgt. *Leonard B. Keller* from

Rockford, Illinois, and twenty-one-year-old Specialist Four *Raymond R. Wright,* from Mineville, New York, raced forward. Leapfrogging through the bunkers, the two gallant youths destroyed one position after another.

Armed with an M-60 machine gun, Keller would take a bunker under fire, pinning down the occupants, while Wright would sneak up to drop in grenades. For over thirty minutes the two fought the VC. Constantly ignoring the enemy fire directed at them, the pair wiped out seven bunkers and killed no less than a dozen of the enemy. Their heroic action drove off a VC platoon intent on destroying their company. With their self-appointed mission completed the two returned to the company where they helped evacuate the wounded.

The courageous pair received their Medals of Honor in a double ceremony held at the White House on September 19, 1968.

BRUCE A. GRANDSTAFF

On May 18, 1967, the CO of Company B, 1st Battalion, 8th Infantry, 4th Infantry Division sent one of his platoons to investigate the sighting of a lone VC on a well-used trail. Contact with the enemy along the Cambodian border in Pleiku Province had been almost continuous since the 4th had started Operation Francis Marion on April 6. This looked like another chance to hurt the NVA. This time, though, the NVA turned the tables.

The K4 Battalion, 32nd NVA Regiment ambushed the platoon, isolating it from the rest of the company. Survivors of that desperate fight told how their leader, Platoon Sgt. *Bruce A. Grandstaff* of Spokane, Washington, organized the platoon in its fight against the NVA. He seemed to be everywhere, throwing grenades, firing his rifle, caring for the injured. Even though he was wounded twice he still managed to destroy one enemy machine gun, then was wounded again. When he realized the NVA were on the verge of overrunning his position he called down artillery fire directly on his location.

Only seven of the thirty-five platoon members lived through the carnage. They told how the NVA walked over the battlefield systematically shooting any American who showed signs of life. The enemy looted and mutilated the bodies before melting into the jungle. The survivors also said it took a direct hit from an enemy rocket to put thirty-two-year-old Grandstaff out of action.

LESLIE A. BELLRICHARD
AND FRANKIE Z. MOLNAR

Two nights later, and just a few miles from where Grandstaff died, the entire 1st Battalion, 8th Infantry, was savagely attacked by three human wave assaults by soldiers from the K5 Battalion, 32nd NVA Regiment. The grunts fought off the enemy but at heavy cost. Two men earned the Medal of Honor in the bitter fighting. Twenty-five-year-old PFC *Leslie A. Bellrichard,* who grew up in Madison, Wisconsin, and who left a wife in San Jose, California, was preparing to throw a hand grenade when an exploding mortar round knocked it out of his hand. Realizing the danger to the four men sharing his fighting hole, Bellrichard dropped down and covered the grenade with his own body. Although mortally wounded by the explosion, Bellrichard struggled to an upright position and defiantly fired his M-16 into the charging enemy until he succumbed to his wounds.

Staff Sgt. *Frankie Z. Molnar* had been among the first to spot the enemy when he cut down five NVA sneaking up on his squad's position. He fought bravely throughout the attack, leaving the relative safety of his spider-hole several times to bring badly needed ammo to his men. As the battle waned Molnar moved among the many casualties, administering first aid. Molnar and several other GIs were moving a severely injured soldier to an evacuation point when a grenade landed at their feet. Rather than dive for cover Molnar dropped on the grenade, shielding the others from the effects of the explosion. The twenty-four-year-old native of Logan, West Virginia, died instantly.

MELVIN E. NEWLIN

Just before midnight on July 3, 1967, one of Marine Lieutenant James B. Scuras's outposts reported movement in front of their position. Scuras's unit, Company F, 2nd Battalion, 5th Marines, 1st Marine Division, provided security to South Vietnam's only producing coal mine at Nong Son in Quang Nam Province. Before the officer could respond the radio crackled, "We're being overrun," then went silent.

Seconds later mortar rounds fell out of the sky; one destroyed the 4.2-inch mortar's supply of ammo. Immediately thereafter, VC sappers appeared at the company's perimeter, throwing satchel charges into the marine bunkers. The attack would have overwhelmed the company if it hadn't been for the valor of an eighteen-year-old marine.

One month after graduating from high school in the Ohio River town of Wellsville, Ohio, in June 1966, *Melvin E. Newlin* enlisted in the Marine Corps. He completed boot camp at Parris Island, South Carolina, then attended infantry training at Camp Lejeune, North Carolina. He arrived in Vietnam in March 1967.

Newlin fought with his company throughout Quang Nam Province in Operations New Castle, Union, and Calhoun. When his company was assigned guard duty at the coal mine it looked like two months of skating—until the night of July 3.

An explosive charge thrown during the initial moments of the attack killed Newlin's four foxhole buddies and seriously wounded him. Ignoring the pain, Newlin kept his machine gun in action, halting two determined attempts to silence him. Then an exploding VC grenade knocked him unconscious.

With the main threat to their attack silenced the VC moved into the center of the outpost, where they destroyed the company's two 4.2-inch mortars and killed their crews. The VC were on the verge of wiping out the marine positions on the opposite side of the perimeter when Newlin came to.

Instead of seeking treatment for his grievous wounds, Newlin remanned his machine gun. Burst after burst of hot lead from his weapon cut holes in the VC ranks. At one point Newlin temporarily shifted his fire to knock out the VC manning a captured 106mm recoilless rifle.

By now the main target of a renewed enemy assault, Newlin never faltered. He continued firing his machine gun until an enemy soldier killed him. Newlin's actions completely disrupted the enemy's attack, allowing the marines a chance to reorganize and for a relief company to arrive.

The posthumous Medal of Honor earned by PFC Newlin was presented to his parents on March 18, 1969.

ROY M. WHEAT

"Liberty Road" was the name given by marines to the Seabee-constructed route connecting Da Nang with the industrial town of An Hoa, twenty-three miles to the southwest. The constant threat of enemy attack on the vital link kept the marines busy.

On August 11, 1967, three marines from Company K, 3rd Battalion, 7th Marines, 1st Marine Division set up a security position adjacent to a Seabee construction site along Liberty Road. Lance Corporal *Roy M. Wheat* volunteered to scout the area to their rear.

As he returned to the position he tripped a booby-trap. Thinking only of saving the lives of his two nearby buddies, the twenty-year-old from Moselle, Mississippi, shouted a warning, then hurled himself on the mine, absorbing the tremendous explosion with his own body.

The most versatile weapon in the Vietnam War was undoubtedly the helicopter. Choppers not only provided the infantryman with previously unknown mobility, but also lifted him to battle, evacuated the dead and wounded, brought in supplies, and helped overcome many of the advantages held by the NVA and VC. Flown by courageous young pilots, the choppers flew so many hazardous missions that extraordinary valor became an everyday occurrence. It took a truly outstanding display of heroism for a chopper pilot to earn a Medal of Honor.

STEPHEN W. PLESS

The UH-1E helicopter (the famed "Huey") piloted by Marine Captain *Stephen W. Pless* on August 19, 1967, was the chase helicopter for an emergency medevac mission. Pless was airborne over southern Quang Ngai Province when his radio crackled with another emergency call: Four soldiers were stranded on the beach north of Duc Pho and were about to be overrun by a large VC force. Unless they were rescued soon, they had no hope of surviving.

With a quick glance at his co-pilot, Captain Rupert E. Fairchild, Jr., Pless broke off from his mission and turned his Huey toward Duc Pho.

Born in Newnan, Georgia, on September 6, 1939, Pless enlisted in the Marine Corps while attending Georgia Military Academy at College Park, Georgia, in 1956. Three years later he was accepted for flight training, earning his wings on April 20, 1960.

Over the next several years he served in a variety of positions, including a tour in Vietnam in 1962. In 1966 he returned to Vietnam to serve as Air Advisor to the Republic of Korea Marine Brigade at Chu Lai. In March 1967 he was transferred to Marine Observation Squadron 6, Marine Air Group 36, as the Assistant Operations Officer.

When Pless brought his chopper over the battleground north of Duc Pho he saw about fifty VC in the open; some were bayoneting and beating the grunts. He flew the chopper in low, guns pounding away. The .50-caliber rounds and rockets killed and wounded a score of VC and sent the others scurrying for cover. Pless came in so low the Huey repeatedly flew through debris thrown up by rocket explosions.

Pless ignored the small-arms fire ripping through his thin-skinned Huey and deliberately set the machine down between the wounded men and the enemy. The two crewmen, Gunnery Sgt. Leroy N. Paulson and Lance Corporal John G. Phelps, leaped from the chopper and raced through enemy fire to the casualties.

Pless then hovered the Huey, sending streams of machine gun fire into the nearby treeline, keeping the VC pinned down. A few did sneak through, however. Fairchild shot three within ten feet of the chopper before he left the ship to help load the wounded.

While Pless skillfully maneuvered the Huey and kept a steady hail of fire directed at the enemy, the three crewmen pulled the wounded soldiers on board. Pless headed the dangerously overloaded Huey out to sea, away from the murderous fire. Four times the chopper settled on the water. Four times Pless nursed the machine back into the air while the crew tossed out all unnecessary equipment. At last, the Huey became airborne and limped back to Chu Lai.

Besides being credited with rescuing his countrymen, twenty VC dead were confirmed for Pless, with another forty as probables. The three crew members were each awarded the Navy Cross. Pless received the Medal of Honor from President Johnson on January 16, 1969.

Promoted to major in November 1967 Pless was considered a sharp, up-and-coming young Marine officer when tragedy struck. On July 20, 1969, his motorcycle plunged off an open drawbridge into Santa Rosa Sound, which separates Pensacola from Pensacola Beach, Florida. His body was fished from the water the next day.

Buried at Barrancas National Cemetery in Pensacola, Pless left a widow and three children.

WILLIAM T. PERKINS

Marine Corps combat photographer Corporal *William T. Perkins* was covering the action of Company C, 1st Battalion, 1st Marines, 1st Marine Division during Operation Medina in the rug-

ged Hai Lang National Forest in southern Quang Tri Province
on October 12, 1967. While waiting at the company command
post for medevac choppers to carry the wounded out from an
earlier brush with the VC the twenty-year-old saw an enemy
grenade land behind the CO. Yelling, "Grenade!" he threw himself on the deadly missile. The explosion killed him.

Perkins is the only combat photographer to earn the Medal
of Honor.

WEBSTER ANDERSON

In the spring of 1967 the elite 1st Brigade of the 101st Airborne
Division was assigned to Task Force Oregon. Organized around
three separate Army brigades (the others included the 196th Infantry and the 3rd Brigade of the 25th Infantry Division), Oregon
was sent into VC-dominated Quang Ngai Province to relieve
Marine units for duty along the DMZ.

Throughout the summer and fall of 1967 Oregon searched
for the 2nd VC Regiment, the primary opponent in the province.
A typical day for Oregon involved light combat action on recon
patrols. On occasion, though, the VC went on the offensive.

At 3:00 A.M. on October 15, 1967, the VC hit Battery A,
2nd Battalion, 320th Artillery (Airborne) at its fire support base
near the coastal city of Tam Ky in Quang Tin Province. The
intensity of the attack stunned the cannoneers. That the battery
did not suffer more was due to the valor of a thirty-four-year-old
staff sergeant from Winnsboro, South Carolina.

Webster Anderson reacted to the furious attack by mounting
the exposed parapet of his howitzer position to direct point-blank
cannon fire on the VC hordes. Two enemy grenades destroyed
his legs, but Anderson never faltered. Despite his crippling injuries and the excruciating pain, Anderson remained in position
to direct the fire of his crew. When an enemy grenade landed
near a wounded comrade, Anderson picked it up and attempted
to throw it out of the position. It exploded before Anderson could
toss it away, carrying away his right hand. Although only partly

conscious, Anderson continued to inspire his men until the attack ended. Only then would he consent to evacuation.

The fourteen-year veteran spent nearly a year recuperating from his grievous injuries. On November 24, 1969, he stood proudly on two artificial legs while President Richard M. Nixon draped the Medal of Honor around his neck.

The Americal Division was formed on September 25, 1967, from the remnants of Task Force Oregon after the 1st Brigade of the 101st was released and the 3rd Brigade of the 25th was re-designated the 3rd Brigade of the 4th Infantry Division (the 4th's 3rd Brigade went to the 25th in the swap). The Americal had its roots in World War II, when it was originally activated on New Caledonia by General Douglas MacArthur for use alongside the 1st Marine Division on Guadalcanal. During its fifteen-hundred-plus days in Vietnam the Americal operated in the 1st Corps area, primarily in Quang Nam and Quang Tri Provinces.

JAMES TAYLOR

The first Medal of Honor recipient from the Americal was 1st Lieutenant *James Taylor,* a twenty-nine-year-old Californian. When enemy forces hit his troop of armored personnel carriers (APCs) from Troop B, 1st Cavalry on November 9, 1967, west of Que Son in Quang Tin Province, Taylor braved heavy enemy fire to rescue fifteen trapped crew members from three burning APCs. He then attacked and killed three NVA manning a machine gun, which had been pouring deadly fire on his men.

The 25th Infantry Division aggressively pursued the VC northwest of Saigon throughout 1967. Although the combat never reached the intensity experienced by the division during Operation Junction City, the action was often sharp.

RILEY L. PITTS

Born in Falles, Oklahoma, on October 15, 1937, *Riley L. Pitts* grew up in Oklahoma City. Even though the prospects for a successful Army career did not look good for a young black man in 1960, Pitts enlisted after graduating from the University of Wichita, Wichita, Kansas, that same year. After completing the tough infantry OCS course at Fort Benning, Georgia, Pitts was commissioned a second lieutenant in February 1961. Before being assigned to the 25th Infantry Division's 2nd Battalion, 27th Infantry in December 1966, Pitts served two years in France.

Like most officers in Vietnam, Pitts's combat command time was limited to six months. He spent his first six months in Vietnam as an administrative officer processing new arrivals into the division. He kept putting in for reassignment to a rifle company but there were more infantry officers available than there were companies.

When Pitts finally took over Company C he proved himself to be a tough, capable, and fair commander. Never one to ask his men to do something he would not, Pitts earned a Silver Star and Bronze Star in his first three months in combat. His heroism peaked on October 31, 1967, during an air assault near Ap Dong in Tay Ninh Province.

The LZ was cold when the unarmed Hueys dropped Company C into the jungle. No sooner had the slicks left than the VC opened up with heavy automatic weapons fire. It was a favorite ambush technique for the VC.

Hastily organizing his men, Pitts overran the VC position, personally killing the gun's crew. Ordered to head north to aid another company under attack by a strong enemy force, Pitts started his company through the jungle. They had not proceeded very far when they were hit from three sides. Pitts dove for cover. Two of the four enemy positions were less than fifteen meters away. He couldn't maneuver the company due to the heavy volume of fire; instead, he took it upon himself to wipe out the bunkers.

While his small command group provided covering fire he tried to knock out one enemy bunker with his M-16. When that didn't work Pitts grabbed a Chinese grenade carried by one of his men and stood up to toss it at the enemy bunker.

To the horror of those watching the grenade rebounded off a tree branch and fell back into the command group. Without hesitation Pitts dropped on it, intent on saving his men.

As he lay there in the jungle, bullets crashing overhead, his men diving for cover, the seconds passed like hours. After what seemed like forever, Pitts realized the grenade was a dud. With a weak laugh he rolled aside, picked up the grenade and tossed it away.

Unable to spare any time to reflect on his release from sure death, Pitts ordered his company to fall back so that he could call in artillery support. When the shells stopped falling, the determined young officer led the company back into battle. He died at the head of his men, urging them on even as he collapsed from multiple gunshot wounds.

Pitts's recommendation for the Medal of Honor worked its way through channels, but some reviewers opposed the award. After all, the grenade had not detonated. In the end, Pitts's supporters won. The fact that the grenade was a dud, they argued, lessened not one bit Pitts's deliberate willingness to sacrifice his own life to save his men. When President Johnson presented Pitts's widow and two children with the posthumous Medal of Honor on October 10, 1968, it was the first ever awarded under such circumstances. It would not be the last.

JOHN A. BARNES

The heaviest fighting in 1967 occurred around the small Central Highlands town of Dak To in Kontum Province about 280 miles north of Saigon, near the Cambodian border. The sparring between the two forces began in June when the 24th NVA Regiment chewed up a company of the 173rd Airborne Brigade's 503rd Infantry. Seventy-six paratroopers died during the two-day fight. The rest of the 173rd and the 3rd Brigade of the 1st Cavalry Division moved into the province to hunt down the NVA.

For the rest of the summer the grunts patrolled the mountainous regions of western Kontum Province. Clashes with the NVA were routine affairs. By the end of October they became more frequent and more intense. On November 4, a battalion from the 4th Infantry Division ran into tough resistance north of Dak To. Forty air strikes were needed to drive the enemy off. Two days later the 4th Battalion, 503rd Infantry (Airborne) battled the NVA on Hill 832 west of Dak To. American losses were heavy.

On November 11, Company C, 1st Battalion, 503rd Infantry under Captain Thomas McElwain patrolled near Hill 823. The presence of the enemy was sensed throughout the day, but none were seen. That night the company, nicknamed Task Force Black, dug deep foxholes in a bamboo grove on a hilltop. Beneath them the red and green lights the NVA used to move troops were visible all through the night.

The following morning McElwain led his company out on a patrol. After traveling but two hundred meters he sensed they were in the midst of the enemy. He ordered his men to open fire. The return barrage from the NVA drove the paratroopers into a tight perimeter. In a few minutes the company was completely surrounded. With little cover and no time to dig foxholes, dozens of men were cut down. The enemy fire slashed across the hillside position like a well-honed scythe.

When two men manning a machine gun were shot down the enemy might have breached the perimeter were it not for twenty-two-year-old PFC *John A. Barnes,* a resident of Dedham, Massachusetts. Serving his seventeenth month in Vietnam, Barnes dashed across the bullet-swept ground, dropped behind the M-60, and opened fire. He killed nine NVA and brought a lull to the battlefield. He was searching for more ammo when he observed an enemy grenade land among several wounded paratroopers. Without thinking of the brutal consequences, he dropped on the grenade as it exploded. His self-sacrifice saved the lives of six men.

Later that afternoon the isolated company was relieved when a sister company broke through enemy lines. The NVA melted back into the jungle. Twenty men from Company C died, 154 were wounded.

On November 18, the 173rd's commander, Brigadier General Leo Scheiter, learned that the NVA 174th Regiment occupied Hill 875, twenty miles southwest of Dak To (on the Cambodian border). He ordered the 2nd Battalion, 503rd Infantry to dislodge them.

The next day Companies C and D started up Hill 875 following artillery and air strikes. Company A protected the rear. At 10:30 A.M., as the two lead companies picked their way gingerly through the vegetation and thick tree trunks mangled by the bombardment, the enemy cut loose. From dozens of concealed bunkers the NVA felled the young American soldiers. Air strikes were called in, but they had little effect. The enemy was too well dug-in.

In the meantime, Company A to the rear also came under attack.

CARLOS J. LOZADA

A three-man squad under Specialist Four James Kelley set up thirty-five meters downhill from Company A to alert the company to any movement to its rear. Over the sounds of gunfire above them the men could hear the NVA coming toward them but the thick foliage prevented any visual contact.

Suddenly, twenty-one-year-old *Carlos J. Lozada* yelled, "Here they come, Kelley!" and started firing bursts from his M-60. His bullets cut down some of the NVA and alerted the rest of the company to the danger.

Kelley joined Lozada and Specialist Four John Steer in sending fire down the hill, but the enemy kept coming.

"Fall back, fall back," Kelley ordered. The enemy attack was quickly overwhelming his small force.

Lozada ignored the order. With the NVA moving in on three

sides Lozada kept up a steady and accurate fire. No less than twenty NVA fell under his fire.

Kelley again called for Lozada to fall back. This time Lozada picked up his M-60, moved a few meters uphill, then dropped behind a fallen tree before opening up on the enemy again.

At this time, the NVA opened up an attack on Company A's west flank. The company was ordered forward to link up with Companies C and D.

Lozada, born in Puerto Rico but raised in New York City, must have realized if he gave up his position the withdrawal of the company would be jeopardized. He elected to stay behind.

"Get out of here," he yelled to Kelley and Steer. "I can handle them." He fired quick bursts at the fleeing NVA.

Just as Kelley started up the trail, his M-16 jammed. As he knelt down to clear the cartridge, Lozada jumped into the middle of the trail, firing his M-60 from the hip, covering Kelley.

Steer joined Kelley, firing downhill alongside Lozada. Lozada continued urging his buddies up the hill, all the time keeping up a steady fire on the NVA.

Just as Kelley and Steer were joined by a relief squad, Lozada ran out of ammo. He turned and raced up the trail, pleased with the knowledge he had saved lives. Lozada had reached the others when an AK-47 round hit him in the head. He died instantly. He would never see his six-month-old daughter back in New York City. His widow accepted his posthumous Medal of Honor on November 18, 1969.

The battle for Hill 875 raged for four more days. That first evening, while the beleaguered defenders hid in hastily dug foxholes, an Air Force jet accidentally dropped a 500-lb. bomb directly on the command group, killing more than thirty troopers and wounding forty-five more.

It took two days before a unit from the 503rd's 4th Battalion fought through the NVA to reach their buddies. Later that night two more airborne companies made it into the lines, bringing critically needed supplies. At last the Americans were able to go on the offensive. They attacked outward from their perimeter, reaching the summit of Hill 875 five days after they'd started up.

In all, the two battalions sustained more than 550 casualties, including 158 dead. Enemy fatalities were estimated at 300.

Even while the battle of Dak To raged, General Westmoreland felt optimistic enough to pay another visit to Washington. When he addressed assembled reporters who met his jet at Washington's National Airport, Westmoreland described the Vietnam situation as "very, very encouraging. I have never been more encouraged in my four years in Vietnam."

President Johnson asked Westmoreland back to Washington in response to the massive anti-war rally held at the Pentagon on October 21–23. More than fifty thousand people participated in the "Stop the Draft" program. The demonstrators peacefully marched to the Pentagon where they held a rally protesting the war. To protect the military bastion the Defense Department flew in ten thousand 82nd Airborne Division troopers from Fort Bragg, North Carolina. Considering the potential for trouble, it turned out to be a peaceful gathering.

General Westmoreland exuded confidence in all his meetings with the press. Appearing on the TV program "Meet the Press," Westmoreland told the audience, "The United States may be able to start withdrawing its troops from South Vietnam in two years or less."

On November 21, Westmoreland told the National Press Club, "We are making progress . . . we have reached an important point where the end begins to come into view."

The situation in Vietnam, as far as President Johnson and his advisors were concerned, was very positive. Even though U.S. forces had been hit hard at Dak To, the administration declared the contest a victory.

While General Westmoreland met with members of the press back in the States, the 1st Cavalry Division pursued the enemy in Binh Dinh Province. Throughout late 1967 a number of brief but violent firefights erupted on the Bong Son Plain. In early December elements of the 9th Cavalry engaged NVA forces near the coastal village of Tam Quan. For several days the fighting raged around Tam Quan and Dai Dong. When the mechanized infantry of the 1st Battalion, 50th Infantry found the fight too tough, reinforcements from the 12th Cavalry's 1st Battalion were called in.

ALLEN J. LYNCH

A year after he joined the Army in November 1964 *Allen J. Lynch* was transferred to Berlin, Germany. It was a cushy assignment, with regular hours and plenty of activities to fill the free time. He could have remained in Germany, safe from the horrors of the growing war in Vietnam, but that wasn't Lynch's style. It was important to him to be involved in the war. And he wanted to see if he could handle combat.

After a forty-five-day leave at home in the south Chicago suburb of Dolton, Specialist Four Lynch reported to Company D, 1st Battalion, 12th Cavalry in June 1967 for duty as a radio-telephone operator (RTO).

By the time Lynch spent six months in combat with the 12th Cavalry, few doubts remained in his mind about his ability to stand up under combat conditions. Any that did were erased forever on December 15, 1967, when Lynch's battalion was sent to Dai Dong to reinforce the worn 50th Infantry.

Company D conducted a sweep near the small village of My An–2. Bordered by rice paddies, bamboo thickets, sugarcane fields, and thick hedgerows, this area of the Bong Son River lowlands crawled with VC soldiers from the 9th VC Regiment. The two point-men for the company were entering a bamboo grove when rifle fire brought down both men. Seconds later, machine-gun fire pinned down the rest of the company, leaving the casualties about fifty meters away across an open field.

Unwilling to leave his wounded buddies at the mercy of the enemy, Lynch dashed out across the open ground, unmindful of the heavy fire. When he reached the casualties he found one man hit in the shoulder, the other in the leg and arm. He patched them up as best he could, then pulled them to cover in a shallow ditch.

While the three men returned the enemy's fire, another grunt tried to reach their isolated position. The enemy cut him down half way to his destination. Lynch rushed out and brought him in.

In pain, but able to fight, the fourth man aided Lynch in holding back enemy probes.

As darkness fell, men from the company called over to Lynch, "Who's over there?"

Lynch shouted back, "There's four of us. Three are wounded." He repeated the words several times but couldn't seem to make them understand his situation. Silently, he watched the company pull out of the village leaving him alone with his three wounded buddies.

For the next two hours Lynch, helped by the three casualties, repulsed several determined enemy movements on his position. A short while later members of his company returned to the village and called for Lynch to run to them while they provided covering fire. He refused. Without him the others would be at the mercy of the enemy.

A few minutes later jets roared in from the east, spraying machine gun rounds, bombs, and napalm on the tree line where the VC hid. Only meters from the carnage, Lynch prayed that the pilots were accurate.

When the jets pulled away an eerie quiet descended on the battlefield. No sound, friendly or hostile, could be heard. Lynch whispered to his buddies, "You guys stay here. I'll go see what's happening."

Alone, Lynch reconnoitered the area around him but found no sign of the enemy. He moved to the small cluster of hootches comprising My An-2, checked each one and the surrounding bush but still found no sign of the VC. Confident the enemy had left the field, Lynch hastened back to the casualties. One at a time he helped the wounded to the village. He left them well-armed under a wide tree while he went in search of a friendly unit.

After following the tracks of an APC for a few hundred meters Lynch found his comrades. They had not expected to see him alive again. Under his direction the three wounded were evacuated.

Lynch was discharged in April 1969. One year later he put his uniform back on to receive the Medal of Honor from President Nixon in White House ceremonies.

Because of his concern over the problems facing Vietnam veterans, Lynch has spent his postwar years as a counselor and advisor for a number of veterans assistance organizations.

CHAPTER
SIX

Tet:
The Turning Point

M ACV started 1968 in a very optimistic mood. General Westmoreland had over four-hundred thousand soldiers and marines at his command to carry out his war of attrition. The multibattalion operations used against enemy strongholds seemed to be working. The body counts faithfully reported every week clearly showed the U.S. ahead.

In nearly every corner of South Vietnam, U.S. troops aggressively went after the NVA/VC. Among the major efforts: the 25th Division's Operation Yellowstone in Tay Ninh Province; the 9th Division's combination with Navy Task Force 117 to beat back the VC in the northern half of the Delta region; and, the 1st Infantry Division's successful efforts to finally reopen Route 13 through War Zone D to Quan Loi.

There were threats against the 26th Marines garrisoning the strategic Khe Sanh base in western Quang Tri Province, but Westmoreland was prepared for that. He shifted the 1st Cavalry Division to the Phu Bai early in January. If the NVA now attacked Khe Sanh, Westmoreland had over half his maneuver battalions in I Corps ready to repulse them.

In spite of the optimistic offensive operations the enemy still initiated much of the ground action.

JERRY W. WICKAM

On January 6, 1968, a heavy barrage of rocket and small arms fire hit Troop F of the 11th Armored Cavalry Regiment's 2nd Squadron while it patrolled south of Loc Ninh in Binh Long Province. At the first sign of trouble, twenty-five-year-old Corporal *Jerry W. Wickam* of Leaf River, Illinois, left his armored vehicle to destroy two enemy bunkers, killing three VC and capturing another in his vicious one-man assault. After an airstrike on the enemy positions, Wickam voluntarily led a patrol back into the area. Attacked again, he destroyed a third bunker and killed two more VC before he was mortally wounded.

That same day, up north at Chu Lai (on the South China Sea in Quang Tin Province), a chopper pilot earned another Medal of Honor for a series of daring rescue operations.

PATRICK H. BRADY

If it hadn't been for a university requirement mandating ROTC participation *Pat Brady* might not have pursued a military career. Brady was born October 1, 1936, in Philip, South Dakota; his parents brought him to Seattle, Washington, when he was three years old. When he enrolled at Seattle University in 1955 to be near his girlfriend, he was quite upset to find out he had to join the ROTC.

"I couldn't believe it," he later said. "Boy, how I hated it. I said, 'This is Communistic!' But they forced me to join."

Brady started out as a poor student. He would have flunked out if he hadn't married his sweetheart, Nancy Parsek. Brady's attitude changed overnight. He graduated with top honors and was voted into the student "Who's Who."

After being commissioned an Army lieutenant in 1959, Brady spent three years as a medical service officer before volunteering for flight training. He earned his wings in 1963. Brady's assignment as a medevac pilot took him to Vietnam in 1964, followed by two tours in the troubled Dominican Republic. In July 1967 he returned to Vietnam with the 54th Medical Detachment, 67th Medical Group, 44th Medical Brigade. By the time he departed Vietnam one year later he had flown over three thousand combat missions and received credit for rescuing over five thousand people. More than fifty of these came on one memorable January day.

In a fogbound valley outside Chu Lai, two seriously

wounded South Vietnamese soldiers desperately needed evacuation. Seven rescue attempts had been made on January 5, but the fog forced the choppers back. The next day Brady volunteered to bring the men out.

Descending below the grey fog, he hovered slowly along a trail using the chopper's rotor-wash to blow away the fog. The flight took incredible flying skills and nerves of steel and Brady had them. He soon found the friendly position. Seconds later the casualties were aboard and Brady lifted his Huey up through the fog.

Soon after delivering those men to an evac hospital, Brady learned of more casualties. A company of the 198th Infantry Brigade suffered sixty wounded during a firefight with the NVA in a fog-shrouded section of Hiep Duc Valley. One dust-off chopper had already been shot down. Brady ignored the danger to race to the scene.

He found a hole in the fog, then dropped down to treetop level to follow a stream to the battleground. Oblivious to heavy enemy fire from as close as fifty meters, Brady brought his chopper in for a load of wounded. With rounds slamming into his craft he made the perilous journey back up the stream.

Three more times Brady made the hazardous trip. Altogether, his fearlessness saved thirty-nine men.

Later, on his third separate rescue mission that day, enemy fire hit Brady's chopper so badly he could barely keep it under control. Lesser men might have called it a day then, but not Brady. He went in anyway and pulled out six casualties. He dropped them at the hospital then picked up a new chopper.

Before the day ended Brady rescued wounded soldiers from two more locations and acquired a third chopper. The ground crews later counted over four hundred bullet holes in the three Hueys he used.

Brady's actions that day were remarkable by anyone's standards but his own. "I had a lot worse days," he said. The Army was sufficiently impressed to recommend him for the Medal of Honor. President Nixon presented it to him on October 9, 1969, while Brady's wife and their four children watched. Brady remained in the Army, receiving his brigadier general's star in 1985.

WILLIAM D. PORT

A divorce sent *William D. Port* of Petersburg, Pennsylvania to Vietnam. The draft wouldn't touch you if you were married and had children. As it was, Port's ex-wife got their two children and the Army got Bill Port. He was inducted in March 1967, six months short of his twenty-sixth birthday.

Following basic training at Fort Benning, Georgia, Port went to Vietnam and Company C, 5th Battalion, 7th Cavalry, 1st Cavalry Division. On January 12, 1968, Port's company battled superior enemy forces in the Que Son Valley of Quang Tin Province. His platoon gave ground under heavy fire. Although wounded in the hand during this movement, Port still helped a more seriously wounded soldier to safety. Later, huddled together with three other casualties, Port saved their lives by covering an enemy grenade with his own body, sustaining severe injuries in the head, chest, arms, and legs.

For two-and-one-half hours the platoon medic worked on Port, but then the VC forced the platoon to retreat. Port, whom the medic reported as dead, was left behind. When the platoon retook the area his body could not be found. The Army carried him as missing in action for four months before changing his status to presumed dead.

But Port was not dead. Grievously wounded but still alive, Port had been taken prisoner by the VC. They treated him at their field hospital for a month before releasing him to a POW camp deep in the jungle.

Never fully recovered from his shattering wounds, Port languished in the primitive camp for ten months before he died on November 27, 1968. In December 1969 the Army listed Port as dead and notified his family for the first time that he had been held prisoner. Not until the POWs came home in 1973 were full details of Port's death and burial in the jungle reported to the family.

In the meantime, Port's posthumous Medal of Honor was approved and presented to his son and daughter by President Nixon on August 6, 1970.

As the years passed the family gave up hope that Port's remains would be found. Then, in August 1985, a team of American investigators, working with a more liberal Vietnamese government, was led to a common gravesite holding the remains of nine American POWs. In October of that year Port's remains were positively identified as one of the nine.

Following funeral services in his hometown, William D. Port was interred in Arlington National Cemetery. He was the last Medal of Honor hero to come home from Vietnam.

For several months beginning in November 1967 the U.S. intelligence network had received information about a pending major North Vietnamese offensive. The evidence led General Westmoreland to conclude the enemy intended to overrun the combat base at Khe Sanh. Accordingly, he shifted his forces northward. He was well-prepared for an NVA attack against the marines holding the base.

On January 31, 1968, in what came to be known as the Tet Offensive, Viet Cong and NVA units struck nearly every major city, thirty provincial capitals, and scores of other towns and villages throughout South Vietnam. Coming on the heels of General Westmoreland's earlier pronouncement of imminent victory, the intensity and ferocity of the attacks stunned the American high command and the American public. The Tet Offensive would prove to be the watershed of American involvement in Vietnam, but first the enemy had to be thrown back.

DREW D. DIX

Two heavily armed VC battalions attacked Chau Phu, the capital of Chau Doc province, completely breaking down the defenses of the city. Special Forces Staff Sgt. *Drew D. Dix,* on the MACV advisory staff for the IV Corps, is credited with single-handedly driving the VC out.

For two days, January 31 and February 1, Dix led repeated attacks against enemy strong points in the city. Leading by personal example, Dix continually inspired his ARVN troops to new heights of heroism. In fierce street fighting Dix knocked out position after position. The Pueblo, Colorado resident captured over twenty VC, killed forty, and rescued no less than twenty U.S. and free world civilians from imprisonment.

EUGENE ASHLEY

Although more than thirty thousand North Vietnamese regulars did ring the Marine base at Khe Sanh the expected major ground attack never materialized. A heavily armed NVA force did move against the Special Forces camp at Lang Vei, just a few miles southwest of Khe Sanh. Using armor for the first time in the war, the NVA overran the small camp, sending the Americans and their Civilian Irregular Defense Group (CIDG) troops reeling.

Sgt. First Class *Eugene Ashley* rallied a group of CIDG survivors and four times led them back against the NVA. Four times the gallant sergeant and his small band were repulsed. Ashley, a thirty-six-year-old from New York City, gathered up the few remaining soldiers for a fifth attack. Halfway to the objective he died at the head of his men. When he fell, the counterattack collapsed. The CIDG fled in terror to Khe Sanh.

In spite of the fact that over one hundred cities were attacked on January 31, for America the epitome of the Tet Offensive was the enemy capture of Hué and the battle for its freedom. The third largest city in South Vietnam and the capital of Thua Thien Province, Hué had great cultural and religious symbolism for the nation. Holding it for even a short period of time would have given the enemy a great propaganda victory. They held it for nearly six weeks. It took twenty-one American and ARVN battalions to pry out the eight enemy battalions entrenched in Hué. Four Americans earned Medals of Honor during the bitter fighting.

FREDERICK E. FERGUSON

On the first day of the attack, Huey pilot *Frederick E. Ferguson,* a chief warrant officer from Phoenix, Arizona, serving with Company C, 227th Aviation Battalion, 1st Cavalry Division, flew low over the city's Perfume River under enemy anti-aircraft fire to rescue the crew of a downed chopper. After landing in the midst of a mortar barrage, Ferguson loaded the five crewmen aboard his craft, then once more flew through the gauntlet of fire along the river. Through his tenacity and courage everyone safely reached friendly territory.

ALFREDO GONZALES

Twenty-one-year-old Sgt. *Alfredo Gonzales,* from Edinburg, Texas, served with the first reaction force sent by the Marines to battle the enemy in Hué. The Marine command had no idea of the magnitude of the enemy involvement in the city. The unit, Company A, 1st Battalion, 1st Marines, 1st Marine Division, was completely overwhelmed by superior enemy forces.

From the morning of January 31, until he was killed on February 4, Gonzales repeatedly exposed himself to danger to rescue wounded buddies and assault enemy positions. Even though seriously wounded on February 3, Gonzales remained in the forefront of the attack. The next day he single-handedly assaulted a series of NVA bunkers. After knocking out a rocket position he was moving toward another when he fell, mortally wounded.

CLIFFORD C. SIMS

Elements of the 101st Airborne Division's 501st Infantry moved into positions outside of Hué to block the escape of enemy forces routed from the city. On February 21, 1968, Staff Sgt. *Clifford C. Sims,* Company D, 2nd Battalion, a twenty-five-year-old career soldier from Port St. Joe, Florida, led his squad into a woodline where other company units lay pinned down. Repeatedly displaying tremendous courage in daring assaults on enemy strongpoints, Sims died when he threw himself on a booby-trap as it exploded. Sims's self-sacrifice saved his squad members from certain death.

During the same fight another career soldier from Sims's company earned a Medal of Honor.

JOE R. HOOPER

After a three year tour in the Navy, *Joe R. Hooper* enlisted in the Army in 1960. Born in South Carolina in 1939 and raised in rural Moses Lake, Washington, Hooper volunteered for airborne assignment upon completion of basic training. He spent the next six years in a variety of airborne units, where he gained a reputation as a tough-as-nails NCO. Several times he requested transfer to Vietnam, but it wasn't until he joined the 501st Airborne Infantry at Fort Campbell, Kentucky, that he knew for sure he was going overseas. Deployment of the 501st to Vietnam was completed just before Christmas of 1967.

The enemy unit that pinned down Company D on the morning of February 21 occupied a series of well-protected bunkers along a river bank a few miles outside of Hué. The company commander requested an airstrike. It was denied; the planes were too busy in Hué.

As rockets, machine guns, and small-arms fire exploded along the company's line, Hooper suddenly turned to his squad. "Follow me!" he commanded.

With several men behind him, Hooper splashed through the water, taking a bunker under fire. In a few seconds he silenced it. While the rest of the company fanned out through the densely wooded area, Hooper took the time to pull several wounded men out of the line of fire. He had finished turning the last of them over to the company medics when he was shot. Instead of seeking treatment, Hooper returned to his squad.

At the forefront of the battle again, Hooper knocked out three more enemy bunkers. Seconds later he killed two NVA who had attacked and wounded the battalion chaplain while the priest was tending the wounded.

Continuing on, he blew up three houses concealing enemy snipers. He was returning to his men when a North Vietnamese officer raced toward him from behind a tree. Hooper killed him with his bayonet.

Later a machine gun pinned down his squad. Hooper flanked the weapon and killed the three gunners with a well-tossed grenade. Suddenly enemy fire erupted from four previously unseen bunkers. Wounded again, Hooper refused to stay down. He gathered up an armful of grenades and raced down a small trench behind the bunkers, tossing grenades into each one as he passed it. All four were silenced by his furious attack. A few minutes later he destroyed three more enemy emplacements.

When he learned one of his men lay wounded and trapped in a ditch, Hooper braved sniper fire to go to the man's aid. Just as he reached the position he came face-to-face with an enemy soldier. Before the NVA could raise his rifle, Hooper pulled out his .45 and shot his foe in the face. He then carried the wounded grunt to safety.

Throughout the rest of the day Hooper continued to set an inspiring example for his men. After the enemy had been driven from the area, Hooper insisted on setting his squad in position before he finally consented to having his wounds treated. Even then he refused evacuation until the following day.

Hooper spent six weeks in the hospital, then returned to the front lines. In the summer of 1968 he was honorably discharged but spent only nine months as a civilian before he reenlisted. On

March 7, 1969, President Nixon presented Hooper the Medal of Honor for his outstanding actions near Hué.

The gallant NCO went back to Vietnam in April 1970, serving with a recon unit. A year later, after finishing his second tour, Hooper received a direct commission to 2nd lieutenant.

Disappointed with the opportunities available in the postwar Army, Hooper resigned in February 1974. He worked for the Veterans Administration for several years before following an ambition to breed racehorses. He was working on his degree in animal husbandry when he died of natural causes on May 5, 1979.

JACK H. JACOBS

In the Delta provinces the U.S. 9th Infantry Division worked with the ARVN 9th Infantry Division to expel the NVA and VC from contested villages. As with all ARVN units, the American advisors worked directly alongside their South Vietnamese counterparts. Since the 9th ARVN was ranked as a weak division its American advisors often had to go to great lengths to motivate its members. That's the situation 1st Lieutenant *Jack H. Jacobs* found himself in on March 9 in Kien Phong Province.

Jacobs assumed command of an ARVN company in the 9th's 2nd Battalion, 16th Infantry, after its CO was wounded and the men started to panic. With blood flowing into his eyes from a serious head wound, the twenty-two-year-old New Jersey resident reorganized the company, rescued several wounded from exposed positions, and single-handedly drove off repeated attempts to overrun the unit. His forceful leadership helped the ARVN defeat the determined enemy.

When the two stateside brigades of the 101st Airborne Division were notified on August 2, 1967 to prepare for movement to Vietnam, they were barely more than training units for men moving on to the war zone. Just to fill the companies to a seventy-five-percent level would require over forty-five hundred men. Other units in the 3rd Army area were ordered to provide personnel to the 101st. As usual in this type of situation, unit commanders got rid of their weakest soldiers first. Some commanders in the 101st resented receiving these problem soldiers, but at least one man sought them out.

PAUL W. BUCHA

When twenty-three-year-old Army lieutenant *Paul Bucha* arrived at Fort Campbell, Kentucky in June 1967 to take command of a rifle company in the 3rd Battalion, 187th Infantry, he had already served six years in the Army but had never commanded troops. The son of an Army colonel, Bucha entered West Point after finishing high school in 1961. Before he graduated in 1965 Bucha would serve as Regimental Commander (the No. 2 position in the cadet chain-of-command), be captain of the swimming team, a member of the water polo team, an All-American swimmer, and the first recipient of the Association of Graduates Award for overall excellence.

Upon graduation from West Point Bucha was selected to attend Stanford University Graduate School of Business in Palo Alto, California, to earn his MBA. Two weeks after he received the degree he reported to Fort Campbell. He arrived there to find his unit, Company D, a company in name only. He was going to have to build it from scratch.

While other company commanders searched through personnel files to weed out disciplinary problems, Bucha welcomed such people with open arms. He said later, "I wanted people no one else wanted. I wanted to build a team; to be able to give my men a sense of belonging. I felt I could do that best by working with people who had no experience or who had had bad experiences."

Says Bucha: "I promised my people I'd do everything I could to bring them all back from Vietnam alive. But we had to work and work hard. While other companies took weekend liberty, my 'clerks and jerks,' as some called us, went on night field

119

maneuvers. I'm sure that that cohesiveness, that teamwork, helped us tremendously in Vietnam."

Bucha's brigade went to Vietnam just before Christmas 1967. Sent to War Zone C northwest of Saigon, his company was the first of the brigade to contact the enemy. "From then on," Bucha said, "we had nearly daily contact with the VC or NVA. Unlike other outfits, we were always in the field. Day after day we hunted the VC. And we found him."

Bucha's emphasis on teamwork paid off. For the first three months, despite frequent firefights with the Communists, Company D suffered no KIAs and no serious wounded. Then came March 18th.

As part of a U.S. offensive operation in Binh Duong Province after Tet, Company D landed near Phuoc Vinh on March 16, 1968. Bucha's men came under enemy fire right from the start. Over the next two days the company battled the NVA, destroying bunkers, supply caches, and an enemy base area. At the end of the third day the hot, tired infantrymen prepared to settle in for the night.

"It was just getting dark," Bucha remembers. "We were moving to a night position when we surprised an NVA battalion preparing themselves for the night. They hit us with everything they had. We tried to hold on until daylight."

Subjected to a veritable hail of heavy automatic-weapons fire, rocket propelled grenades (RPGs), Claymore mines, and small-arms fire, Bucha functioned throughout the night with one thought uppermost in his mind: to keep his promise to his men.

Even though most of the company was pinned down, Bucha moved to the most threatened positions to direct his men's fire against the NVA. When he realized that one particular machine gun was doing most of the damage to his men, Bucha low-crawled through heavy foliage to destroy it with a well-placed grenade. Wounded while returning to his company, Bucha pulled his men into a tighter perimeter when he saw the outlying squads could not repel the human wave assaults sent by the enemy.

As the battle wore on through the night, Bucha doubted his company's chances of survival. It seemed that at any minute the enemy would overwhelm his beloved men. Before his feelings of despair took over, Bucha's RTO, a new man experiencing his first combat, turned to him and said, "Sir, we're really kicking hell out of 'em, aren't we!"

The youngster's naive confidence inspired Bucha. "Yes," he answered, "I guess we are."

When enemy sappers probed his perimeter to learn its exact location Bucha radioed his platoon leaders. "Knock off the noise. I'll do the firing from here," he told them. He reasoned his single weapon, firing from a central location, would keep the NVA from learning his unit's boundaries. That would prevent them from rushing a weak spot. It would also keep his men from taking more casualties.

Bucha's brigade commander, in constant radio contact with him, told him he was sending in reinforcements. Bucha declined the help. Since the nearest units were more than one half-mile away, their movement would unnecessarily endanger more lives. Company D was on its own.

During a lull in the fighting Bucha sent a squad out to retrieve casualties. Almost instantly the NVA cut them off. Unwilling to risk more wounded, Bucha radioed the squad members to hug the dirt while he called in artillery around their position. It was risky, but it had to be done.

A few hours before daybreak Bucha called in medevac choppers to pull out his casualties. Completely ignoring the fire from enemy snipers and unwilling to risk the lives of any of his men, Bucha moved into a clearing where he used flashlights to direct the choppers down. Three were needed to carry away the wounded.

At daybreak the enemy broke contact, allowing Bucha to recover the dead and wounded members of his cut-off squad. His company had suffered its first killed in action, eleven in total, fifty-four more were wounded. Without the spirit of teamwork instilled in the company members by Bucha it would have been worse.

Bucha spent two more months in the field before being rotated to a staff position in brigade headquarters. In November

1968 he returned home. Following a six-month course at Fort Knox, Kentucky, Bucha was assigned to West Point as an instructor in the Social Services department. He was serving in that capacity when he received word he had been awarded the Medal of Honor.

"I thought a mistake had been made and I wanted to straighten it out," he recalls. "I just didn't think there was anything unusual about my actions that night."

Bucha tried to reach an officer in the Pentagon but a senior NCO in his office cut him off. "Sir, with all due respect, your men put you in for that medal. It's the highest symbol of respect they could give you. Don't disappoint them."

Bucha didn't. He accepted his award from President Nixon on May 14, 1970. In his view he holds the Medal on behalf of his company. "I am as proud of them as I am of the Medal," he says. "I feel I accepted the award more for them than myself."

Further honors awaited Bucha. In recognition of his military accomplishments and his efforts to establish a job placement program at West Point for civilian ex-drug addicts, Bucha joined such notables as entertainer Elvis Presley and Presidential Press Secretary Ronald Zeigler as one of the Jaycee's Ten Outstanding Young Men of 1971. He was the youngest so honored and the only military man on the list.

A desire to attend law school so that he could aid returning Vietnam veterans led Bucha to resign his commission in August 1972. He was prepared to enter Harvard when he met Texas businessman H. Ross Perot.

Perot offered Bucha a job running his fledgling computer programming business in Europe. Bucha jumped at the chance. For the next six years he lived abroad, developing and overseeing the growth of Perot's business from nothing to one producing millions of dollars in annual revenue.

In 1980 Bucha started his own international marketing consulting firm. Today, a millionaire several times over, he frequently reflects on the events that brought him the country's highest award for valor: "I think medals are often awarded for actions one gets involved in which, if he had done a better job to begin with, wouldn't have resulted in anyone being called a hero or anyone being hurt."

The U.S. military considered the Tet Offensive a resounding defeat for the enemy. In some ways they were correct. The Viet Cong suffered such severe losses they never again posed a serious threat in South Vietnam. And none of the attacking forces managed to secure even one military objective.

Regardless of the military losses, Tet was a definite political victory for North Vietnam. Even the most diehard supporters of U.S. war policy began expressing doubts about her ability to win the war.

The administration's advocates themselves expressed shock when General Westmoreland asked for two-hundred-and-six thousand more troops on March 10. Just four months previously he had all but announced a victory.

America's efforts in South Vietnam stood at a crossroads.

President Johnson announced a halt to the bombing of North Vietnam on March 31. He further startled the nation by announcing he would not seek another term as president. General Westmoreland would get some of his requested reinforcements, but nowhere near the amount for which he had asked.

The Joint Chiefs of Staff cabled Westmoreland on April 16, ordering him to begin shifting more of the burden of war to South Vietnam. The term "Vietnamization" would not be coined by Defense Secretary Melvin Laird for nearly a year, but the process had already begun.

The presidential decision to halt the bombing of North Vietnam led to the commencement of peace talks in Paris on May 10, 1968. Five more years of tough combat faced American troops, though, before the negotiations finally brought peace.

Despite political assassinations, student riots, a bitter presidential campaign, and dwindling support for their sacrifices, young men continued to battle the enemy in South Vietnam.

As part of General Westmoreland's post-Tet counter-offensive the 1st Cavalry Division went into the rugged A Shau Valley in western Thua Thien Province. Literally untouched by U.S. troops since 1966, except for Special Forces operations, this remote area harbored not only NVA units but was liberally sprinkled with anti-aircraft guns. Two battalions of the 7th Cavalry were air-assaulted (brought by chopper) into northern A Shau Valley on April 19. For the next five days, under dense fog and intermittent thundershowers, the cavalrymen sparred with the NVA. A brisk firefight occurred on April 26, when Company D of the 7th's 5th Battalion bumped into a retreating NVA battalion. It was an indecisive part of the overall battle, but it brought a Medal of Honor to a young first lieutenant.

JAMES M. SPRAYBERRY

Aboard the slicks (unarmed choppers) bearing the men of the 7th Cavalry's 5th Battalion into the LZ near the Chaine Annamitique mountains on the Laotian border was twenty-year-old 1st Lieutenant *James M. Sprayberry*. Wounded in the fighting in Binh Dinh Province in January, he'd only recently rejoined his company.

A native of Sylacauga, Alabama, Sprayberry enlisted in April 1966 after spending a year at the local junior college. "I was bored with school," Sprayberry explains. "I was looking for some excitement. And I was tired of being a pacifist."

He completed basic training at Fort Benning, Georgia, then Advanced Infantry Training at Fort Jackson, South Carolina, before entering armor OCS at Fort Knox, Kentucky. He was commissioned in January 1967. Then he went back to Fort Benning before going to the 7th Cavalry in Vietnam in November 1967.

Even though he was as young as or younger than most members of his platoon, Sprayberry quickly earned their respect. He was a tough but fair officer, who never needlessly risked a life.

Company D spent the first four days of Operation Delaware marching through monsoon rains in pursuit of the elusive foe.

Signs of the NVA were everywhere. The troopers destroyed tons of equipment and supplies found in caves dotting the craggy hills.

A surprising discovery was hundreds of pounds of heroin found neatly stacked on pallets in one cave. "That explained why many of the NVA we encountered would keep on coming after being shot repeatedly," Sprayberry said.

On April 24, Sprayberry celebrated his 21st birthday. After a brief party and congratulations from his men they went back to the war. Late the next day the CO, Captain Frank Lambert, took his command group and the 1st Platoon on a patrol down a thickly vegetated finger of a steep mountain. Lambert was looking for a main supply road used by the NVA.

What Lambert didn't know was the NVA were retreating from other 7th Cavalry units further down the road. Lambert ran smack into them. They pinned him down near the end of the finger. Wounded troops started to pile up.

At a medevac pad three hundred meters east of the stranded platoon, Sprayberry sprang into action. He led his platoon forward, hoping to rescue the others. Vicious enemy automatic-weapons fire drove him back. He had only one option left.

"I figured the only way to save the men was to go for them after dark," Sprayberry recalls. "I asked for volunteers to go with me."

Every man in the platoon offered to go. He picked ten. Around 8:00 P.M. he loaded up with grenades and led his rescue party down the mountain.

"It was pitch dark," Sprayberry said. "We moved slowly down the trail. Cover was scarce because of all the recent bombing. I knew the enemy was out there, I just didn't know where."

The NVA found him. Tongues of fire spat from a machine gun, searching for the Americans. Sprayberry moved his men to cover, then crawled towards the bunker. From fifteen meters away he tossed a grenade. The firing stopped.

The rescue party continued forward. A number of one-man spider-holes were encountered. Sprayberry single-handedly destroyed them with grenades.

As he drew closer to the site of the surrounded platoon, Sprayberry send some of his men to bring in scattered U.S. soldiers. "The soldiers were hiding all through the area. In the dark they didn't know if we were friend or foe, so it took a good deal of courage for my troopers to move into the dark."

Some groups of wounded soldiers were led to Sprayberry's position by radio directives. Those without radios had to be rounded up by hand. When he had gathered up six or seven men, he sent them back up the trail to the perimeter. Those too badly wounded to walk were placed on litters.

Several times, while venturing out from his position, Sprayberry happened upon an enemy fortification. He destroyed no less than ten bunkers, killed a dozen NVA, and eliminated two machine-gun positions in his quest to save his friends.

When convinced he had found all the beleaguered soldiers, he formed up the column and then moved them back through the night to the medevac pad. During the seven-hour foray, Sprayberry rescued forty men, including Lambert.

Sprayberry finished his Vietnam tour in October 1968. He came back to the States and was serving at Fort Polk, Louisiana when the Medal of Honor was awarded on October 9, 1969. He was the youngest officer to earn the medal since World War II.

He remained in the Army even though he never felt completely at home there. "I was even more uncomfortable with the outside environment," he explains, "so that's why I stayed in the Army."

JAY VARGAS AND
JAMES E. LIVINGSTON

Following the brutal battles in Hué, Khe Sanh, and other northern cities, the marines continued to stymie NVA movement across the DMZ. The 3rd Marine Division was prepared to go on the offensive near Dong Ha when the NVA brought the battle to them. On April 29, 1968, the 320th NVA Division chewed up an ARVN regiment near the village of Dai Do, two miles from

Dong Ha, then ambushed the marine battalion sent to aid them. Another marine battalion, the 2nd of the 4th Marines, was fed into the foray. In the five-day battle that followed, two of its officers earned Medals of Honor.

Captain *Jay Vargas,* a twenty-seven-year-old career officer from Winslow, Arizona, ignored painful wounds to stay at the helm of G Company through three days of tough fighting. Isolated for a day and a night in Dai Do, Vargas rallied his marines to beat off three determined NVA counterattacks. Reinforced the next morning by Company E, led by twenty-eight-year-old Captain *James E. Livingston,* the two officers combined their forces to drive the enemy from Dai Do. The two then consolidated their positions and allowed a third company to pursue the NVA into the adjacent village of Dinh To. When the NVA hit that unit with a furious counterattack, Livingston gathered up the effective men of his company and led them back into battle. Even though he was immobilized by a third wound during this bold maneuver, he continued to direct the advance. Only when the NVA had been repulsed did Livingston agree to evacuation.

ROBERT M. PATTERSON

In Phuoc Long Province, north of Saigon along the Cambodian border, Specialist Four *Robert M. Patterson* of the 101st Airborne Division's 2nd Squadron, 17th Cavalry, earned a Medal of Honor on May 6, 1968, near the hamlet of La Chu. B Troop's 3rd Platoon was attacking enemy bunkers when interlocking machine-gun fire pinned down the leading squad. Unwilling to wait for someone else to do something, Patterson sprang into action. Covered by rifle fire from two buddies, Patterson raced into the open to destroy two bunkers with M-16 fire and grenades. When he spotted another bunker, Patterson went after it and didn't stop until he'd wiped out all enemy resistance. By official count the twenty-year-old North Carolinian had knocked out five enemy strongpoints and killed no less than eight VC.

In mid-May 1968 a strong Communist force besieged the Special Forces camp at Kham Duc, 45 miles southwest of Da Nang, on the Laotian border. After three days of intense battle, the high command elected to air evacuate the one thousand friendly troops. C-123s and C-130s pulled out the men while fighters raced overhead to provide cover. By the afternoon of May 12 the evacuation was complete. Or was it? Somehow, three men had been left behind.

JOE M. JACKSON

On Mothers Day, May 12, 1968, Lieutenant Colonel *Joe M. Jackson* was taking his semi-annual check-ride in a C-123 cargo plane. No matter how long a pilot had been flying, the Air Force demanded that he take a proficiency test twice each year. After twenty years of service Jackson was used to the requirement. This check-ride was to be an easy trip north from Da Nang to a strip near the DMZ to deliver some supplies, then back to Da Nang. Everything seemed routine.

By 3:00 P.M. that Sunday Jackson had satisfactorily completed the check-ride. He was returning to Da Nang when his radio crackled with voices from Kham Duc. They needed help. Another C-123 had tried to land to bring out the three remaining ground personnel. Under heavy enemy fire the pilot had aborted the approach. Now he was low on fuel. He pleaded for someone else to try and get the soldiers out.

Jackson turned to the flight examiner in the right seat, Major Jesse Campbell, and said, "We're going in."

Twenty years and thousands of hours as a fighter pilot had prepared the forty-five-year-old Jackson for this moment. When he reached the vicinity of Kham Duc he was at nine thousand feet. Reasoning the enemy gunners would expect him to make the same approach as the first C-123, Jackson resorted to an unorthodox approach.

Banking his plane over to lineup with the six-thousand-foot-long runway, Jackson chopped power, dropped full flaps, and pushed the nose down. The rate of descent rapidly reached a terrifying four thousand feet per minute. It was the stomach-churning rollercoaster ride of a lifetime.

The book says you don't fly a C-123 that way—and Jackson knew it. He said later: "I was afraid I'd reach the 'blow-up' speed, where the flaps, which were in the full down position for this dive, would be blown back up to the neutral position. If that happened we'd pick up additional speed and not be able to stop."

As it was, Jackson barely had enough time to bleed off the extra speed he did carry. One quarter-mile from the runway, he brought the huge cargo plane out of its dive—inches above the tree tops. He had only a few seconds to set up for touchdown when he crossed the runway threshold. He was down! He jammed his feet on the brakes, hoping to stop the big bird before she collided with a wrecked helicopter twenty-two hundred feet down the runway. With screaming tires the heavy plane skidded to a halt just short of the debris.

Before Jackson or his crew could even look for the stranded men, the three raced from a ditch alongside the runway. A crewman, Staff Sgt. Manson L. Grubbs, pulled them aboard. Amidst hugs and back-slapping, Grubbs radioed Jackson they were safely aboard. He could take off.

But Jackson had more problems. He and Campbell watched helplessly while an enemy soldier fired a 122mm rocket directly at them. Down the runway it raced, its deadly tip packed with explosives. Halfway to the airplane the rocket hit the asphalt and broke in two, the pieces skidding to a halt just twenty-five feet away. They didn't explode.

"Let's get out of here," Jackson said. With the throttle jammed full forward, and dodging debris as they picked up speed, Jackson lifted the plane off the ground through a cross-fire of tracer rounds. "We were scared to death," he remembers.

Climbing at maximum power until beyond range of the enemy's weapons, Jackson set a course for Da Nang. He'd been on the ground at Kham Duc less than one minute. Miraculously, not one enemy round hit a crewmember or the plane.

Jackson was born on March 14, 1923, in Newnan, Georgia,

where his family was friendly with that of Marine Major Stephen Pless. Jackson left home in 1941 to enter the Army Air Force. He served throughout World War II as a crew chief on a B-25 bomber. After the war he took flight training and earned his wings. In Korea he flew 107 fighter sorties, picking up a Distinguished Flying Cross in the process. In the late 1950s he was among the first Air Force pilots to fly the U-2 spy plane. He received his well-earned Medal of Honor on January 16, 1969. Two years later he retired as a full colonel.

ROBERT C. BURKE

One of the first reinforcing units to reach Vietnam after the Tet Offensive began was the 27th Marine Regiment. On February 17, the unit landed at Da Nang, where it provided security until it was sent home in September of 1968. Even though they were only in Vietnam for six months the 27th clashed with the VC several times. A particularly fierce fight occurred on May 17 at Le Nam hamlet, on Go Nai Island in southern Quang Nam Province.

As Company I approached a dry riverbed fronting a treeline they came under heavy fire from a well-concealed VC force. Half a dozen marines dropped in the open. The others scrambled for cover—except for one.

An eighteen-year-old PFC from Monticello, Illinois, picked up his M-60 and began a one-man assault against the enemy. *Robert C. Burke* never hesitated. He raced to the waist-high bank and sent burst after burst of machine-gun fire into the VC positions. While he kept the enemy pinned down other marines moved the wounded to safety. When his own weapon jammed, Burke picked one up from a casualty and moved deeper into the VC area, killing five more. In the meantime, another marine fixed the M-60. Burke took it back. He stepped into the open, firing deadly bursts into the VC bunkers until he was killed.

Burke was the youngest recipient of the Medal of Honor for service in Vietnam.

Air crewmen shot down over enemy territory had a good chance of avoiding capture if the crews of Search and Rescue teams could reach them. Highly professional and extremely dedicated, SAR crewman were a special breed. Called on to fly over enemy-held terrain, the SAR crews were frequently the targets of enemy fire themselves. The North Vietnamese and VC often used a downed air crew as bait to lure in slow-moving SAR aircraft. When the rescue chopper came within range the enemy gunners would shoot it down, sometimes using that crew as additional bait. Unmindful of the hazard, SAR crews exhibited tremendous courage in their daily struggle to save American lives.

CLYDE E. LASSEN

Clyde E. Lassen always demonstrated energy and zeal. Born March 14, 1942, in Fort Myers, Florida, Lassen enlisted in the Navy in 1961 after graduating from the Venice, Florida, high school. Although enlisting as an aviation mechanic, Lassen had his sights set on naval aviation. Through four years of enlisted service he worked hard, took courses at junior colleges in San Diego and Pensacola, and proved to the Navy he had the skills to be a flier.

After successfully completing flight school Lassen received his wings and an ensign's commission. Two years later he was a SAR pilot aboard the USS *Preble* off the coast of North Vietnam.

On the evening of June 19, 1968, Lassen hovered his UH-2 Seasprite chopper over the water a few miles off North Vietnam's coast. He patiently awaited word of two downed naval aviators. There had been no contact with them since they had jumped from their disabled plane an hour earlier. Just when it seemed the pilots would be given up for lost Lassen's co-pilot, Lieutenant Clarence L. Cook, received their map coordinates over his radio. They sat on the side of a steep, heavily wooded hill surrounded by tall trees and enemy soldiers. The NVA were closing in on them. They had to be taken out—and fast.

Lassen set course for the site. An overcast sky cut visibility. When he arrived there was no sign of the pilots. Lassen was sure he had missed the location, but suddenly a flare flashed through the inky sky.

Moving toward the illumination he looked for a pickup spot. A rice paddy at the bottom of the hill looked promising. Lassen relayed his plan to the downed airmen, then hovered a few feet over the muddy water. This maneuver drew the fire of nearby NVA. A shower of small arms fire flew at the chopper. Lassen's door gunners, Aviation Machinist Mates Bruce B. Dallas and Donald N. West, returned the fire. Lassen made up his mind to sit out the enemy fire, but then word reached him that the pilots couldn't get down the hill. The brush was just too thick.

After pulling back momentarily, Lassen decided that if the stranded sailors couldn't get to him, he'd go to them.

Cautiously, mindful of the tall trees and of enemy fire, Lassen nursed his craft up the hill. Calling for flares from an overhead plane to illuminate the area, Lassen found a good pickup spot between two trees. Dallas and West dropped the rescue hoist into the darkness below.

Just as rescue seemed likely, the last of the overhead flares died out. Lassen immediately lost his depth perception. "Look out for the trees!" one of the gunners screamed into the intercom. A severe jolt shot through the chopper as its rotor blades slammed into a tree trunk.

Lassen fought for control of the ship with every ounce of strength and all of his skill. It vibrated heavily. Somehow the intrepid pilot managed to right his craft.

As if the damage to his helicopter didn't make things difficult enough, Lassen realized he was running low on fuel. And the overhead plane reported it had run out of flares.

It would have been acceptable for Lassen to abandon his mission at this point—but he didn't. He hadn't completed the rescue, and he was determined to do so.

He radioed for more flares, then once again directed the aviators to make their way downhill. His door gunners could keep the enemy marksmen at bay, but Lassen wanted nothing more to do with those tall trees.

He hovered out of range until another flare ship arrived. Then he went back to the paddy. The volume of enemy fire increased as he grew closer to the rescue site. Hits riddled the chopper's thin skin. Amazingly, no rounds hit the crew.

With only thirty minutes of fuel left Lassen began his descent toward the anxious pilots. He was fifty feet over the paddy when the flares died out. Once again, it seemed like his luck had run out.

With no time left for the overhead plane to circle back to drop another flare, and determined to save the men, Lassen turned on his landing light. The high-powered beam cut a bright swath through the night, a perfect target for enemy gunners. Lassen ignored the withering fire. His door gunners sent streams of bullets into the night as he set the chopper down. Seconds later the two pilots, homing in on the landing light, burst out of the jungle. Eager hands pulled them aboard the chopper. Once satisfied that the two pilots were safe onboard Lassen pulled his injured chopper into the sky. He set a course for the sea.

Dangerously low on fuel, Lassen landed on the first vessel he reached. Crewmen from the guided missile frigate *Jouett* later found less than five minutes of fuel left in the Seasprite's tanks.

Each member of the crew was decorated for his role in the daring rescue: Lassen received the Medal of Honor, Cook the Navy Cross, and Dallas and West each received the Silver Star. Lassen continued his career in naval aviation, eventually attaining the rank of commander.

On June 3, 1968 General Westmoreland, recalled to The States to serve as Army Chief of Staff, turned over command of MACV to his deputy, General Creighton W. Abrams. Under Abrams, the strategy of large scale search-and-destroy operations shifted to one of smaller, company-sized maneuvers. Already the U.S. was attempting to reduce its losses. Any battalion-sized or larger operations would be left mainly to the ARVN.

Even with the reduction in offensive operations, service in Vietnam was replete with dangers, for those in traditional noncombat roles as well as for combat troops. Truck convoys were particularly vulnerable to enemy ambush. Criss-crossing South Vietnam in a never-ending round of deliveries, the convoys presented enticing targets to the VC and NVA. This was the case when a convoy traveling from the massive American supply base at Long Binh outside Saigon, 60 miles to the northwest, was ambushed near Ap Nhi on August 25, 1968.

WILLIAM W. SEAY

Rockets, grenades, automatic weapons, and small arms fire wracked the deuce-and-a-half trucks from the 62nd Transportation Company. One of the drivers, nineteen-year-old Sgt. *William W. Seay,* sprang from his cab to take up a position behind the wheels of the vehicle in front of him. He blazed away with a M-16, dropping two of the enemy a scant thirty feet away. Twice he left his position of relative safety to retrieve enemy grenades and throw them back at the advancing NVA. On his second try an enemy round tore into his right wrist.

He pulled back to the safety of a ditch, where he waited for a medic. Suddenly he spotted three enemy soldiers preparing to fire at the casualties huddled around him. Seay shouted a warning, then stood. With his right hand limp at his side, he fired his rifle with his left. He killed the three soldiers but an enemy sniper mortally wounded the Brewton, Alabama, native.

NICKY D. BACON

On August 26, 1968, the 1st Platoon of Company B, 4th Battalion, 21st Infantry, Americal Division ran into trouble while on routine patrol with an armor unit west of Tam Ky in Quang Tin

Province. A twenty-two-year-old squad leader from Phoenix, Arizona, *Nicky D. Bacon,* took his men forward in an assault on an enemy bunker line. Minutes later the platoon leader fell with a severe wound. Bacon, who served with the 1st Infantry Division in Vietnam in 1966, took charge of the platoon. Under his expert leadership the men surged forward to attack the enemy.

When the nearby 3rd Platoon lost its leader Bacon assumed command of it, too. The intrepid soldier led both platoons against the reinforced bunkers. Unable to destroy a particularly well-defended bunker, Bacon climbed aboard the rear deck of a tank. Completely exposed to hostile fire he poured a hail of bullets into the enemy ranks, driving them off.

In the Fishhook area of War Zone C, northwest of Saigon, the 1st Infantry Division spent the fall of 1968 searching for the 1st NVA Division. During the last week of October members of the Big Red One clashed repeatedly with the enemy. 1st Division artillery supported all these actions. From fire support bases scattered throughout the region massive fire power poured down on the enemy.

On one memorable night the division's 5th Artillery Regiment severely damaged an NVA unit crossing the nearby Cambodian border. One of the shells hit an enemy ammo depot, causing 128 secondary explosions. It was probably this action that resulted in an enemy attempt to destroy the responsible fire support base (FSB).

CHARLES C. ROGERS

Fire Support Base Rita was manned by the 155mm howitzers of the 1st Battalion, 5th Artillery commanded by Lieutenant Colonel *Charles C. Rogers.* Almost nine hundred meters in diameter, Rita had been painstakingly carved out of the jungle adjacent to the Cambodian border by sweating soldiers the previous summer. Night after night the artillerymen sent H&I (harassing and interdiction) fire missions slamming into NVA units crossing the border. As long as Rita remained operational the NVA were not safe.

Colonel Rogers was serving his twelfth month in-country. He volunteered for duty in Vietnam because service there was critical to his well-thought-out career plans. "I wanted the combat experience, and I felt it was imperative to my career to get a combat command," he says.

The son of a coal miner, Rogers was born in Claremont, West Virginia, on September 6, 1929. Following his 1951 graduation from West Virginia State College Institute, where he took degrees in chemistry and mathematics, Rogers was commissioned a 2nd lieutenant through the college's ROTC program. Fifteen years of routine assignments preceded Rogers's arrival in Vietnam in the fall of 1967.

Rogers had been scheduled to depart Vietnam in mid-November but he had extended to take a MACV staff position. It was an excellent opportunity to add more experience to his already brilliant career. Now, on Halloween, he had just two weeks to go before he gave up his command.

For the previous three nights, FSB Rita had been heavily mortared. Halloween night was no different. As soon as the sun dropped below the horizon, rockets and mortars fell from the sky.

All this mortaring had kept Rogers from getting much rest over the past few nights. This night he was determined to get some sleep. At 12:30 A.M., November 1, 1968 he crawled into his sleeping bag under the radio complex in his Tactical Operations Center. Fifteen minutes later the base erupted in a "mad-minute" (at irregular intervals every weapon on a base is fired outward in an attempt to catch an attacking enemy unaware).

The noise awakened the colonel. When the firing did not stop after a minute Rogers called one of his battery commanders'.

"Captain Dan Settle told me the enemy had broken through the wire and was all over the position. So I grabbed my steel pot and flak jacket and headed over," Rogers recalls.

What he saw outside the TOC astonished him. "All the armored personnel carriers on the west flank had been hit by rocket-propelled grenades. I instantly realized there was nothing there to stop the enemy but my batteries."

Rogers raced through the carnage toward his battery. On the way he shot at several NVA soldiers running through the base. When he reached the howitzer position Rogers found most of his men huddled in their bunkers to avoid the murderous fire. Going from bunker to bunker the officer ordered the men to their weapons, then gave fire commands to the crews.

While so occupied, he was hit in the face by a ricocheting round. The slug struck the left side of his nose and lodged in his palate. Choking on the swell of blood, Rogers reached into his mouth.

"I pulled the bullet from the roof of my mouth and threw it on the ground; the wound continued to bleed profusely."

Still full of fight, Rogers advanced on several NVA hiding behind a log pile. Before he reached them an RPG went off at his feet. A nearby enlisted man died and Rogers took shrapnel in both legs from the explosion, but he didn't give up. Crawling forward, he killed the enemy with grenades.

Over the next several hours, using an M-14 as a crutch, Rogers moved throughout the FSB, directing his men in repulsing the fanatical enemy. Wherever the fighting seemed the hardest, that's where Rogers went.

On one of his visits to a howitzer position he found the cannoneers hiding in their bunkers. Rogers ordered them back to their guns. "Sir, we can't come out. We'll all be killed out there," one private answered.

Rogers shouted back, "Dammit! Don't you see me standing here? I'm not getting killed. Now, get your butts out of that bunker."

Sheepishly, embarrassed by the colonel's bravery, the crew crawled out. A few minutes later their howitzer was back in action.

On through the night the NVA came. No matter what the

Americans threw at them, the enemy kept coming. "I was amazed," says Rogers. "I just couldn't understand it. As fast as we cut them down, why here comes another row of them."

All the batteries were firing, knocking down enemy soldiers by the score. Rogers stood in a howitzer emplacement helping the crew fire the weapon into the screaming horde of enemy soldiers. Mortars crashed down around him. "They were hitting all around, and then I saw a series of rockets being walked in my direction. One hit seventy yards east of me, the next thirty. I thought, 'I bet the next one is coming right into this parapet . . . '"

Rogers came to in an upside down position against the bunker. His mind was filled with vague images of flying through the air and the howitzer falling over. Both his legs were badly injured; he couldn't walk. Then a medic appeared. "The Old Man's been hit again. We need a litter." Seconds later strong hands lifted him on the litter then carried him to the TOC.

Still fully conscious, Rogers barked orders to those around him. He called in air strikes, directing their fire to within one hundred yards of the perimeter wire. "I've never seen the guys lay it on so close and effective," Rogers said later.

Helicopter gunships arrived at daylight. Their massed firepower finally broke the enemy attack. The NVA retreated into the jungle, pulling along their wounded. At least 328 enemy dead were later counted around FSB Rita.

Medevac choppers flew in to take out the dozens of American casualties. Rogers refused to leave. He stayed on, evaluating reports from the gunships. He wanted to be sure the enemy was gone. Only when convinced the fight was over did he let the medics place him on the chopper.

After three months of recuperation in Japan, Rogers asked to return to his job at MACV. The doctors refused, but Rogers persisted. He won. Three days after being released from the hospital, Rogers flew back to Vietnam. "I still had a job to do," he explains. He finally returned to the States in July 1969.

On May 14, 1970, Rogers received his Medal of Honor from President Nixon. He stayed in the Army, graduating from the prestigious Command and General Staff School and the Army War College. He also managed to earn a Masters Degree along the way. The highest-ranking black ever to earn a Medal of Honor, Rogers received the second star of a major general in 1980.

The 1st Cavalry Division left northern I Corps in November 1968 to take up positions along the Cambodian border in Binh Long Province north of Saigon. Almost from the moment they arrived in the area the First Team was in contact with the enemy. The firefights were frequently brief—but always bitter.

JOHN N. HOLCOMB

The men of Company D, 2nd Battalion, 7th Cavalry, 1st Cavalry Division were anxious for December 3rd to end. This was to be their last air assault before Christmas. After sixty straight days in the field they all looked forward to a much-needed break. In honor of the approaching holiday some GIs sported tiny Santas on their rucksacks. Others carried Christmas wreaths.

It was supposed to be a routine assault, if any combat action can be termed "routine." Out on the choppers, a ground sweep of the area around the LZ, then a flight back to the base camp.

Among the men waiting to board the choppers was twenty-two-year-old Sgt. *John N. Holcomb.* A native of Richland, Oregon, he had enlisted in October 1966. His first duty station after basic training was Germany. In March of 1968, with MACV screaming for replacements, Holcomb was transferred to Vietnam.

On December 3rd he was a short-timer with less than ninety days left to serve on his tour.

As the troop-laden Hueys approached the LZ, Holcomb could see artillery rounds prepping the open meadow. Helicopter gunships criss-crossed overhead, zipping rockets and machine-gun bullets into the surrounding jungle.

The slicks touched down. The grunts spilled onto the ground. They raced to set up positions on the LZ's perimeter, anticipating the crack of enemy rounds. They didn't come. The LZ was cold.

Holcomb set his squad up in defensive positions. The last chopper rose from the meadow. Then it happened. An RPG flew from the jungle toward the chopper. It exploded with a deadly roar. An enemy force, estimated at battalion size, opened fire on Company D. Holcomb's squad lay directly in the path of the main enemy attack.

In the first few minutes of the fight an RPG wounded Holcomb's M-60 machine gunner. Fully aware that the enemy was concentrating fire on that position, Holcomb nonetheless picked up the weapon, moved forward, and sent belt after belt of ammo into the enemy ranks, forcing them to pull back.

During the lull that followed, Holcomb reestablished his men into a tighter defensive position. Concerned only for their welfare, he carried the wounded to safety, giving them what first aid he could.

When the enemy returned for a second attack, Holcomb was ready. Supported by one rifleman, he took up the most exposed position. Again his accurate fire forced the charging enemy back. Just as he was preparing to go for more ammo an RPG hit his machine gun, destroying it and grievously wounding him.

Undaunted by the pain, Holcomb crawled back to his men through grass set on fire by mortar explosions. As the last surviving leader of the decimated platoon, Holcomb radioed the enemy's location to the overhead gunships. Then he went forward a third time.

A survivor of that fight, Stephen Benko, remembers Holcomb's last minutes "We didn't know each other very well and didn't like each other very much but he died keeping me alive. John died in my arms after sprinting across twenty meters of open ground to bring a new machine gun to my position. Before that, he'd been racing around the LZ with ammo and bandages for the score of wounded and dying. Together, we'd succeeded in stopping an all-out ground attack by the North Vietnamese, who had us outnumbered and surrounded."

Benko recalls "being very angry at Holcomb for charging across that clearing. I was mad because I needed him alive; because he was a good soldier and I was scared. He must have known he couldn't make that run. All the enemy fire was being focused on us because we were among the few firing back.

"His big body must have made a huge target for the NVA," Benko says. "John was a brave man. But he was more than that. He was a man who made others brave."

Holcomb's posthumous Medal of Honor was presented to his parents on February 16, 1971.

While the Army and marines fought their ground actions in late 1968 throughout South Vietnam, the Studies and Observation Group continued its clandestine operations in Laos and Cambodia. On one of these, a remarkable Green Beret added the Medal of Honor to his long list of decorations.

ROBERT L. HOWARD

When choppers dropped Sgt. First Class *Robert L. Howard,* an officer, and a small force of Nungs into a small clearing in Laos on December 30, 1968, the twenty-nine-year-old NCO was in the middle of his third tour in Vietnam. A deeply religious man, Howard was also extraordinarily devoted to his men—earning him a well-deserved reputation as one of the most courageous men to serve in Vietnam.

"When things really got bad," he said later, "I'd try to think about my men. Thinking about what I could do to help them kept me from giving up or getting scared."

Wounded fourteen times during fifty-four months in Vietnam with the Special Forces, Howard earned every possible combat decoration, including eight Purple Hearts.

Howard had left his Opelika, Alabama, home twelve years earlier to enlist. He was serving in a quartermaster outfit when the war in Vietnam heated up, and he immediately volunteered for Green Beret training. His first Vietnam tour started in July 1965.

One-and-one-half years later, on his second tour, Howard earned a Distinguished Service Cross. On November 21, 1967, during a furious battle with North Vietnamese soldiers guarding a large supply dump, Howard personally destroyed two heavily defended bunkers. When he went to inspect one of them, a survivor opened fire. Pinned down directly in front of the automatic weapon with the barrel just six inches above his head, Howard calmly threw a grenade through the opening, killing the gunner.

Now, in late December 1968, Howard was on a mission to find a missing American soldier. And the enemy was waiting.

No sooner had the helicopters headed back across the border than the NVA opened up. In the blaze of small-arms fire and grenades the platoon leader fell, badly wounded. The Nungs fled into the jungle, firing wildly. A grenade exploded near Howard, driving shrapnel deep into his legs and ruining his rifle.

Unable to stand, and in excruciating pain, Howard thought only of his lieutenant. Ignoring the bullets snapping overhead Howard crawled through the underbrush, his bleeding legs dragging behind him.

Somehow he managed to reach the officer. Just as he started administering first aid an enemy round hit one of the lieutenant's ammo pouches. Howard ducked for cover as the rounds exploded, then returned to the unconscious officer.

Summoning up a reserve of superhuman strength, Howard pulled the man to safety. He then set about reorganizing his small remaining force.

Crawling from position to position, the indomitable NCO moved his men into a better defensive arrangement. Over the next three-and-one-half hours Howard directed the Nungs in holding off the enemy. He called in air strikes, directing them to within fifty yards of his position. Finally, Howard felt secure enough to call in choppers for evacuation.

He'd been wounded in the legs, stomach, foot, and buttocks, but refused to board the chopper until all his men were safely aboard. Only then would he allow himself to be pulled up.

After recuperating from his injuries Howard spent eight more months in Vietnam before rotating back to an instructor's position at Fort Bragg, North Carolina. In August 1970 he went back to Vietnam for a fourth tour.

He was still there when word came he was to receive the Medal of Honor. "At first, I wasn't sure what the Medal was being awarded for," he recalls. "I'd been told I was put in for a decoration for a fight in November 1968, but that wasn't it."

Actually, Howard had been recommended three times for the Medal. The first was downgraded to the Distinguished Service Cross. When the decorations board reviewed the second and third recommendations they elected to award a Silver Star for the second, the Medal of Honor for the third.

Some board members felt Howard should have had three Medals of Honor, but regulations wouldn't allow it.

When the blue ribbon was placed around his neck on March 2, 1971, Howard was sporting lieutenant's bars. He'd received a direct commission in December of 1969.

Since the end of the war in Vietnam Howard has spent most of his time teaching at the Special Forces school at Fort Bragg. "A lot of guys I served with in Vietnam made it possible for me to be here because they gave their lives for me," Howard says. "So I feel that for as long as I'm able, I have an obligation to train young soldiers to survive in combat."

Howard has continued his own training, too. He completed his undergraduate degree, then in 1980 received a Masters in Public Administration from Central Michigan University.

CHAPTER SEVEN

Medics and Chaplains at War

A man wounded in Vietnam had an excellent chance for survival—better than ninety percent. In most cases a casualty was in an evacuation hospital within thirty minutes of being hit. Once there, the survival rate soared to nearly one hundred percent. Never in the history of warfare had soldiers received such excellent care.

The first and most important link in this chain of care was the medic or corpsman attached to Army and Marine units. These youngsters, many of whom had never given a career in medicine much thought before starting their military service, found themselves the sole source of medical treatment in hostile territory.

Charged with daily life-and-death decisions at a young age, many medics assumed an overly protective attitude toward the men in their unit. They frequently became so involved with their "patients" that they went to extraordinary lengths to save them.

During the course of U.S. involvement in Vietnam fourteen medics earned Medals of Honor. Only six survived to wear their decoration.

In addition to the medics, three Catholic chaplains earned Medals of Honor in Vietnam, two posthumously. Although considered noncombatants, chaplains accompanied combat units into the field, where they not only provided spiritual support but also assisted the medics in treating the wounded. Armed only with their courage, the chaplains often faced the same dangers as the grunts.

DONALD W. EVANS

A twenty-three-year-old medic from Covina, California earned a posthumous Medal of Honor in Kontum Province on January 27, 1967, by saving the lives not only of men from his own

147

platoon but also from another nearby platoon. Specialist Four *Donald W. Evans*'s platoon of Company A, 2nd Battalion, 12th Infantry, 4th Infantry Division had not yet been committed to the battle near the hamlet of Tri Tam when he heard that an adjacent platoon had taken casualties.

Without hesitation Evans charged forward through one hundred yards of open ground, mercifully untouched by exploding mortars and small-arms fire. After treating a half-dozen casualties, two of whom he carried back to his platoon, Evans was hit by grenade fragments. He ignored his wounds to rejoin his own platoon as it entered the battle. Twice more he carried wounded out of the line of fire. He was running toward another when the enemy shot him down.

CHARLES C. HAGEMEISTER

After a year at the University of Nebraska, nineteen-year-old *Charles Hagemeister* decided that the war raging halfway across the world demanded his attention. It didn't seem right for him to be enjoying college life while other people his age were dying in rice paddies. He enlisted in the Army on May 19, 1966.

Following basic training at Fort Polk, Louisiana, where he qualified as an Expert on the rifle range, Hagemeister went to Fort Sam Houston, Texas. All Army medics received their training there, at the Brooke Army General Hospital. Courses in Anatomy, Biology, Chemistry, and Physiology, coupled with hands-on training in the hospital's wards, prepared the fledgling doctors for their work in Vietnam.

Hagemeister went overseas, to the 1st Battalion, 5th Cavalry, 1st Cavalry Division, in November 1966. He saw action in scores of fights during which he received credit for saving dozens of lives. His toughest fight, though, came on March 20, 1967, as part of Operation Pershing in northern Binh Dinh Province.

On March 19, the 1st Battalion, 8th Cavalry ran into a tough force from the 18th NVA Regiment. Two battalions of the 5th

Cavalry, including Hagemeister's 1st, were sent in as reinforcements. The next day the NVA attacked his company.

Fire from enemy small-arms and machine guns ripped into the walking troopers from three sides. Hagemeister raced to treat two casualties from the lead squad. A few minutes later word reached him that his platoon leader had been hit.

Hagemeister crawled rapidly through the blistering enemy fire. He reached the officer, treated him and several others, then prepared to evacuate them. At that moment the crack of a sniper's rifle sent a round singing past Hagemeister's ear. He jumped for cover, his eyes searching the treetops for the deadly foe. He spotted him.

The other soldiers were unable to bring their weapons to bear on the sniper, so the Hagemeister picked up an M-16. His Expert rating with the weapon back at Fort Polk paid off. Hagemeister killed the enemy with one shot.

Seconds later he killed three enemy soldiers trying to outflank his position, then exchanged rounds with an NVA machine gunner. Hagemeister won that duel.

His private battle over, Hagemeister raced through the enemy fire to contact a nearby platoon. He brought them into his perimeter where he personally placed riflemen in defensive positions. Under their covering fire the gallant medic moved the casualties to positions of safety.

The Medal of Honor was presented to Specialist Four Hagemeister in ceremonies at the White House on May 14, 1968. He remained in the Army, received a direct commission, and in 1985 entered the Army's prestigious Command and General Staff School at Fort Leavenworth, Kansas.

In addition to tending to the religious needs of the men in the field, chaplains were crosstrained in medicine. Although they were not expected to function as medics in battle, they could help the medics tend the wounded. The three chaplains who earned Medals of Honor in Vietnam received their decorations for rescuing wounded men under fire.

VINCENT R. CAPODANNO

Ironically, the three chaplains all earned their medals during one sixty-day period in the fall of 1967. The first was a Navy chaplain from Staten Island, New York.

One of nine children, *Vincent R. Capodanno* was ordained as a Maryknoll priest in June of 1957. He devoted the next seven years of his life to missionary work in the Far East. He then transferred to Honolulu where he applied for service with the Navy Chaplain Corps. He specifically requested duty with the marines in Vietnam. As a Navy lieutenant Father Capodanno joined the 1st Marine Division in April 1966.

Twenty months later, after serving in eight military operations, he went to Company M, 3rd Battalion, 5th Marines for Operation Swift. Father Capodanno told the battalion commander, Lieutenant Colonel Peter L. Hilgartner, that he wanted to be with M Company so he "could get to know the men as well as he did those in the other companies," of the 3rd Battalion.

On September 4, 1967, M Company was hit while moving across a rice paddy near Chau Lam–1 in the Que Son Valley in Quang Tin Province. Two platoons were quickly isolated. The commander, Lieutenant John D. Murray, pulled his other platoons back to a small knoll.

As soon as word reached Father Capodanno of the plight of the two stranded platoons, he left the company's command group to help the wounded. Completely ignoring the heavy volume of enemy fire, the intrepid chaplain moved across the battlefield, gave aid to the wounded, and administered Last Rites to the dying.

When a mortar round severely wounded the priest in the arms and legs, and nearly severed his right hand, he pushed aside the corpsman trying to treat him. "Take care of the others," he said.

The padre moved in the direction of the heaviest fighting. At every stop he gave comfort to the wounded as well as the fighting men. He spotted a marine trying to pull a wounded corpsman to safety. At the same time he saw an enemy machine gunner aiming at the pair. Father Capodanno dashed forward. His movement drew the enemy's fire. . . . After the battle Father Capodanno's bullet-riddled body was found just inches away from the mortally wounded corpsman.

CHARLES J. WATTERS

In an interview given a few months before he was killed in action, Chaplain (Major) *Charles J. Watters* told a reporter he volunteered to go on combat patrols, "just to get a little exercise. You haven't lived until you've crawled on your hands and knees through thick overgrowths of bamboo."

A tall, lean man, Father Watters had wanted to be a priest every since he was in the fourth grade in Jersey City, New Jersey. After high school he entered Seton Hall University, then attended the Immaculate Conception Seminary in Darlington, New Jersey.

His first parish assignment after his ordination in 1953 was to St. Mary's Church in Rutherford, New Jersey. He later spent seven years at a parish in nearby Paramus. There he learned to fly, eventually earning a commercial license and instrument rating.

In the early 1960s Father Watters decided he wanted to serve his country as well as his God. He enlisted as a chaplain with the New Jersey National Guard. In 1965 he requested transfer to the Army and active duty.

Never a man to shrink from danger, Father Watters—at age thirty-eight—volunteered for airborne training. He spent some time with the 101st Airborne Division at Fort Campbell, Kentucky, before being sent to the 173rd Airborne Brigade in Vietnam.

He loved the camaraderie among his paratroopers. "They may be a bit crazy in many ways but you have never seen more spirit and drive than from these boys. And, most importantly, in combat, they never leave a man behind," he noted.

Asked if he carried a weapon in combat, Father Watters smiled and answered, "I'm the peaceful kind. All I shoot is my camera and if they start to shoot at me I yell, 'tourist!' Seriously, a weapon weighs too much and, after all, a priest's job is in taking care of the boys. But if we ever get overrun I guess there'll be plenty of weapons lying around."

Father Watters estimated he'd been in at least fifty engagements with the enemy. And he was one of three chaplains to make the combat jump near Katum during Operation Junction City. He said it was the only one of his seventeen jumps on which he had "no uneasy feelings. There was too much else to think of."

His one-year tour of duty ended in June 1967, but Father Watters wasn't ready to go home. His "boys" needed him. He extended for another year of service.

He never completed it. He died on November 19, 1967, during the battle for Dak To.

Father Watters was in the forefront when the paratroopers of the 2nd Battalion, 503rd Infantry became embroiled with the NVA on Hill 875. Moving among the battling troopers he gave encouragement and first aid to the wounded. When he noticed a wounded paratrooper standing in shock between the two forces Father Watters ran into the open, hoisted the man onto his shoulders, and carried him back to safety.

During that brutal afternoon the airborne chaplain left the safety of the perimeter at least five times to retrieve casualties. When he was satisfied that all of the wounded were inside the perimeter Father Watters busied himself helping the medics, applying bandages, gathering up and serving rations, and providing spiritual and mental strength and comfort.

According to reports later filed by survivors of that grim battle, Father Watters was on his knees giving the Last Rites to a dying paratrooper when, at dusk, an American bomber accidently dropped a 500-lb. bomb in the center of the paratroopers. Father Watters died in the blast.

His two brothers accepted his posthumous Medal of Honor on November 4, 1969.

CHARLES LITEKY

On December 6, 1967, a small force of Company A, 4th Battalion, 12th Infantry, 199th Light Infantry Brigade scoured the jungle thirty miles north of Saigon in Bien Hoa Province. The night before the VC had dropped mortars on the company's position. If the GIs found the mortar site, maybe they could also find evidence of the men who operated it.

Walking in the middle of the column with the company commander, Captain Bruce Drees, was the battalion chaplain, Captain *Angelo Liteky* (Angelo was his ordination name). Father Liteky had been in Vietnam for eight months. In that time he'd been in a number of brushes with the enemy, but nothing too serious. He was glad for that.

The men snaked their way cautiously through the dense jungle. Suddenly three VC briefly appeared on the trail ahead. A deadly pall of silence covered the jungle—then a cacophony of weapons fire erupted. RPGs streaked out of the trees. Claymore mines filled the air with deadly steel balls. Machine guns chattered. The GIs hugged the ground for cover.

Liteky made his way to two wounded men. The first was a young medic who had told Father Liteky the night before that he was going to start a rock 'n' roll band after he got home in a few weeks. Now his leg was nearly blown off. Only gristle and bone remained where his knee had been.

"Did you say a prayer for me, Father?" the medic asked.

"Of course I did. You'll be all right, you'll make it," Liteky told him. Then Liteky pulled him and the other man to safety.

A witness to Father Liteky's bravery later said: "When Captain Liteky went out there the first time, we thought we'd never see him again. By the end of the day we just knew he could walk on water."

When the chaplain came upon one casualty the savage enemy fire kept him from getting the man to safety. Determined to save the man's life, he flipped over on his back, manhandled the bleeding man onto his chest, then, using his elbows and heels, pushed himself thirty yards toward an evacuation site. Once out of the line of fire he carried the man to safety.

All afternoon Father Liteky brought up stretchers, ammo, and rations. Helmetless, he moved upright through the battlefield, annointing the dying, giving aid to the wounded.

At one point, after giving the Last Rites to a man with a huge hole in his back, Father Liteky came upon an abandoned M-16. He picked it up. For a moment he was ready to use it to defend himself and the wounded, but then he thought better of it. If a priest is going to buy it today, he told himself, they won't find a rifle on him.

Later, in the face of rockets and small-arms fire, the priest stood exposed in an open area to guide in medevac helicopters. Under his directions the medics loaded up the wounded.

The fight lasted from early afternoon to late evening. Chaplain Liteky, despite painful wounds in the neck and foot, rescued twenty wounded soldiers. Many would have died without his help.

After he completed his Vietnam tour in October 1968 Father Liteky was sent to Fort Bragg, North Carolina. In early November of 1968 he learned he was to receive the Medal of Honor. He had mixed feelings about the award.

"The company commanders who write up these medal nominations, they know how to pump it up," he said. "I'm not saying some of these things didn't happen. I'm just saying it makes *them* look good, too."

Despite his misgivings, Father Liteky accepted the medal from President Johnson on November 19, 1968.

Liteky returned to Vietnam in 1970. What he saw there greatly disturbed him. "When I got back over there I really got turned off by the war," he later said. "I thought we should get out of there with all possible speed. I really got disgusted with things I saw. The insensitivity toward life; the emphasis on body counts—a mania."

It was about this time, too, that Liteky acknowledged another problem—his vocation. "One of my biggest problems in the priesthood all along was that my identity had pretty much gotten swallowed up," he said.

Born Charles J. Liteky on February 14, 1931, in Washington, DC, he grew up in Jacksonville, Florida. As a youth he had been a good football player. He was being groomed for the starting quarterback slot at the University of Florida when he decided to enter the priesthood. Ten years after his 1956 ordination, he entered the Army.

Upon return from his second Vietnam tour Liteky decided to face both his problems. He resigned his Army commission and left the priesthood. He worked at a variety of jobs, including pumping gas, then ran a halfway house in Cleveland for drug-addicted vets. For a while he lived in a shack on a deserted Florida beach. He even spent time working as a benefits counselor for the Veterans Administration.

Today, the ex-priest is decidedly anti-war. He works to ban nuclear weapons; he organizes protests against American involvement in Central America. He is the coordinator of the National Federation of Veterans for Peace, a group of fifteen veterans' organizations advocating non-violence.

In a well-publicized demonstration of his opposition to President Reagan's Nicaraguan policy, Liteky renounced his Medal of Honor in July 1986. Liteky placed his medal at the base of the Vietnam Veterans Memorial in Washington, DC. To the assembled reporters Liteky said, "I find it ironic that conscience calls me to renounce the Medal of Honor for the same basic reason I received it—trying to save lives."

CLARENCE E. SASSER

During a recon-in-force mission in Dinh Tuong Province on January 10, 1968, 9th Infantry Division medic PFC *Clarence E. Sasser* repeatedly ignored enemy fire to bring the wounded from his unit to safety. Even when an exploding mortar shell immobilized his legs, the twenty-year-old from Angleton, Texas, never stopped. He crawled one hundred meters through exposed terrain to reach one casualty. He dragged that man to safety, then called to a group of others to work their way to him. For the remainder of the action—five hours—Sasser dragged himself from casualty to casualty, treating their wounds. When medevac choppers finally made it in, Sasser refused evacuation until all the other wounded were pulled out.

Sasser spent ten months in the hospital recovering from his painful injuries, but on March 7, 1969, he stood proudly as President Nixon awarded him the Medal of Honor.

DONALD E. BALLARD

On May 18, 1968 in Quang Tin Province, Corpsman *Donald E. Ballard,* from Kansas City, Missouri, had just finished evacuating two heatstroke victims when his outfit, Company M, 3rd Battalion, 4th Marines, 3rd Marine Division, was surprised by a VC ambush. Immediately racing to the aid of a casualty, Ballard applied a field dressing and was directing four marines in the removal of the wounded man when an enemy soldier tossed a grenade into the group. Yelling "Grenade!", Ballard vaulted over the stretcher. In one swift motion he pulled the grenade under his body.

It was a dud.

Calmly picking himself off the jungle floor, Ballard sent the stretcher bearers on their way and continued treating the wounded.

It wasn't until a few days later that the impact of his brush with death hit him. "I was pretty shook up," he said.

Ballard is only the second man whose valor was not discounted because the deadly missile he chose to cover with his own body to protect others did not explode.

THOMAS W. BENNETT

During the Vietnam War conscientious objectors were allowed to choose between military service as a medic or community service, usually in a local hospital. When twenty-one-year-old

Tom Bennett received his draft notice in the summer of 1968 he immediately applied for CO status.

Because of his deep-seated religious convictions, the Morgantown, West Virginian's application was approved. When the draft board offered him the choice between military and civilian service, Bennett selected the Army. Though he was a pacifist, young Bennett felt he could contribute to his country by caring for the casualties of war.

Bennett spent six months training at Fort Sam Houston in Texas before being posted to the 4th Infantry Division. He arrived in Vietnam in January 1969. Three weeks later, following three days of intense combat, Corporal Bennett was killed in action.

On February 9, his unit, Company B, 1st Battalion, 14th Infantry, was on a sweep of the Chu Pa region of Pleiku Province. When the NVA ambushed another company Company B was sent to their aid. They walked into a trap.

The enemy fire hit Bennett's unit as it closed on its sister company. Three members of the point platoon fell, seriously wounded. The cry of "Medic!", "Medic!" travelled down the line of men.

From his position near the company command group Bennett bounded forward, ignoring the enemy bullets flying through the air. His only concern was the wounded.

Bennett dressed the casualties' wounds. He then made three trips across the battlefield to carry the men to an evacuation site.

The intense fusillade of fire pinned down Company B through the night and into the next day. Foregoing rest, Bennett moved constantly among the injured. Several times he left the safety of the perimeter to bring wounded back into the lines.

On February 11, after a night of relative calm, Company B set off in pursuit of the elusive foe. In a repeat of the previous action the men were again ambushed. Five GIs dropped in the initial blast of rifle fire.

Bennett reached the first man. He patched him up and sent him to the rear. The next man lay in front of the company, between it and an enemy machine gun. Bennett started forward.

A sergeant stopped him. "Don't go out there. You'll never make it."

"I've got to get him," Bennett said. "He's hit bad. I've got to get him."

Pushing the sergeant aside, Bennett half-ran, half-crawled toward the wounded man. The NVA gunner easily picked up the moving target. Corporal Bennett was killed just short of the man he tried to save.

The Medal of Honor presented to Corporal Bennett's parents on April 7, 1970, was the only one earned by a conscientious objector in Vietnam.*

DAVID R. RAY

An NVA human wave assault ripped into the fire support base at Phu Loc 6 near An Hoa in Quang Nam Province manned by cannoneers of Battery D, 2nd Battalion, 11th Marines, 1st Marine Division during the early morning hours of March 19, 1969. Ignoring NVA sappers racing through the wire, Corpsman *David R. Ray* went from parapet to parapet treating the wounded. Even though he'd been hit by flying shrapnel himelf, Ray continued caring for other casualties. While he huddled over one man two NVA surprised him. Ray killed one and wounded the other with two well-placed pistol shots. Later, when an enemy grenade landed near a patient, Ray threw himself over the casualty, protecting him from the explosion. The twenty-four-year-old former University of Tennessee student died from the wounds he received in the blast.

GARY D. BEIKIRCH

Deep in a remote section of Kontum Province the Special Forces established an outpost to interdict NVA supply lines reaching

---

*Another medic, Desmond T. Doss, is the only other CO to ever earn the award. His was presented for service on Okinawa in World War II.

across the Laotian border. Manned by twelve Green Berets and 450 hill tribesmen known as Montagnards, or "'Yards" the camp had a definite effect on NVA troop movement into the Province.

The Green Berets could tell their strategy was working because NVA attacks on their outpost were increasing.

The medic attached to Camp Dak Seang was twenty-two-year-old Sgt. *Gary D. Beikirch*. In 1967 Beikirch quit college in his native Greece, New York, to join the Green Berets. "To broaden my experience," is the way he puts it.

After arriving in Vietnam in July 1969, Beikirch became intensely involved in the war because he believed in it. In addition, there were numerous worthwhile medical projects that could be carried out among the primitive Montagnards. Beikirch developed a deep personal commitment to the people he worked and fought beside.

"I was chided for going 'native'," he says. "I'd do things like take the kids down to the swimming hole for an afternoon of fun."

He also remembered being on patrols near the Laotian border, all alone except for his 'Yards. A rare mutual trust existed between the two diverse peoples. At times Beikirch's life was completely in their hands. He never worried.

All through March of 1970 evidence mounted that the NVA were planning a major attack on the camp. Routine patrols were fired on with more frequency. Jungle trails indicated the presence of large bodies of enemy soldiers. The Green Berets knew that the NVA were coming—it was just a question of when.

They came on April 1, 1970.

Beikirch instinctively knew when the first mortar shell crashed down it was no ordinary attack. Seconds later the crack of rifles and the chatter of machine guns filled the air. Rocket-propelled grenades and hand grenades added their explosions to the din. From positions well-concealed in the jungle around the camp the NVA launched a full-scale attack designed to annihilate the defenders.

Beikirch grabbed his medical kit and went to work. Threading his way through the barrage of mortars he moved to the wounded. In full view of the enemy he patched up wounds, offered encouragement, and carried casualties to the safety of the medical bunker.

Midway through the eight-hour battle Beikirch learned that an American officer lay unconscious and dangerously exposed on the battlefield. Thinking only of saving the man's life, Beikirch immediately ran to the officer's aid.

A mortar shell exploded directly behind him. Flying metal ripped into Beikirch's spine and right hip. A third red-hot chunk pierced his back and exploded out through his stomach.

Though stunned by the intense pain, Beikirch still thought only of the wounded officer. Somehow he made his way to the man, applied a field dressing, and then carried him to safety.

After applying bandages to his own wounds, Beikirch returned to the bullet-swept camp. He searched for and evacuated the other wounded. He was hit again as he dragged a Montagnard soldier to safety—while at the same time giving him mouth-to-mouth resuscitation. Beikirch's determination saved the man's life.

Finally, as the battle waned and the NVA pulled away from the battle site, Beikirch collapsed from loss of blood.

When he awoke seven days later Beikirch went through a crisis of spirit which changed his life.

"I was a Green Beret, the epitome of ego and self-sufficiency, lying in a hospital bed with my guts hanging out, cauterized, I.V.s stuck into both arms and both sides," he recalls. "I was battling for life and I looked for strength inside myself. I couldn't find it and I was scared."

Beikirch began praying. Through prayer he found peace and calmness. "I felt someone was there who cared for me. I knew some kind of God was real."

After eight months in the hospital Beikirch finished his military obligation—and then began his "trek." He explored Eastern philosophies and tried meditation. For a time he worked with quadraplegics in a VA hospital. Finally, he returned to college to study counseling.

160

By the time he received his Medal of Honor on October 15, 1973, Beikirch knew where he was going.

He became a minister in the United Baptist Fellowship. He now works as a guidance counselor at a private Christian school and at a community veterans outreach center.

The North Vietnamese victory in South Vietnam in 1975 dashed Beikirch's hopes of returning to the Central Highlands as a missionary. However, he has returned to Vietnam, becoming the only Medal of Honor recipient to do so since the war ended.

As an elected officer of the Vietnam Veterans of America Beikirch travelled to Hanoi in May of 1982. While the other delegates talked to North Vietnamese officials in general terms of friendship and the MIA (missing-in-action) problem, Beikirch asked only whether missionaries would someday be allowed in Vietnam.

The answer was noncommittal, but, he says, "It did give me hope."

DAVID F. WINDER

The final Vietnam Medal of Honor earned by a medic was post-humously presented to PFC *David F. Winder* on July 17, 1974, for an action in which he participated in Quang Ngai Province on May 13, 1970.

Winder's unit, Company A, 3rd Battalion, 1st Infantry, Americal Division, was searching for an NVA company when it was ambushed. Responding instantly to the frantic cries of "Medic!" Winder, the son of a Mansfield, Ohio, doctor, low-crawled toward the casualty through a rice paddy.

He was hit, but kept going. Somehow, he reached the man and gave him treatment. Undaunted and oblivious to the pain of his own wound, he set off toward another casualty.

A second bullet slammed into him. He went down. Unable to ignore the call for help, Winder rose again. Struggling forward slowly, but with tremendous determination, he made it to within ten meters of the casualty before a burst of machine-gun fire killed him.

Inspired by Winder's selfless concern for others, his company broke from cover, attacked and overran the NVA positions.

CHAPTER EIGHT

The War Winds Down

1 969 was a year of transition in U.S. involvement in South Vietnam. The tactic of battalion-sized sweeps against the VC and NVA in a specific land area, General Westmoreland's "search and destroy," would no longer be employed.

Instead, American forces operated from fixed bases strategically located along well-travelled routes to thwart the NVA infiltration of South Vietnam. Although there were offensive operations throughout the year, most combat actions came as a result of aggressive patrolling by company-sized, or smaller, units. This was consistent with the new policy of Vietnamization.

President Richard M. Nixon had been elected after promising to end American involvement in South Vietnam. Popular support for the withdrawal of American troops continued to grow. Under "Vietnamization," major responsibility for military conduct of the war would be turned over to the ARVN.

U.S. units worked closely with their ARVN counterparts to improve their battlefield techniques as the armed forces of South Vietnam were trained to shoulder the offensive burden against the enemy. Self-sufficiency of ARVN units was a major goal of the Nixon administration.

In early June 1969, President Nixon announced the first withdrawal of American military units. One battalion of the 9th Infantry Division left the rice paddies of the Mekong Delta for the pine forests of Ft. Lewis, Washington. By the end of the year, the rest of the 9th, and most of the 3rd Marine Division, had left Vietnam. American troop strength had been reduced by fifteen percent.

Those troops remaining in Vietnam faced a perplexing situation. Fully aware that their country no longer supported their efforts, they still had to fight a determined and dangerous enemy. The beginning of the end of America's presence in Vietnam was not accompanied by a lessening of the brutality of the war.

Indeed, some of the most bitter fighting lay ahead. Fifty-three American soldiers earned Medals of Honor during 1969. Despite the daily hardships they experienced as part of an unpopular war, young Americans repeatedly covered themselves in glory.

DON J. JENKINS

One of 1969's first Medals of Honor was earned by PFC *Don J. Jenkins,* a twenty-year-old from Quality, Kentucky. On January 6, using an M-16, an M-60 machine gun, two anti-tank weapons, and a grenade launcher, the gallant Jenkins destroyed several enemy bunkers that had pinned down his unit, Company A, 2nd Battalion, 39th Infantry, 9th Infantry Division during a patrol in Kien Phong Province. Undeterred by a severe shrapnel wound, Jenkins then went to the aid of a squad isolated only a few meters away from the enemy's line. Jenkins pulled three casualties to safety before his wounds caused his collapse. He survived to wear his Medal of Honor.

On January 11, 1969, seven armored personnel carriers from Troop A, 1st Squadron, 11th Armored Cavalry Regiment escorted a column of fuel and supply trucks along Route 13 to Quan Loi in Binh Long Province. Since this route was considered a hotbed of NVA activity, the tankers felt lucky to have made the run without any trouble. If only the return trip could have gone as well.

HAROLD A. FRITZ

Leading the column of APCs was a twenty-four-year-old 1st lieutenant from Lake Geneva, Wisconsin. *Harold A. Fritz,* the executive officer of Troop A, had volunteered the previous evening to take the place of a sick officer. Fritz was an experienced officer, serving his twelfth month with the 11th ACR. The previous August he had earned a Silver Star as the CO of an M-48 tank platoon.

Now, as he raced back down Highway 13, he felt something was about to happen.

A sudden explosion threw Fritz violently against the side of his APC. His flak jacket was blown off his body. Red hot shrapnel ripped into his back and legs. At first he thought he'd hit a mine. A barrage of explosions, crippling the other vehicles under his command, told him it was an ambush—and a well-executed ambush, as he soon discovered. NVA bunkers lined both sides of the road for a half-kilometer in either direction. The twenty-nine soldiers manning the APCs were caught in a deadly crossfire.

As flames leaped over the front of his APC, Fritz pulled his driver from the wreckage. He thrust a rifle into the man's hand, then set about to organize a defense.

One of the first things Fritz learned was that all of his radios had been knocked out. He couldn't report his situation or call for help. He was on his own.

Dashing back and forth among the blazing APCs, Fritz put his men into position, passed out ammo, and treated wounds. He pulled all the weapons and ammo he could off of the APCs; he knew his unit didn't have a lot of ammunition—so he wanted to ensure they gathered every round possible.

The enemy continuously probed Fritz's defenses. They would have overrun one position if he hadn't stood up, completely exposed to the enemy, firing a machine gun cradled in his arms. His accurate fire sent the NVA scurrying.

A few minutes later another NVA probe threatened to over-run the medic's position. Yelling, "Come with me!" to a small group of GIs, Fritz, armed only with a .45 and a bayonet, waded into the NVA.

Slashing and blazing away at pointblank range, Fritz drove the NVA back into the jungle.

By 11:30 A.M., after the battle had raged for over an hour, Fritz knew the situation was desperate. Only he and five others remained standing. His RTO had tried to fix one of their radios, but had no idea whether it worked. Ammo was low. There were few choices left.

During a brief lull in the enemy's firing Fritz explained the options to his men. "We can try pulling back through the jungle," he told them, "or we can stand and fight it out."

To a man, they elected to fight it out.

Fritz was ready to lead another charge when he spotted a cloud of dust coming down the road. "It was a scene right out of a John Wayne western," Fritz recalls. "Our radio had worked. Headquarters sent out a relief column."

It stopped one hundred meters away, unable to distinguish friend from foe in the melee. Fritz ran toward them, intent on deploying the tanks. Out of his view behind him an NVA sapper team prepared to fire a rocket at the lead tank. The tank fired first.

"The muzzle blast blew me twenty-five feet off the road into the bushes," Fritz remembers. "I thought they were shooting at me. My ears were ringing like crazy when I ran up yelling at the tank commander."

Fritz used hand signals to set the tanks into offensive positions. They still weren't enough. Two full companies of infantry from the 1st Cavalry Division were needed before the NVA broke contact.

Fritz was medevaced to safety that afternoon, but later in the evening went AWOL from the hospital, stole a jeep, and made his way back to his unit. It took a direct order from his CO to send him back for treatment.

Up until three years earlier Fritz had run his own successful contracting business in Lake Geneva. With a pregnant wife he wasn't too concerned when his draft notice arrived. Certainly he was entitled to a deferment. He took his case to the local draft board.

To his surprise, Fritz says, one of the board members was a man he'd recently taken to court over an outstanding debt. There's no way you're going to win this one, he told himself.

He was right. His appeal was denied.

To avoid the random process of conscription Fritz enlisted

in April 1966. One year later he was commissioned a second lieutenant.

After receiving his Medal of Honor on March 2, 1971, Fritz decided to make the Army his career. "With my experiences I felt I could help soldiers. And, I enjoyed the military life," he says.

Fritz was promoted to lieutenant colonel in 1984. When he retires he plans to enter the field of school administration.

THOMAS P. NOONAN

Thomas P. Noonan was born in Brooklyn, New York, on November 18, 1943. He graduated from Grover Cleveland High School in 1961 (one of his classmates was marine hero Robert O'Malley), then entered Hunter College in the Bronx.

When he graduated with a Bachelor degree in Physical Education in June 1966 Noonan could have sought a commission in any branch of the service. Instead, he enlisted in the Marine Corps. He went to Vietnam as a rifleman in June of 1968. He served initially with the 1st Marine Division, then was transferred to Company G, 2nd Battalion, 9th Marines, 3rd Marine Division.

In late January 1969 the 3rd Marine Division launched Operation Dewey Canyon against a main NVA infiltration route in the A Shau Valley along the Laotion border in Thua Thien Province. The marines faced combat in a rugged mountainous area covered with thickly woven jungle.

Noonan's company was ordered to a new site on February 5. Torrential rain poured down as the marines worked their way through the forests. The lead elements of the company were moving down a rain-slicked slope when the enemy forces opened up. Four marines were hit. Repeated attempts to rescue them were repelled by heavy fire.

Unable to stand the cries for help from his buddies, Lance Corporal Noonan broke from cover. Ignoring calls from his squad leader, Noonan nimbly made his way down the slippery slope. He found cover behind an outcropping of rocks just a few meters away from the nearest casualty.

"Hang in there," he yelled. "I'm coming to get you. Just hang on."

Noonan's fellow marines sent out a heavy volume of fire, forcing the NVA to take cover. Noonan raced out from behind the rocks. In a few steps he reached the first marine.

"I've got you, buddy. You're going to be okay."

The ground proved too slippery for Noonan to carry the casualty so he started pulling the man to safety. An AK-47 cracked. Noonan spun to the ground, blood gushing from a deep wound.

Rather than seek cover Noonan turned back to the man whose life he was determined to save. He offered words of encouragement, then resumed pulling the man to cover. He'd almost reached safety when a burst of machine gun fire stopped him. He died with his hands still clenching the wounded marine's fatigues.

Outraged at the slaughter, the other marines charged down the slope, rifles blazing. They drove the enemy off. The original four casualties lived.

Noonan's parents accepted his posthumous Medal of Honor on February 16, 1971.

The North Vietnamese response to the unilateral bombing halt of November 1, 1968, was to rush a torrent of supplies south to support a new offensive. The attacks began on February 22, 1969. Aimed primarily at U.S. logistical bases, the offensive was designed to disrupt the allied supply lines.

Unlike the 1968 Tet Offensive, these attacks lacked the depth necessary to do any lasting harm. Damage was minimal and American casualties were light. Regardless of their duration, the offensive actions once again demonstrated the enemy's ability to dictate where and when the battle would be joined.

Eight Medals of Honor were earned in one particularly tough four-day period of the offensive. From the rugged mountains of Quang Tri Province in the north, to the interior of Laos, to the swampy lowlands of the Delta region, soldiers and marines battled the enemy. Three medals were earned in the fighting on February 22 alone.

WESLEY L. FOX

In the A Shau Valley 1st Lieutenant *Wesley L. Fox,* a former enlisted marine, ignored painful wounds to continue to lead his battered company against NVA attackers. With all other officers wounded, Fox personally led his men in a grenade charge that drove the enemy off. Under his spirited leadership the men of Company A, 1st Battalion, 9th Marines, 3rd Marine Division pursued the NVA, destroying a large bunker complex, and capturing a large quantity of supplies.

GEORGE C. LANG

Specialist Four *George C. Lang,* a draftee from Hicksville, New York, led his squad of Company A, 4th Battalion, 47th Infantry, 9th Infantry Division in an attack on enemy locations in Kien Hoa Province. Repeatedly exposing himself to hostile fire, Lang wiped out three bunkers and captured a large cache of enemy weapons. As he examined the weapons retaliatory VC rockets crashed down around him. In spite of severe wounds that left him permanently paralyzed, Lang directed his men in an assault on the enemy location.

ROBERT D. LAW

On a long-range recon patrol deep in enemy territory in Binh Long Province north of Saigon, twenty-four-year-old Specialist Four *Robert D. Law* threw himself on an enemy grenade to save his patrol members of Company I, 75th Infantry, 1st Infantry Division. He died in the blast.

OSCAR P. AUSTIN

During the early morning hours of February 23, the NVA hit an observation post outside Da Nang manned by marines from Company E, 2nd Battalion, 7th Marines, 1st Marine Division. PFC *Oscar P. Austin,* a twenty-one-year-old from Phoenix, Arizona, went to the aid of a fallen marine. As he neared the man a grenade hit the ground nearby. Austin threw himself between the injured marine and the grenade. He caught the full effect of the explosion. Still concerned only with the other man, Austin was turning toward him when he saw an enemy soldier aiming a rifle at the marine. Austin deliberately placed himself in front of the man. He died from the burst of rifle fire.

ROBERT W. HARTSOCK

At almost the same time Austin was dying the VC hit the 25th Infantry Division's base camp at Dau Tieng in Hau Nghia Province. A twenty-four-year-old dog handler with the 44th Scout Dog Platoon, Staff Sgt. *Robert W. Hartsock* spotted a sapper team advancing on the tactical operations center. Accompanied by his platoon commander, Hartsock set up an ambush for the enemy. When he opened fire the VC tossed a satchel charge at the two men. Hartsock fell on it as it exploded, protecting the officer. Gravely wounded, he continued firing at the enemy until he succumbed to his wounds.

LESTER W. WEBER

On the afternoon of February 23, 1969, the 2nd Platoon of Company M, 3rd Battalion, 7th Marines, 1st Marine Division went to the rescue of a squad pinned down by the enemy in Bo Ban village in Quang Nam Province. While moving through a rice paddy it, too, came under attack. Lance Corporal *Lester W. Weber* set off on a single-handed assault that broke the enemy's attack and cost him his life. Twice the twenty-year-old wrestled with Viet Cong soldiers, killing them in hand-to-hand combat. He destroyed four enemy emplacements and was moving on a fifth when a burst of machine-gun fire killed him.

"Puff the Magic Dragon" was the name given by ground troops to the specially equipped C-47s used by the Air Force in Vietnam. First flown in 1935, the C-47 had been the backbone of the Air Force in World War II. Now flying in its third war, the plane saw service as a passenger plane, a supply plane, on leaflet dropping missions, and for loudspeaker broadcasts.

Late in 1965 the C-47 assumed a new role. Three 7.62mm machine guns were mounted in the cargo door. Their combined firepower was a devastating six thousand rounds per minute. This awesome display of might denied the enemy the cover of night. While tracer ammunition cut a neon-like path of light toward the target, the plane's loadmaster dropped high-intensity flares overboard. The flares were twenty-seven pounds of magnesium that burned at four thousand degrees F., illuminating the countryside with two million candlepower of light. "Puff" became a welcome friend during night combat.

JOHN L. LEVITOW

On the evening of February 24, 1969, a C-47, "Spooky 71," took off from Bien Hoa Air Base north of Saigon. Several Army compounds in the Long Binh area were receiving fire from aggressive VC forces. Spooky 71 had been called in to help the perimeter guards repulse the hostiles.

For four-and-a-half hours pilot and aircraft commander Major Ken Carpenter flew his craft over the Long Binh–Bien Hoa area in response to calls for help from the ground. Flying tight circles at altitudes averaging only a thousand feet above ground level, Spooky 71 sent thousands of rounds burning into the enemy positions below. The crew dropped dozens of flares giving their comrades below the light they needed to defend their positions.

The crew of Spooky 71 would have been pleased to hear the cheers of the guys on the ground.

In the rear of the plane Airman First Class *John L. Levitow,* the loadmaster, performed his duties routinely. After 180 missions Levitow could do his job in his sleep. He'd remove the Mark 24 flare from its rack, set the ejection and ignition controls, then pass the volatile missile to the gunner.

Spooky 71's gunner, Airman Ellis C. Owen, attached the flare to a lanyard. On command Owen pulled a safety pin, then tossed the armed flare out the cargo door. Twenty seconds later it erupted in a blinding flash of light.

It was a routine the crew performed dozens of times each mission.

Major Carpenter was banking his C-47 into a left turn when it was suddenly jarred by a tremendous explosion. A brilliant burst of light surrounded the plane.

They didn't know it, but a VC mortar round had hit the plane's right wing, exploding inside the wing frame. Thousands of pieces of shrapnel ripped through the plane's thin skin.

In the cockpit Carpenter and his co-pilot wrestled to regain control of the wildly yawing plane. Carpenter wasn't sure he could right the craft.

The cargo compartment was in even worse shape. Shrapnel had wounded four of the crew. Levitow had forty holes in his right side. "It felt like a large piece of wood had struck against my side. I really didn't know what it was," he recalls.

Airman Owen was down, too. But he was suffering from an agony far greater than his wounds.

Owen had been ready to toss a fully armed flare out the cargo door at the precise instant the mortar hit. As he fell backwards it slipped from his grip. The deadly flare rolled crazily along the floor. In less than twenty seconds it would erupt, incinerating the crew and destroying the plane.

Levitow had just finished pulling a casualty away from the open cargo door when he spotted the errant flare. With no idea of how long it had been free, he only knew that he had to get it out of the plane.

Three times Levitow reached for the flare. Three times it slipped from his hand. Desperately he threw himself on the metal cylinder, trapping it under his body. Inch by painful inch Levitow dragged the flare toward the open door. A thick smear of blood marked his path along the plane's aluminum floor.

At last the door was within reach. With a superhuman effort Levitow heaved the flare out the door. A split second later the flare erupted. Levitow collapsed in a heap.

In the cockpit Major Carpenter managed to stop the wild gyrations of the wounded plane, then brought the plane back to Bien Hoa and a safe landing. The ground crew later counted over thirty-five hundred holes in the plane, some exceeding three feet in length.

"After the mission," Carpenter relates, "I was able to reconstruct what happened by the blood trail left by John. I had the aircraft in a thirty-degree bank and how Levitow ever managed to get to the flare and throw it out I'll never know.

"In my experience, I have never seen such a courageous act performed under such adverse conditions. The entire eight-man crew owes their lives to John."

Levitow recovered from his wounds after a brief hospital stay. He was discharged from the Air Force in August 1969 and returned to his home in Glastonbury, Connecticut.

When President Nixon presented Levitow with the Medal of Honor at the White House on May 14, 1970, the gallant airman became the first enlisted man since World War II, and the youngest Air Force hero ever, to receive the top award.

In the A Shau Valley of Thua Thien Province the marines of the 2nd Battalion, 9th Marines had taken a beating for several days. Repeatedly, the NVA hit the marines, caused extensive damage, then faded back across the Laotian border less than 2 kilometers away. Finally the marines had had enough.

At night fall on February 21, 1969, the 9th Marines' Company H crossed the border. They ambushed an NVA truck convoy, completely surprising the enemy. General Abrams gave permission two days later to continue the incursion. The marines stayed in Laos for several weeks.

WILLIAM D. MORGAN

He enlisted in the Marine Corps to go to sea. That's what he had put on his enlistment papers when he signed up in November of 1966. Following completion of his basic training in March 1967 *William D. Morgan* was sent to Sea School in Portsmouth, Virginia.

In July 1967 the nineteen-year-old Pittsburgh, Pennsylvania native joined the Marine Detachment aboard the USS *Newport News*. The next year passed too quickly for Morgan. He greatly enjoyed the spit-and-polish discipline aboard ship. Travelling across the seas as part of an elite unit was duty that many envied.

But there was a war on. Like all marines, Morgan was first and foremost a rifleman. In July of 1968 he joined the 2nd Battalion, 9th Marines as a machine gun section leader.

Like the other marines in Company M, Morgan was deeply frustrated at the Laotian sanctuary enjoyed by the NVA. It seemed totally unfair that the enemy could have that protection. He chomped at the bit to strike back. When his company commander gave the order to cross the imaginary line, Morgan was ready and willing.

The marines pursued the NVA up and down Laotion Route 922. Unaccustomed to such violations of their privileged ground, the NVA fought back with tremendous ferocity.

On February 25, 1969, heavy fire from a well-concealed NVA bunker pinned down a squad of marines. Two of the wounded lay dangerously close to enemy fire.

Repeated attempts to pull the men to safety were stopped by heavy bursts of machine gun fire and rocket-propelled grenades (RPGs). Unwilling to leave his fellow marines at the mercy of the NVA, Morgan sprang into action.

Crashing through the jungle, Morgan made his way to the road in front of the enemy bunker. He yelled to nearby marines, "Pull 'em in," then charged across the road, directly at the bunker, his M-60 blazing.

In full view of the enemy, Morgan sent a stream of hot lead into the bunker. Other NVA positions took him under fire. He fell, mortally wounded in a hail of bullets.

Although it lasted only a few moments, Morgan's charge allowed other marines to pull the casualties to safety. His deliberate self-sacrifice inspired the other marines to crush the NVA defenders.

When Morgan's parents accepted their son's posthumous Medal of Honor on August 6, 1970, they were not told he had died in Laos. Instead, the citation pinpointed the action as occurring in "Quang Tri Province, Republic of Vietnam . . . southeast of Vandergrift Combat Base."

It was years before they learned the truth.

Throughout America's gradual withdrawal from Vietnam, MACV's Study and Observation Group continued its clandestine operations. The Navy's SEALS were an integral part of SOG's forces. The equivalent of the Army's Special Forces, SEALS are elite counterinsurgency forces skilled in underwater demolition and parachuting. Operating both inside Vietnam and across its borders, SEALS played a vital role in the war.

JOSEPH R. KERREY

To the men who served with him in Vietnam, *Bob Kerrey* was an "operator's operator." He excelled at making quick decisions in the field and continually exhibited coolness and courage under fire. As one of his team later said, "Kerrey could handle anything put before him."

Kerrey would have many more chances than most men to put that statement to the test.

A native of Lincoln, Nebraska, Kerrey took a degree in Pharmacology at the University of Nebraska in 1966. In the fall of that year he enlisted in the Navy. He completed Officer Candidate School and received an ensign's commission on June 9, 1967. Two weeks later Kerrey reported to Coronado, California for the first stage of the grueling SEAL course.

Kerrey entered the Underwater Demolition Class with 141 others. Sixty-eight graduated. Of those, fourteen were selected for further SEAL training.

Physical strength was an important asset to SEAL candidates, but not as important as determination and drive to reach a goal. Kerrey possessed all three. As one trainee said of him, "There was never a task or duty Kerrey couldn't perform."

When he graduated from the tough course in December of 1967 Kerrey was assigned to SEAL Team One. A year later he arrived in Vietnam.

Once assigned to leadership of a platoon in SOG, Kerrey quickly gained a reputation as an officer deeply concerned about his men, and very professional in the field. He made every effort he could to protect them from injury. The respect Kerrey earned from his teammates was summed up by one former platoon member who said, "The enlisted guys would jump on a grenade to save Mr. Kerrey's life."

Kerrey spent his first three months in-country in the Mekong Delta region running a variety of guerilla operations against the local Viet Cong infrastructure. In March 1969 his team was sent to the mountainous province of Khanh Hoa along the South China Sea.

Soon after their arrival reliable intelligence reported the presence of several key local VC political figures on an island in Nha Trang Bay. Kerrey's group was selected to kill or capture them. They set out on the night of March 14.

In order to surprise the enemy Kerrey led his small team straight up a 350-foot sheer cliff. After several hours of arduous climbing—in complete darkness—the team silently gathered on a rocky ledge above the enemy's location. Through prearranged hand signals and hushed whispers Kerrey split his team into two elements. The treacherous descent to the enemy's camp began.

As they neared the end of downward maneuver, Kerrey's pointman bumped into an enemy soldier's hammock in the dark. The VC's shouted warnings instantly brought a heavy barrage of small-arms fire onto Kerrey and his men.

Kerrey was maneuvering his team into defensive positions when an unseen grenade suddenly exploded at his feet. The force of the blast threw Kerrey savagely against the jagged rocks. It also shattered his right leg beyond repair.

Suffering excruciating pain, Kerrey still managed to direct his team's efforts in repulsing the enemy. He gave his radioman clear, precise instructions that brought his second team through the darkness to a position where they could help by delivering a telling crossfire on the VC.

Using only the flashes of tracers cutting through the night Kerrey and his men defeated the VC and captured a number of prisoners. Weak from a massive loss of blood, Kerrey overcame his shock to organize an extraction site and defend it against VC snipers. Choppers came in and pulled the SEALs to safety. Kerrey was rushed to the hospital.

His ordeal was only beginning.

In an interview given in *The Wall Street Journal* in 1985, Kerrey revealed how the ending of his proud life as a SEAL affected him. The "operator's operator" was permanently crippled in a brief, violent moment.

"Flash, there was no health," he said. "All the bravado, all that high self-esteem was gone. Tuck a bed pan under you a few times and it brings you right down to earth."

It took seven months in the hospital for Kerrey to recover and learn to walk with an artificial leg. On December 1, 1969, he took his discharge from the Navy.

Recovery from the pain of his war experience and his personal suffering gave Kerrey time to reflect. He began to have misgivings about the war and his role in it. His hurt caused him to think of the hurt he caused.

When word came of the Medal of Honor award Kerrey thought of rejecting it as unwarranted and unwanted. Instead, he accepted it as a symbol of the valor of his comrades.

Kerrey drove himself harder than ever before to overcome his handicap. He took up running to build up the strength in his leg. Through mile after painful mile of work he again proved himself to be the "operator's operator." Eventually, he was able to participate in marathon races.

Determined to achieve similar success in the business world Kerrey developed a chain of popular restaurants in the Omaha area.

In the early 1980s Kerrey turned his attention to politics. Summing up his philosophy, Kerrey said: "It is important to make a judgement about what is right and wrong, and then fight for those things you believe are right. You may be proven wrong but you will have made an effort."

In November 1982, Democrat Bob Kerrey was elected the Governor of Nebraska.

TERRY T. KAWAMURA

On March 20, 1969, the nineteen-year-old son of a career Army sergeant deliberately sacrificed himself to save his fellow soldiers. On that night a group of VC sappers attacked the 173rd Airborne Brigade's base camp at Camp Radcliff at An Khe in Binh Dinh Province. When the enemy took his barracks under fire, Corporal *Terry T. Kawamura* grabbed his rifle and returned the fire. A mortar crashed through the roof, the explosion stunning and wounding several soldiers. A split second later a demolition charge came flying through the roof. Kawamura realized his buddies were not going to be able to escape the impending explosion. Unhesitatingly, Kawamura threw himself on the explosive, dying so others might live.

JAMES L. BONDSTEEL

Army Staff Sgt. *James L. Bondsteel,* a native of Allen, Michigan, served in Vietnam for four straight years. He spent his first two years as a communications specialist with the Signal Corps. In December of 1967 he transferred to Company A, 2nd Battalion, 2nd Infantry, 1st Infantry Division. He remained with that unit until February 1970. On May 24, 1969, near An Loc in Binh Long Province, Bondsteel displayed tremendous courage in a vicious one-man assault on a series of enemy bunkers. In a violent four-hour battle Bondsteel personally destroyed ten enemy bunkers and killed over a dozen of the enemy. Wounded twice, he successfully rescued a number of casualties, carrying them to safety.

JIMMY W. PHIPPS

Near An Hoa in Thua Thien Province on May 27, 1969, Marine PFC *Jimmy W. Phipps* of Santa Monica, California, serving with the 1st Engineer Battalion of the 1st Marine Division, was defusing a 175mm artillery round planted by the VC as a booby trap. After he realized that the shell was attached to a secondary explosive device Phipps elected to destroy it with a hand grenade. He had just prepared the grenade when the fuse of the secondary device ignited. Instantly sensing the lethal danger to those around him, Phipps dove forward, covering the secondary device and the artillery shell. He absorbed the full and tremendous explosion with his own body, saving the lives of his fellow soldiers.

MICHAEL F. FOLLAND

The 199th Infantry Brigade's Company D, 2nd Battalion, 3rd Infantry was attacking an enemy bunker complex that had pinned it down in the dense jungle in Long Khanh Province on

July 3, 1969. Corporal *Michael F. Folland* and his company commander crawled forward to take a bunker under rifle fire. A grenade landed near them. Folland screamed, "Grenade!" His CO picked it up and threw it away. A second later another grenade dropped near them. This time the officer couldn't reach it. Folland, a twenty-year-old from Richmond, Virginia, dove for the missile. He was mortally wounded in the explosion, but his actions saved his CO's life.

GORDON R. ROBERTS

Two weeks before his eighteenth birthday, on June 14, 1968, *Gordon R. Roberts* left his home in Lebanon, Ohio, to enlist in the Army. Trained as a rifleman, Roberts spent six months in Europe with the 8th Infantry Division before going to Vietnam in April 1969.

Roberts joined the 101st Airborne Division's 1st Battalion, 506th Infantry in time to fight at the bloody battle for Ap Bia Mountain, otherwise known as "Hamburger Hill", in the A Shau Valley, one mile east of the Laotion border, on May 10–20. He earned a Silver Star by displaying coolness and courage in that intense fight.

On July 11, 1969, Roberts's unit, Company B, moved along a ridgeline in Thua Thien Province on its way to help another company under heavy enemy fire. Suddenly, from a nearby hill, the NVA unleashed a fury of small-arms fire and RPGs. Company B hit the dirt, unable to move.

With incredible courage Roberts crawled through the grass toward the nearest gun emplacement. He jumped to his feet, rifle blazing, and headed straight into the enemy's fire. His accurate fire killed the two gunners. He paused to load a fresh clip in his M-16, then moved toward a second bunker. A burst of enemy fire knocked the rifle from his hands.

He raced back down the hill. Yelling, "Gimme that," he grabbed a rifle from a buddy, then took off back up the hill.

The second bunker fell to his onslaught, and he knocked out a third with an accurate grenade toss. He was cut off from his platoon now, but continued on, adrenaline pumping through his veins. A fourth bunker fell.

Because his single-handed assault had carried him so far ahead of his own unit, Roberts worked his way through the jungle to join another company. He fought with them until the enemy pulled back.

The young soldier finished his one-year tour in Vietnam in April 1970. On March 2, 1971, the slight-framed Roberts stood alongside his beaming parents as President Nixon draped the Medal of Honor around his neck.

Roberts later graduated from the University of Dayton and earned a Masters degree from the University of Cincinnati.

JOHN G. GERTSCH

A week after Roberts's display of bravery another 101st Airborne trooper earned a posthumous Medal of Honor for gallantry over a three-day period. On July 16, Staff Sgt. *John G. Gertsch* took command of his platoon of Company E, 1st Battalion, 327th Infantry after his lieutenant was killed during heavy fighting in the A Shau Valley. Over the next two days Gertsch repeatedly risked his life to maneuver his men against the enemy. He was wounded on the 18th but refused to be evacuated. His concern for his men overcame any feelings he had for his own welfare.

He proved that beyond any doubt on July 19. In the middle of vicious firefight, Gertsch saw an enemy rifleman firing at a medic treating a wounded officer. He raced through a barrage of small-arms fire to position himself between the two men and the NVA soldier. Under Gertsch's covering fire the medic pulled the officer to safety. The NVA directed their fire toward Gertsch, killing him.

JOSE FRANCISCO JIMENEZ

A twenty-four-year old Mexican-born marine staged a one-man assault on August 28, 1969, destroying two enemy bunkers, an anti-aircraft gun crew, and killing a number of NVA before being himself mortally wounded. *Jose Francisco Jimenez* moved to Eloy, Arizona, in 1956, when he was ten years old. Although he never became a citizen, Jimenez enlisted in the Marines because he wanted to "show America how grateful" he was for all it had given him and his family.

When his Company K, 3rd Battalion, 7th Marines, 1st Marine Division stumbled across the NVA in southern Quang Nam Province near Hoi An that August afternoon, Jimenez went to work. Over and over he moved alone against the enemy's strongpoints until he was hit too many times to continue. When his fellow marines caught up to him they found Jimenez mortally wounded, only ten feet away from a trench of dead NVA.

Throughout most of 1969 the 1st Cavalry Division operated northwest of Saigon. Repeatedly clashing with NVA units trying to slip across the Cambodian border, the cavalrymen fought in dozens of brief but violent firefights.

DONALD S. SKIDGEL

He tried to enlist several times in 1967, but neither the Army nor Marines would take him. *Don Skidgel* was married with one daughter and a pregnant wife. The military establishment wasn't interested in young married men—at least not yet.

Born on October 13, 1948, in Caribou, Maine, Skidgel grew up in Plymouth, Maine. The rural area around Plymouth was an excellent place for a boy to mature. Through the dense green forests of central Maine he hunted small game from the time he was old enough to hold a rifle. Under his father's tutelage he developed a keen instinct for the outdoors.

Skidgel always looked for excitement and adventure. School

didn't offer him enough, so he quit at age sixteen. Within a matter of weeks he was off on his own, working in Connecticut.

He took up riding motorcycles for the thrill they provided. Barreling down the backroads of rural Maine, he would crank a two-wheeler up as fast as he could. He was always looking for more excitement.

In 1966 he married—another adventure. A year later his daughter was born. He was so excited that he could hardly stop talking about her.

As proud as he was of being a father, Skidgel still sought excitement. He thought he could find it in the military—but they weren't interested.

At least not until January 1968. After the Tet attacks the Army reached out for anyone it could find. Skidgel soon received his draft notice. With his wife expecting the following month, Skidgel reported for induction in February 1968.

Skidgel completed his basic training and was training as a tank crew member at Fort Knox, Kentucky, when a recruiter from the Airborne School at Fort Benning, Georgia, made a pitch to Skidgel's class.

To Skidgel airborne training was just another adventure. Besides, it paid fifty dollars a month more. Along with several of his buddies Skidgel said, "Why not?" and signed up.

Skidgel earned his wings in August 1968. By that time one of his adventures had ended—his marriage ended in divorce.

Skidgel arrived in Vietnam in May 1969. Although airborne-qualified, he went to the 1st Cavalry's Troop D, 1st Squadron, 9th Cavalry. They needed men more than the airborne units did.

On September 14, 1969, Troop D provided road security to a truck convoy near Song Be in Binh Long Province. An NVA battalion lay concealed in the grass alongside the road. When the deuce-and-a-halves came into range the enemy opened up. Small-arms fire and RPGs raked the column. Trucks and APCs swerved from side to side, seeking an escape.

All but Skidgel's.

Skidgel ordered the driver of his APC to steer the vehicle off the road directly into the middle of the enemy force. From his position atop the vehicle Skidgel sent repeated bursts of machine gun fire into the NVA ranks.

After he knocked out one key position he dismounted the APC. He grabbed an M-60 machine gun, then ran through the bulletswept field to a better firing position.

For more than fifteen minutes he stayed in the open, dueling with the enemy. His one-man attack diverted the enemy's attention long enough for the rest of the convoy to organize a defense.

When he ran out of ammo Skidgel headed back to his APC for more. He had finished loading up when a cry for help came over the radio. The command element's APC was under strong attack.

Ordering "Let's go," to his driver, Skidgel boarded his vehicle. Using the machine guns with brutal effectiveness he knocked out several more enemy positions. He was still urging the driver forward when an RPG hit, blowing him out of the gunner's seat and onto the rear fender.

With blood streaming from multiple wounds, Skidgel crawled back to his gun. His driver called for him to quit but Skidgel wouldn't. This was an adventure he wanted to finish.

Onward they pressed. Skidgel's selfless actions had the desired effect. The NVA turned their attack from the command vehicle to the lone APC moving on them. They concentrated their fire on Skidgel, at last shooting him off his perch.

In the meantime, the command vehicle withdrew to a better position. There it reorganized the elements of the convoy into a counterattacking force that drove the enemy off the field.

Skidgel's bravery had saved the convoy.

On December 16, 1971, Vice President Spiro Agnew, in the presence of Skidgel's parents, presented Skidgel's posthumous Medal of Honor to his son, three-year-old Terry D. Skidgel.

MICHAEL J. NOVOSEL

Mike J. Novosel flew off to war for his country for the first time in 1945, when he was the twenty-two-year-old pilot of a B-29 bomber bound for Japan. He spent the last four months of World War II flying bombing missions, then served another two years in the South Pacific commanding a bomber squadron.

It was pretty heady stuff for a youngster who had grown up in the Pittsburgh suburb of Etna, Pennsylvania. He vividly recalls his homecoming six years after he'd enlisted: "The treatment was unbelievable. Everyone was so grateful for what we had done over there."

Novosel went to Florida to serve as a test pilot at Eglin Air Force Base before he departed active duty in 1949. When the Korean War broke out a year later he owned a very successful restaurant in Fort Walton Beach, Florida, was a partner in an appliance store, and a major in the Air Force Reserve.

That didn't keep him from volunteering for active duty, however.

"I didn't get into combat—not that I didn't want to," he says. "It's just that the Air Force didn't pick me up until 1953. And then it was to attend the Air Command and Staff School."

When the Air Force released him in 1955 as a lieutenant colonel, Novosel became a pilot for a major commercial airline. It was a way for him to spend more time with his growing family.

Less than ten years passed before Novosel again went on active duty—and found himself in his third war.

"I was a great fan of John Kennedy. I took him at his word when he said to do something for your country. When I found out there was a war going on in Vietnam I volunteered," he said.

The Air Force didn't have much use for forty-two-year-old lieutenant colonels, so Novosel went to the Army. "They were desperate for pilots, so they took me," he said.

Newly commissioned Army Warrant Officer Mike Novosel spent a year in the States flying choppers with the Special Forces before he was sent to Vietnam as a medevac pilot.

He finished his twelve months in January 1967. This time when he came home there were no bands. "There wasn't even anyone to say 'Hello' or 'Congratulations, you made it back from 'Nam after a year.'"

Novosel spent two years training new helicopter pilots before he decided to resume his civilian flying career. Fate changed his plans. His separation physical revealed that he had glaucoma.

"For civilian airlines it's a grounding condition. But the Army gave me a waiver and let me continue flying."

In March 1969 Novosel started his second tour of duty in Vietnam. He went to the 82nd Medical Detachment, 45th Medical Company, 68th Medical Group at Binh Thuy, upriver from Can Tho, about 75 miles southwest of Saigon.

On October 2, 1969, Novosel had already been at the controls of his chopper for seven hours when word came that three ARVN infantry companies had stumbled across an NVA training area in the Plain of Reeds, Kien Tuong Province, near Cambodia's Parrot's Beak. There were heavy casualties. They needed to be pulled out.

Novosel turned to his co-pilot, WO2 Tyron Chamberlain, and said, "Let's go get them."

On the flight to the battle site Novosel learned the heavy enemy fire had already brought down two Cobra gunships and hit two F-100 Air Force jets. But that didn't lessen his determination to save the wounded.

Once at the battleground, an open area alongside the Cambodian border covered with six-foot-tall elephant grass, Novosel flew slowly looking for the wounded. The thick vegetation made it difficult. "We spotted the first one," he recalls, "and all of a sudden we started seeing others all over."

Back and forth across the battlefield Novosel flew, picking up wounded. His crew chief, Specialist Four Joseph Horvath remembers: "I never heard so much enemy fire before. I saw gun flashes from bunkers all around us."

Completely disregarding the fire, Novosel hovered while Horvath and the medic, Specialist Four Herbert Heinold, pulled the wounded aboard.

"As soon as we touched down we started receiving fire," recalls Heinold, "but Mr. Novosel stayed until we got the wounded aboard. Several times the intensity of the fire forced us out. At one point I saw gun flashes from at least a half dozen places."

Six times enemy fire forced Novosel to pull back. Six times he came in from another direction. Each time his ruse worked.

As soon as he had a full load of wounded, nine or ten men, Novosel flew them to medics waiting at the Special Forces camp at nearby Moc Hoa. Then he flew back into the carnage. Three times during the two-and-one-half-hour ordeal Novosel made the round trip.

Novosel had decided it was getting too dark to find more casualties when a wounded ARVN stood up, waving his shirt. From twenty meters behind the man an NVA machine gun fired at the chopper. Novosel never hesitated.

In order to save the ARVN, and to protect the wounded already filling his ship, Novosel brought his Huey in low, then began backing it up. He wanted as much metal between him and the machine gun as possible.

Horvath had started pulling the casualty into the chopper when an enemy rifle round slammed into the cockpit. Plexiglass and bullet fragments flew through the compartment, some embedding themselves in Novosel's right calf and thigh. Shock, and the impact of the shrapnel, caused him to lose control of the Huey.

"Aw hell! I'm hit," Novosel remembers saying. He was afraid he would pass out, but managed to regain control of the chopper, climbing rapidly out of the area. Horvath finished pulling the ARVN aboard sixty feet above the ground.

Altogether, Novosel made fifteen extractions, bringing twenty-nine casualties to safety. With his wounds patched up he returned to flying the next day. "I didn't think much of it at the time. I've had other missions just as tough," he says of the rescues.

During his two tours of duty in Vietnam Novosel received credit for extracting more than fifty-five hundred casualties. Few men have amassed such an enviable record.

Before Novosel left Vietnam in March 1970 his oldest son,

Michael J., Jr., joined the unit as a medevac pilot. They have the unique distinction of having rescued one another. "My son was shot down one day and I picked him up," Novosel recalls. "When I was shot down the same week, he picked me up."

Once Stateside again, Novosel served three years as the aviation officer and pilot for the Army's prestigious Golden Knights parachute team. He was with them when he was summoned to the White House on June 15, 1971, to receive his Medal of Honor. He is the oldest recipient for Vietnam service.

When Novosel retired after forty-four years of service to his country in March 1985, he was the last military aviator on active duty who had flown combat missions in World War II.

CHAPTER NINE

POWs Fight Back

A merican soldiers who were captured and held as prisoners of war were a very special group of warriors who engaged the enemy on a different level. Over seven hundred men spent up to eight-and-one-half years in the hands of the VC or North Vietnamese. They were held in camps ranging from isolated VC outposts in South Vietnam to the infamous "Hanoi Hilton"—the block-long French-built prison complex in downtown Hanoi, named by the North Vietnamese, Hao Lo, or "Fiery Furnace." While in captivity the POWs were subjected to incredible brutality and deprivation.

Throughout their period of confinement most POWs lived in a small cell. Only a handful were fortunate enough to have a cellmate. A concrete slab served as a bed, an old bucket as the toilet. Meals were served but twice a day. Usually they consisted of a thin watery soup along with a meager portion of rice. Meat, or any protein, was available only rarely.

Although isolated from one another, the POWs developed elaborate methods of communication. By tapping on walls or using hand signals, they laboriously sent messages. Thus they could keep each other informed and organize against their captors. To be caught sending messages, though, invited swift and inhuman torture.

Resistance to the enemy's attempts to extract military information proved to be a difficult task. Some men completely resisted the North Vietnamese interrogations, revealing only their name, rank, and service number. Most, though, held out only as long as they could endure the pain of torture. Even then they were often able to give their captors false information.

The four POWs who earned Medals of Honor displayed unique valor. They were cited for *sustained* bravery rather than for specific acts of gallantry. Overcoming unimaginable hardships, these heroic men repeatedly resisted the enemy. They demonstrated great courage in organizing their fellow captives against their captors, and although horribly injured they attempted to escape. Their indomitable courage provided dramatic inspiration to the other POWs.

DONALD G. COOK

Born in Brooklyn, New York, on August 9, 1934, *Donald G. Cook* grew up in Burlington, Vermont. An avid football player, he played on teams both at his high school and at St. Michael's College in Winooski, Vermont.

After graduating from St. Michael's in June of 1956, Cook enrolled in Marine Corps OCS. He went on active duty in January 1957 and received his commission as a second lieutenant five months later.

Cook selected the field of communications as his specialty, and drew an assignment with the 1st Marine Division. When he showed a talent for languages the Marine Corps enrolled him in the U.S. Army Language School in Presidio, California. The Mandarin Chinese course required one year of intense study, but Cook persevered, graduating in May 1961. Cook next attended the Army Intelligence Course at Fort Holabird, Maryland. In September of 1961 he returned to the 1st Marine Division as head of its Interrogation Team.

On December 11, 1964, Cook left his Hawaii duty station with eight other marines for a temporary thirty-day assignment in Vietnam. The VC captured him on December 31, 1964.

Years passed without any further word of Cook. Only when the other POWs came home in 1973 did the story of Cook's heroism while a prisoner become known.

Cook served as the senior marine advisor to a South Vietnamese marine battalion. On that last day of December, while his unit conducted an offensive sweep in coastal Phuoc Tuy Province, the VC shot down a U.S. helicopter. Cook led a platoon toward the crash site. The VC sprang an ambush.

Most of the Vietnamese marines ran. Cook tried to organize the few remaining South Vietnamese into a workable defense but took a round in the left leg before he could get them into position. The rest of the marines took off. Alone and immobile, Cook was carried off by the VC.

As soon as he arrived at the first POW camp Cook established himself as the commanding officer of all the POWs. His assertiveness thwarted VC efforts to break down military discipline among the prisoners. Even though he was beaten and tortured by sadistic guards, Cook still refused to step aside. He insisted on acting as the POWs' CO and demanded the appropriate respect.

According to one former POW, Cook "wouldn't even give the VC the time of day."

In their propaganda meetings the VC characterized American officers as members of the elite class, unwilling and unable to perform manual labor. Cook undermined that effort by organizing calesthenic classes for the POWs, leading them himself. On other occasions Cook purposefully stepped up the pace of work details in order to embarrass the VC interpreter working alongside him.

The results not only proved Cook's point, but earned him more physical abuse.

Cook's courage also impressed his captors. The VC forced Cook to hike several hundred miles through jungle and mountain terrain to a new camp in Phuoc Long Province even though he was weak with malaria. Witnesses expressed amazement at Cook's stamina. His deteriorating health caused him to stagger, yet he refused to accept help or to allow anyone to carry his pack. He would not show weakness to the enemy. Once at the new camp, the VC commander praised Cook for his perseverance.

During his stay at the new site Cook used his limited medical knowledge to give first aid to his fellow prisoners. At times he even gave heart massages to revive malaria victims. More than once Cook shared his meager rations with those sicker than himself. Other times he sacrificed his small allowance of penicilin so that another man might benefit from a larger dose.

Cook recognized the need for maintaining communication among the prisoners. He set up message drops and developed a simple code. Always his message contained the theme: Resist.

One time the guards caught him passing a message. Furious at his constant insubordination, they knelt him in front of the other prisoners. A VC officer held a pistol to Cook's head. To the amazement of the other prisoners and the VC, Cook defiantly recited the pistol's nomenclature in a calm, strong voice. The guards gave up.

In spite of Cook's mental strength, disease extracted its inevitable toll. Unable to counter the crippling effects of malaria, Cook died on December 8, 1967. The other POWs buried him in a jungle grave.

Though repatriated POWs reported Cook's death and the Provisional Revolutionary Government of South Vietnam confirmed it in January 1973, his widow refused to accept the news. Without his body, she held out hope he might still be alive. At her insistence, the Department of Defense listed him as Missing In Action.

A Medal of Honor recommendation had been prepared for Colonel Cook, who was promoted regularly while carried as MIA, soon after reports of his courage were verified. It was approved, but the award held in abeyance at the family's request.

On February 26, 1980, with his widow's approval, the Defense Department officially declared Cook deceased. Mrs. Cook accepted her husband's posthumous Medal of Honor from Navy Secretary Edward Hidalgo on May 16, 1980.

JAMES B. STOCKDALE

When anti-aircraft fire blew his Skyhawk jet apart on September 5, 1965, ice-cold fear gripped Navy Commander *James B. Stockdale*'s stomach. It wasn't fear of capture that hit him—after all, as a Navy fighter pilot on his two hundred and first mission over North Vietnam, Stockdale had learned to accept the risks of being shot down and captured.

It was far worse than that. "I had the most damaging information a North Vietnamese torturer could possibly extract from an American prisoner," he remembers.

Stockdale knew the truth about the Gulf of Tonkin incidents.

Thirteen months earlier Stockdale had been the CO of Fighter Squadron 51 aboard the carrier *Ticonderoga*. On August 4, 1964, Stockdale scrambled into the air in response to a call for help from the destroyers *Maddox* and *Turner Joy*. They reported an attack by North Vietnamese PT boats.

For two hours Stockdale flew his jet back and forth above the black waves. He fired his rockets where the destroyers fired. He searched where the destroyers' radar said the enemy boats should be. Always his eyes, and his radar, told him the same thing: there was nothing out there.

When he returned to the *Ticonderoga* he threw his helmet against the bulkhead in disgust. "Nothing but a damn Chinese fire drill!" he swore. "Spooked operators and spooked equipment."

In spite of what Stockdale reported, President Johnson ordered reprisal attacks against North Vietnam. A few days later Johnson's Gulf of Tonkin Resolution sailed through Congress. The U.S. was at war—an undeclared war, to be sure—but still a war.

If the North Vietnamese could pry that information from Stockdale they would possess tremendous ammunition for their propaganda.

Born in the small central Illinois town of Abingdon on December 23, 1923, Stockdale entered Annapolis with the class of 1947. His frustration at missing out on action during World War II peaked when his cousin, Robert H. Dunlap, received a Medal of Honor for heroism as a marine officer at Iwo Jima in 1945.

A stateside instructor's berth kept Stockdale out of the Korean War. Sometimes he thought he'd never get a fighter command. Finally, in February of 1963, his assignment to a fighter squadron came through.

Now, as he drifted below his parachute, Stockdale vowed not to reveal what he knew.

He hit the ground hard, discovering for the first time that the force of the ejection had shattered his left knee and broken his left shoulder. Before he could pull himself free from his chute a crowd of peasants descended on him. They beat him with clubs and their fists until North Vietnamese soldiers pulled him away—eventually transferring him to the notorious "Hanoi Hilton."

Eight years would pass before Stockdale again knew freedom. Three of those years would be spend in solitary confinement; one would be spent in complete isolation. For two years he stayed locked in leg irons. His injured leg never received treatment. As a result, he has a permanent limp.

"If you really want to turn a person to putty," he says, "isolation is best. I spent a month blindfolded. The Vietnamese never knew how close I came to giving up and spilling my guts."

But he didn't. As senior POW Stockdale organized the others into military units. Commanders were appointed. Orders were issued. The chief order demanded defiance of the enemy. Captives were expected to resist torture as long as they could.

Stockdale devised a simple but effective code for communication. "It was a tap code keyed to a five-by-five matrix. Through tapping we could pass messages, keep each other's morale up," he recalls.

Stockdale knew the value of rituals for maintaining control. Without discipline, the group would fall apart. He had to provide an example of resistance so that the others would know what was expected of them.

Early in 1969 the North Vietnamese made it clear they were going to use Stockdale in propaganda pictures. To foil their efforts, Stockdale beat his own face to a bloody pulp with a wooden stool; he used a razor blade to tear up his scalp. The result: no pictures.

According to Stockdale, the North Vietnamese applied fear, guilt, pain, solitude, and degradation to turn prisoners against each other and to pry loose military information. Whenever they caught a prisoner in any act considered a violation of the Hanoi Hilton's many petty rules, the guards cruelly tortured the offender. The worst crime was to cause other prisoners to oppose the camp authority.

Almost as soon as his imprisonment began Stockdale was

recognized as a leader of the resistance. Twice the guards identified him as the organizer of elaborate secret resistance groups. Each time a dreadful purge followed. Stockdale and the other leaders were horribly tortured, then cast into solitary. The other prisoners suffered as well. At least one died during the purges.

"In September 1969 I had been caught in a third prison bust. I was at the end of my string. I had been through thirteen different torture sessions. I didn't want any more men to suffer as a result of my actions," Stockdale recalls.

Stockdale feared he would reveal the names of his fellow conspirators. He took a drastic step to prevent that. When left alone in the small room used for torture sessions Stockdale crawled to its tiny window. Hampered by the leg irons cutting deep into his flesh, Stockdale somehow managed to break the glass, and slash his wrists with the shards.

"It was clear to me I had to stop the interrogation. If it cost my life, it cost it," he says matter-of-factly.

The North Vietnamese found him before he bled to death. Stockdale's willingness to sacrifice his own life deeply impressed his captors. And, the publicity-conscious North Vietnamese could not afford to have the world learn of the senior POW's suicide.

They turned off the torture machine. While Stockdale's ordeal would not completely end until his release on February 12, 1973, the North Vietnamese did treat him with considerably more respect after this incident.

For his "valiant leadership and extraordinary courage in a hostile environment," Stockdale received the Medal of Honor from President Ford on March 4, 1976. Stockdale looked forward to resuming his naval career, but it was not to be. His one dream—to command an aircraft carrier—never materialized. "They patted on three stars and patronized me. I'd been away too long. I was destined to be on the second team."

After thirty-three years of active naval service, Admiral Stockdale retired in 1977. He spent three years as the president of The Citadel Military Academy in Charleston, South Carolina, before accepting a position as a senior research fellow at the

Hoover Institute on War, Revolution, and Peace at Stanford University in Palo Alto, California. He also lectures at Stanford University.

GEORGE E. DAY

On August 26, 1967, Major *George E. Day,* also known as "Bud," flew an F-100 on a forward air control mission about fifty miles north of the DMZ. A pilot since 1952, Day had over five thousand hours of flying time, with forty-five hundred hours in single engine jets. His experience included time in almost every jet fighter in America's arsenal.

Day was no stranger to the military, either. Born in Sioux City, Iowa, on February 24, 1925, he left there to enlist in the Marine Corps in 1942. He spent thirty months as a noncommissioned officer in the South Pacific during World War II.

He returned to Iowa to earn his Bachelor's degree, then took a law degree from the University of South Dakota in 1950. He also accepted an Air National Guard commission as a second lieutenant.

After the hostilities erupted in Korea, Day was called to active duty and selected for flight training. By the time the Korean War ended Day had spent two tours there as a fighter-bomber pilot.

In April of 1964 Day went to Vietnam to serve as an F-100 squadron's assistant operations officer at Tuy Hoa Air Base. Later, he went to Phu Cat Air Base to organize and command the first squadron of F-100s used as forward air controllers (FACs).

The F-100, a vintage Korean War jet, was used as a high speed FAC on missions where slower FAC planes proved too vulnerable to ground fire. His men called themselves the "Huns."

On that hot August day ground fire hit the head Hun. Day knew immediately he'd have to bail out. On ejection he slammed into the plane's fuselage. The impact broke his right arm in three places and sprained his left knee. He was captured as soon as he touched down.

For two days the North Vietnamese tortured and interrogated him. He suffered intense pain from his untended injuries but still thought about escape. All he needed was the right opportunity.

On the third day an enemy medic crudely set his broken arm. Day thought the cure was worse than the injury.

Day's captors were members of the local militia. Mostly teenagers, they were undisciplined and easily deluded. Day convinced his guards that his injuries left him incapable of moving. As a result they left his hands untied, securing only his feet.

On the sixth day after he was shot down Day undid the knots and headed south.

He walked for two days, going without sleep the first night out of fear the enemy would find him. On the second night, he crawled under a bush to sleep. In the middle of the night, a bomb, rocket, or artillery shell (he never did know which for sure) exploded at close range. Red-hot shrapnel ripped into his right leg. The concussion ruptured his sinuses and eardrums. He vomited blood.

Day holed up for two days until he regained his senses. Then he restarted his southbound trek.

As he drew closer to the Ben Hai River, which marked the DMZ, the land grew rougher. Where before he had traversed rice paddies, he now walked through heavy jungle.

The only food he had during this odyssey was a few raw frogs he caught and berries he found growing on bushes along his route.

Day knew that he was close to starving when he began to hallucinate and talk out loud. Still, he pressed onward.

At last he reached the river. By using a bamboo log as a float, Day waded across.

Growing more delirious with each passing hour, Day found it increasingly difficult to maintain his bearings. The no-man's-land of the DMZ was harsh country, pock-marked by numerous bomb craters. Day stumbled and fell frequently, weak from hunger.

One day two FAC pilots flew directly overhead. Day screamed, shouted, and jumped around. They didn't see him.

Near the end of his ordeal Day heard choppers nearby. He headed toward the sound. He didn't know it but the choppers were picking up a Marine patrol a short distance away.

He limped through the underbrush, every fiber of his body intent on reaching the choppers. As he got closer he yelled, but his voice couldn't be heard above the noise. He burst into the LZ just as the last chopper disappeared over the trees.

Filled with despair, Day staggered back into the jungle—still determined to find help.

Perhaps if he hadn't been so weak, so unable to orient himself, Day might not have stumbled into the VC ambush a few days later. He'd been able to avoid other VC by going around them. This time he used a trail well-worn by American patrols. Before he knew it he walked right into the middle of a VC ambush position.

Day always figured he must have scared them as much as they scared him. Here he was, an unexpected apparition stumbling out of the jungle, with matted hair, filthy skin, clad in shorts and staggering around like a drunk.

The VC hesitated before reacting. When they called to him, Day ran into the jungle. The VC opened fire. He got about thirty feet before bullets hit his left hand and thigh.

His escape attempt was over.

Day never did know exactly how long he had stayed on the run. The closest he could ever determine was somewhere between eleven and fifteen days.

What he does remember is it took the VC only a day and a half to return him to the original prison camp.

Cruel torture awaited Day. A starvation diet dropped his weight from 170 to 110 pounds. The North Vietnamese refused Day all medical treatment for his gunshot wounds. They festered and became infected.

Day met with stoic resistance all attempts by the North Vietnamese to extract information. He simply refused to talk.

The North Vietnamese resorted to two full days of barbaric

torture to try to break Day, but he still resisted. At one point they bound his hands behind him, tied a rope to his wrists, then used that rope to hoist him off the ground, suspending him from an overhead ceiling beam. His shoulders dislocated. When he still would not cooperate the interrogation officer ordered a guard to twist Day's mangled right arm. The pop of the wrist bone could be heard across the room.

Stretched to the limit of human endurance, Day agreed to talk. The North Vietnamese were sure they had broken the stubborn lawyer.

But they hadn't. Even though he knew he faced death if discovered, Day answered his captors' questions with false information, revealing nothing of military significance.

When Day arrived at Hoa Lo Prison in Hanoi two months later, he was a complete physical wreck. Even though he couldn't perform the simplest tasks for himself the North Vietnamese continued to torture him.

His ordeal continued until his release on March 14, 1973.

Day's incredible resistance to the unspeakable cruelties of the North Vietnamese was rewarded with the Medal of Honor on March 4, 1976.

Colonel Day is one of the most decorated men in Air Force history. Among his sixty decorations and awards—which include forty for combat—are: the Air Force Cross, the Distinguished Service Medal, two Silver Stars, the Legion of Merit, the Distinguished Flying Cross, ten Air Medals, three Bronze Stars, and four Purple Hearts.

Today, retired Air Force Colonel Bud Day lives in Florida, where he practices law.

LANCE P. SIJAN

"Sijan! My name is Lance Peter Sijan!"

The voice, raspy and filled with pain, spoke defiantly to a North Vietnamese interrogator. For over two hours the enemy officer had tortured the downed pilot. He'd say to the POW,

"Your arm, your arm is very bad. I am going to twist it unless you tell me."

The prisoners in nearby bamboo cells would hear the unseen Air Force officer say, "I'm not going to tell you, it's against the code of conduct." Then they would hear him scream. They knew the guard was twisting his arm.

The other prisoners had no idea of their fellow captive's identity. All they had seen was a badly beaten and emaciated body thrown into a cell. Then the questioning started.

Amazingly, the prisoner threatened his captor. "Wait till I get better, you SOB," he told the North Vietnamese, "you're really going to get it."

They couldn't believe a man could be so bold.

At last, when they thought their fellow prisoner was about to break, he shouted out his name, rank, and serial number.

That was how they met Air Force Captain *Lance Sijan*.

During his senior year in high school Sijan received an appointment to the U.S. Air Force Academy. The eighteen-year-old left his hometown of Milwaukee to join the class of 1965 in Colorado Springs, Colorado.

Sijan quickly proved himself a leader. He excelled not only academically, but also on the gridiron. He spent two years on the varsity team as a substitute end.

Following graduation Sijan entered flight training. He earned his pilot's wings in November 1966. Seven months later he was sent to Vietnam and joined the 480th Tactical Fighter Squadron at Da Nang.

On November 9, 1967, Sijan flew in the back seat of an F-4 Phantom piloted by Colonel John W. Armstrong, CO of the 366th Tactical Fighter Squadron. It was a routine bombing mission near Vinh, North Vietnam until ground fire hit their plane. Armstrong ordered an ejection.

Armstrong was never seen or heard from again. Sijan suffered a skull fracture, a mangled right hand with three fingers bent back to the wrist, and a compound fracture of the left leg. To add to his ordeal, he had no survival equipment.

Sikorsky HH-3 Search and Rescue choppers, the famous Jolly Green Giants, raced to the area as soon as they received word of the shoot-down. They made radio contact with Sijan almost immediately. The SAR crews learned of his injuries. Sijan was down, but not out. By the sound of their rotors Sijan directed the helicopters over the thick jungle canopy.

Suddenly, one Jolly Green Giant crew heard Sijan transmit, "I see you. I see you. Stay where you are. I'm coming to you."

Ignoring the increasingly heavy ground fire the chopper hovered in place, its rescue line disappearing into the jungle below. Bullets crashed into the chopper, a few at first, then more. After half an hour, with no further voice contact, the chopper pulled out.

But SAR didn't give up. Over one hundred aircraft were used in the search the first two days, fourteen more on the third. Enemy fire brought down one plane and several helicopter crewmen were wounded by ground fire, but the search was in vain. No further word was heard from Sijan.

Where was he?

The trauma of Sijan's injuries had overwhelmed him within a few feet of the rescue line. For the next three days he passed in and out of consciousness from the excruciating pain.

When he at last regained consciousness Sijan realized that his freedom depended on his strength. Unable to stand or use his legs to crawl, Sijan pulled himself backwards through the jungle. Foot by painful foot, Sijan dragged himself along.

One of his cellmates, Captain Guy Gruter, recalls that "Sijan said he'd go for two or three days—as long as he possibly could—then he'd be exhausted and go to sleep. As soon as he'd wake up, he'd be off again."

Sijan evaded the searching enemy for six full weeks. For almost forty-five days, without food and with very little water, Sijan moved over the rugged terrain. He was so emaciated that every bone in his body protruded through his gaunt skin.

He finally collapsed along a dirt road. He lay there for more than a day before a truck passed by and found him.

As Sijan later told Gruter, the North Vietnamese gave him shelter and food. After a few days, with his strength returning, Sijan's thoughts again turned to escape.

One day a single guard served him food. Sijan beckoned him over. When the guard bent down, Sijan told Gruter, "I just let him have it. Wham!"

After knocking the guard unconscious Sijan pulled himself back into the jungle. This time only a few hours passed before they found him. The guards severely beat him.

On New Years Day 1968 the North Vietnamese threw Sijan into a cell near Captain Gruter. That very night the others heard him scream his name in defiance at his interrogators.

Over the next several days, according to Gruter, "the guy was always trying to push his way out of the bamboo cell. They'd beat him back with a stick. We could hear the cracks."

Finally, the North Vietnamese were ready to transport their prisoners to Hanoi. Gruter and Colonel Bob Craner were detailed to care for Sijan.

"When I got a look at the poor devil, I retched," says Craner. "Maybe twenty percent of his body wasn't open sores or raw flesh. He was so thin; every bone in his body was visible."

Gruter picked Sijan up to carry him to the truck. "He looked like a little guy, but when I picked him up I told Craner, 'This was one big sonofagun.'"

On the trip to Hanoi Gruter realized he had met Sijan at the Academy. "I have never had my heart broken like that," says Gruter, who remembered Sijan as a 220-pound football player. Now, Sijan "had no muscle left and looked so helpless."

Not once during the grueling, bouncy four-day truck ride to Hanoi did Sijan complain. Lucid for varying periods of time, Sijan responded weakly to Gruter's and Craner's questions about his forty-five-day ordeal.

Craner recalls that through it all, Sijan never gave up his desire to seek freedom. "One of the first things he mentioned in Vinh was how we were going to get out. 'Have you guys figured out how we're going to take care of these people? Do you think we can steal a gun?'

"He had to struggle to get each word out. It was very, very intense on his part that the only direction he was planning was escape. Even later, he kept dwelling on the fact that he had made it once and he was going to make it again."

When they finally reached Hanoi, the three were tossed into a dank, unlit cell. A pool of water covered most of the cement floor. And it was cold. Craner remembers, "It was the first time I suffered from the cold. Guy Gruter and I started getting respiratory problems right away. I couldn't imagine what it was doing to Lance.

"Through it all Sijan never talked about pain. In fact, I never heard him complain. He was so full of drive whenever he was lucid. It was always positive for him, pointed mainly toward escape."

Craner remembers one night in particular. "A guard opened the little plate in the door and looked in. Lance beckoned to him. I recognized it as the same signal he had given the guard in the jungle. It was clear what was on his mind."

Near the end, Sijan asked for help to exercise so he could build up his strength for another escape attempt. "We got him propped up and waved his arms around a little," Craner says. "That satisfied him. Then he was exhausted."

About eight days after they arrived at the Hanoi Hilton, Craner knew the end had come. Pneumonia gripped Sijan's lungs. He started making strangling sounds. His two roommates rushed to sit him up.

"Then, for the first time since we'd been together his voice came through loud and clear," Craner recalls. "He said, 'Oh my God, it's over,' and then he started calling for his father. He'd shout, 'Dad, Dad, where are you? Come here, I need you!'

"I knew he was sinking fast. I beat on the walls, calling for the guards, hoping they'd take him to a hospital. They finally came and took him away. As best as I could figure it was January 21. It was the last time we saw him."

On a detail a few days later a guard told Gruter, "Sijan die."

When they were released in early 1973, Craner and Gruter immediately initiated a recommendation for Sijan to receive a

Medal of Honor. Craner says it was because "Sijan survived a terrible ordeal, and he survived with the intent, sometime in the future, of picking up the fight. There is no way you can instill that type of performance in an individual."

On March 4, 1976, after presenting Medals of Honor to Admiral Stockdale and Colonel Day, President Ford turned to Mr. and Mrs. Sylvester Sijan of Milwaukee. "I deeply regret," he said, "that one of the awards today is posthumous."

Then he handed the father his son's medal.

CHAPTER
TEN

America
Withdraws

T he main U.S. effort in the final three years of the war,
1970–73, concentrated on pushing the South Vietnamese Army
into battle as fast as possible—and withdrawing American units
even faster. Though several U.S. divisions occupied potentially
volatile territory along the Laotian and Cambodian borders, they
were there primarily to train the ARVN.

Over three-hundred-and-eighty thousand troops were in
South Vietnam at the beginning of 1970. Twelve months later
only two-hundred-and-sixty-five thousand Americans remained.
In 1970 the 1st Infantry Division, most of the 4th Infantry Division, the 25th Infantry Division, and several separate infantry
brigades all departed Vietnam.

The withdrawal of troops and the deemphasis on American
involvement resulted in a reduction of combat deaths in 1970 to
4,221 from the 9,414 suffered in 1969. This was the lowest level
since 1966, when 5,008 Americans were killed in action.

The major combat in 1970 came during the invasion of Cambodia in May and June. Elements of the 25th Infantry, 1st Cavalry, and 4th Infantry Divisions penetrated up to thirty kilometers
into the previously off-limits area. While the invaders recorded
no major military victories, they did destroy huge quantities of
supplies—seriously hampering the NVA's ability to wage war.
The incursion had the secondary objective of enhancing the
South Vietnamese military's self-confidence. That goal was only
partly met.

The Cambodian invasion produced no Medals of Honor. Almost all the Medals earned during the final three years of U.S.
participation in Vietnam came during static defense missions
performed by American troops.

There were combat battalions engaged in recon-in-force
missions in areas hotly contested by the NVA, but most units
were assigned security roles near towns, roads, and military in-
stallations. The days of aggressive offensive operations were in
the past.

211

The Studies and Observation Group did maintain an offensive schedule. Its elite counter-intelligence troops continued their efforts behind enemy lines, and across international borders.

FRANKLIN D. MILLER

A twenty-four-year-old staff sergeant from SOG's Command and Control-Central, *Franklin D. Miller,* led one such mission into Laos on January 5, 1970. From the LZ in Kontum Province Miller headed his American-Vietnamese long-range recon patrol across the border. No stranger to combat in Vietnam, Miller wore a Purple Heart earned on one of his two previous tours.

Soon after they moved into Laos, one of the Vietnamese Rangers tripped a booby trap, wounding four. Within minutes an NVA platoon arrived to investigate the explosion. Miller sent his team up a hill into a defensive position, then turned to meet the enemy. Twice the Sante Fe, New Mexico, resident single-handedly fought them off.

Miller led his team to an evacuation site but the NVA hit a third time. Their fire drove off the rescue chopper and wounded the rest of the team, including Miller. Alone and unaided he repulsed three more attacks before a relief force reached them. Through his gallant efforts seven lives were saved.

RUSSELL A. STEINDAM

During the final days of the war patrolling and ambushing occupied most of the average grunt's combat time. Unable to offensively engage the NVA, American troops were not ready to concede the countryside to him, either. As long as they were there the troops would battle the enemy.

First Lieutenant *Russell A. Steindam* of Plano, Texas, led one of his squads from Troop B, 3rd Squadron, 4th Cavalry, 25th Infantry Division to an ambush site in Tay Ninh Province on the night of February 1, 1970. Before they reached the site, enemy fire ripped into their ranks, wounding several. Steindam ordered his men to return fire, then helped move the casualties to the safety of a bomb crater. He was radioing to his CO when an enemy grenade landed among the wounded. He shouted a warning, then jumped on the grenade. He died saving his men.

JOHN P. BACA

Ten days later Specialist Four *John P. Baca* jumped on a grenade to save eight men but—amazingly—he survived his grievous wounds. The 1st Cavalry trooper was on a night ambush in Phuoc Long Province along the Cambodian border with his platoon from D Company, 1st Battalion, 12th Cavalry when a fragmentation grenade landed near him. He whipped off his helmet, covered the grenade with it, and fell on the helmet as the grenade exploded. Baca spent a year in the hospital recovering from his wounds.

Throughout the Vietnam War incredible acts of heroism often occurred during tough fights that had no lasting consequence. This was the case when a company of Chinese Nungs— with Special Forces leadership—attacked a strategic mountain pass in Chau Doc Province on the Cambodian border.

BRIAN L. BUKER

Only twenty-years-old when he died, Special Forces Sgt. *Brian Buker* was one of thousands of soldiers who served a second tour in Vietnam. He'd been there before as a paratrooper with the 173rd Airborne Brigade in 1968 and 1969.

What he witnessed on that first tour convinced him of the need to stop the spread of Communism before it engulfed all of Southeast Asia. He'd also learned that conventional warfare had little impact on the North Vietnamese insurgents. The only way to aid the South Vietnamese seemed to be at the village level. The native tribesmen needed training to resist the VC and the NVA. The Special Forces offered the type of training Buker felt would let him help the South Vietnamese help themselves.

During his first tour in Vietnam Buker volunteered for the Special Forces. He entered training in July 1969. By November he was back in Vietnam; this time he wore the coveted Green Beret.

Buker joined Detachment B-55, which controlled the Mobile Strike Force Companies. Organized around South Vietnamese and ethnic minorities, these companies operated in battalion-sized combat operations in difficult terrain.

For years the NVA had reigned supreme in a mountain fortress just inside the Vietnamese border. As long as they were there, Chau Doc Province would never be free. Buker's company was going to try to change that.

Although technically an advisor, on this mission Buker took charge of a platoon. Up through the rugged mountains, through a series of enemy strongpoints, he pushed his troops forward. He repeatedly exposed himself to enemy fire while setting an example of personal heroism for his men.

Buker and his men fought the enemy all day long. Bunker after bunker fell to the platoon's onslaught. By late afternoon the battle-weary troops cleared the pass and established a hold on the crest of the mountain.

But Buker felt that the enemy wouldn't give up the site easily—and he was right. Before he could complete preparation of his defensive positions the NVA counterattacked, quickly reoccupying two bunkers.

Buker could have sent one of his squads out after the bunker, but that wasn't his style. He went himself.

Bounding forward, ignoring the enemy's fire, Buker closed on the first bunker. He knocked it out with a grenade.

He moved toward the second bunker but was shot by an enemy machine gun. Even that didn't stop him. He crawled on. He got to within grenade range and destroyed that bunker, too.

Rather than stop for badly needed medical attention, Buker began to organize his men for a drive on the remaining pockets of resistance. An enemy RPG killed him before he could complete his task.

Without Buker's dynamic leadership the attack faltered. Under heavy fire the Nungs pulled back. By that evening the NVA again controlled the mountaintop.

Buker's widowed mother, from Albion, Maine, accepted her son's posthumous Medal of Honor on December 16, 1971.

A special program that the Marine Corps used to promote Vietnamization was the Combined Action Platoon, where groups of three or four volunteer marines lived in villages among the South Vietnamese. In addition to providing security, the marines were expected to train the local males to defend their homes. Vigorous patrolling kept the nearby area free of VC and the NVA. Obviously, the enemy did not like this marine efforts to undermine their propaganda. They frequently targeted CAP villages for attacks.

MIGUEL KEITH

When Marine Lance Corporal *Miguel Keith,* from Omaha, Nebraska, arrived in Vietnam in November of 1969 he volunteered for the CAP program. To him it seemed like a good way to help the South Vietnamese.

During the early morning hours of May 8, 1970, the NVA hit Keith's village in Quang Ngai Province. Wounded twice in the opening barrage, he still managed to support several defensive positions manned by the locals. Later, he single-handedly attacked five VC who were approaching the command post, killing three and wounding the others.

Determined to protect the South Vietnamese he had come to know and respect in the past six months, Keith ignored a third wound to charge twenty-five NVA massing in the dark for another attack. His accurate fire killed four and sent the rest scurrying for cover. Seconds later, though, an enemy soldier shot and killed Keith.

The remarkable bravery of eighteen-year-old Keith, the last marine to earn a Medal of Honor in Vietnam, completely disrupted the NVA's plans for overrunning the village.

LOUIS R. ROCCO

Sgt. First Class *Louis R. Rocco,* from Albuquerque, New Mexico, volunteered to accompany a medical evacuation chopper going to the rescue of eight ARVN soldiers critically wounded near Katum on May 24, 1970. Rocco manned one of the door guns as the chopper headed for the LZ but his accurate fire didn't keep the NVA from shooting the machine out of the sky.

Rocco broke his wrist and a hip in the crash. Unmindful of the pain, he began pulling the others from the burning wreckage. Alone and completely unaided, Rocco carried the three casualties into the ARVN perimeter. There, he administered first aid until he collapsed from loss of blood.

Fortunately, Rocco survived his wounds, and today he serves as New Mexico's State Director of Veteran Affairs.

ROBERT C. MURRAY

Unlike the typical soldier who went to Vietnam—a high school graduate with a working-class background—*Robert Murray* left Harvard's Graduate School of Business to join the U.S. Army. Raised in upper-class Tuckahoe, New York, Murray had graduated from Fordham University in New York City with a Bachelors degree in June of 1968 before entering Harvard that fall.

As an undergraduate Murray had been entitled to a draft deferment, which he lost when he entered graduate school.

He'd already received his notice from the draft board when his brother enlisted in the Army Reserves. That inspired Murray to accept the inevitable and get his military obligation out of the way. On October 29, 1968, he enlisted in the Army.

Murray could have used his education to go to OCS and get a commission in a noncombat field. Instead, in his own quiet, determined way, he elected to serve as an enlisted man. A well-trained one, too. He volunteered for Ranger training after basic.

"Even though he didn't participate in organized sports in college, Bob was always very athletic," his mother, Mrs. James P. Murray, said. "Ranger training was just a way for him to show he was as good at soldiering as he was at studying."

Murray excelled throughout the difficult and rugged Ranger and airborne training. His selection as the outstanding graduate of his class earned him a meritorious promotion to staff sergeant.

In November 1969 he went to Vietnam. He joined Company B, 4th Battalion, 31st Infantry, Americal Division, in Quang Nam Province, as a squad leader. The division performed mostly security missions, operating out of fire support bases strategically placed throughout the province.

The daily patrols and nightly ambushes kept Murray's squad busy. He worked particularly hard at preventing casualties. Like everyone else, he knew the war was winding down. He didn't want anyone from his squad to be the last man killed in Vietnam.

On June 7, 1970, Murray's squad was patrolling near Hiep Duc Village. They were hunting an elusive enemy mortar that had dropped harassing fire on their position for several days. In the thick jungle one man tripped a grenade rigged as a booby trap.

"Take cover!" he yelled.

Murray realized several of his squad couldn't get out of the way in time. Concerned only with their safety, he flung himself on the grenade. He died in the blast, but saved his squad members from death or serious injury.

"It was just like Bob to die for his men," his mother said when she accepted his posthumous medal on August 8, 1974. "He was always so worried about them."

Unfortunately, Murray's father never learned of his son's high honor: he had died in 1971.

GLENN H. ENGLISH, JR.

On September 7, 1970, four APCs carrying members of Company E, 3rd Battalion, 503rd Infantry, of the venerable 173rd Airborne Brigade moved down a jungle road in the Phu My District in Binh Dinh Province. A mine suddenly blew up the lead vehicle. Seconds later, automatic weapons fire ripped into the APC, setting it on fire.

Thirty-year-old Staff Sgt. *Glenn H. English, Jr.* leaped from the vehicle, his fatigues afire. Without stopping, he rallied several nearby soldiers, leading them in a vicious counterattack that routed the enemy.

English returned to the road, where the cries of three men trapped in the burning APC caught his attention. Ignoring the threat of explosion from stored ammo, English climbed inside the APC. As he lifted a wounded man to safety, the ammo blew up. The explosion killed English and the men he was trying to save.

Based on the success of the Cambodian incursion, MACV planned an invasion of Laos for early 1971. This time, however, the main thrust would be made by ARVN troops. Americans would provide only artillery and aviation support.

Beginning on January 30, 1971, U.S. combat engineers opened Route 9 through Quang Tri Province. On February 8, ARVN tanks rolled across the border in Operation Lam Son 719.

MICHAEL J. FITZMAURICE

In support of the ARVN, Troop D, 2nd Squadron, 17th Cavalry, 101st Airborne Division regarrisoned Khe Sanh. On the night of March 23, 1971, NVA sappers infiltrated the base. They tossed three satchel charges into a bunker occupied by Specialist Four *Michael J. Fitzmaurice* and three other soldiers.

In 'the dim light Fitzmaurice, from Cavour, South Dakota,

managed to throw two of the charges out of the bunker. When he came upon the third, he covered it with his flak jacket and his own body.

The subsequent explosion seriously wounded and partially blinded Fitzmaurice, but he continued fighting. He charged out of the bunker and fired at the enemy until an exploding grenade wrecked his rifle. While searching for another weapon he killed a sapper in hand-to-hand combat. Fitzmaurice then returned to his bunker where he manned a machine gun until the enemy fled.

Fitzmaurice spent thirteen months in the hospital recovering from his wounds. A well-deserved Medal of Honor was presented to the twenty-one-year-old on October 15, 1973.

For the first few weeks of Operation Lam Son 719 the South Vietnamese soldiers performed well. By the time they reached Tchepone, however, NVA resistance stiffened. MACV decided to pull the ARVN units out of Laos.

Instead of an orderly withdrawal, however, the movement turned into a rout. Whole ARVN units broke and ran. Medevac choppers were mobbed by able-bodied troops. Equipment was abandoned.

The first major offensive under Vietnamization was a disaster.

Yet withdrawal of American units continued. In early 1971 the 11th Armored Cavalry Regiment, the Americal Division, and most of the elite 1st Cavalry Division returned home. In August 1971 the 173rd Airborne Brigade left Vietnam. The 173rd had been the first Army combat unit to enter Vietnam—and its departure symbolized the end of American involvement. In January of 1972 the 173rd was inactivated.

The colors of the 5th Special Forces Group were returned to Fort Bragg, North Carolina in March 1971. Most of its personnel, though, remained in Vietnam, performing the same functions for newly created agencies.

One of the new units established after the 5th Special Forces Group officially withdrew was the Vietnam Training Advisory

Group. Like their brothers from the early days of the war, these Green Berets still provided guidance and leadership to ARVN units.

JON R. CAVAIANI

When he took his Selective Service physical in 1962 *Jon Cavaiani* learned he was 4-F. His allergy to bee stings meant that the Army didn't want him. That was fine with Cavaiani—he had a family and a good job selling agricultural chemicals. He didn't want the Army either.

Born on August 2, 1943, in Royston, England, Cavaiani immigrated to America with his parents in 1947. The family settled in Ballico, California, where they operated a very successful farm. After college Cavaiani took a job as a district sales manager in central California.

Cavaiani was well on his way to middle-class success when he took and passed his citizenship test in 1968. "After that, I felt a profound sense of responsibility to the country that had been so good to me," he says.

Although he had two daughters, Cavaiani enlisted in the Army in May 1969. He selected Special Forces training to prove a point after his toughness was questioned in basic training. Cavaiani proved his detractors wrong—he graduated with the Green Beret while they did not.

With his farm background and his military specialization in medicine, the 5th Special Forces assigned Cavaiani to duty as the agricultural advisor to I Corps when he arrived in Vietnam in August 1970. He travelled to the different Special Forces camps, helping the CIDG troops properly grow their crops and raise their stock.

He enjoyed that role until the NVA destroyed an orphanage where he spent his off-duty time. The savagery of the slaughter sickened Cavaiani. His life would never be the same. He volunteered for SOG's Command and Control-North (later Vietnam

Training Advisory Group). Soon, he was leading clandestine cross-border operations, taking his revenge on the NVA.

Soon after the Laotian invasion Cavaiani took command of the security platoon at radio relay station Hickory, north of Khe Sanh in Quang Tri Province. Composed of Special Forces, Montagnards, ARVNs, and communications specialists, the camp operated deep within enemy-dominated territory.

For several days at the end of May 1971 Cavaiani's patrols reported the presence of large numbers of the enemy in the vicinity. He himself had seen hundreds walking boldly through the jungle in broad daylight.

"We knew we were going to get hit; it was just a matter of when," Cavaiani says.

The night of June 3–4 witnessed a torrential downpour that kept the defenders in their bunkers. The outposts could see only a few feet in the driving rain.

At dawn Cavaiani and another American set out to check the perimeter. Unknown to them, NVA sappers had converged on the camp in the rain. A deadly ring of Claymore mines surrounded the Allied compound.

Halfway through his rounds Cavaiani detected movement to his front. "Get down," he yelled to his companion.

A Claymore detonated. The lethal steel balls flew harmlessly by. The battle for Station Hickory was on.

For the rest of that fateful day Cavaiani led the seventy defenders in a spirited fight. While mortar shells crashed down, RPGs flew through the air, and small-arms fire cracked overhead, Cavaiani raced back and forth through the camp. He put people in position, cared for the wounded, distributed ammo, and manned a variety of weapons.

At one point he fired a twin .50-caliber machine gun into the enemy's ranks until an RPG blasted him off the position.

"You could see the RPGs coming in, they were so slow," he remembers. "When I'd see one I'd just slip off the weapon to cover. One time, I miscalculated."

The exploding grenade wounded him, but Cavaiani never

221

slowed down. He continued his valiant leadership, inspiring those around him.

By noon, he knew he couldn't hold out. He called for evacuation.

Under continual heavy fire Cavaiani guided choppers into the camp. Inclement weather hampered the movement. By four that afternoon Cavaiani and fifteen others still remained on the ground. If they could make it through the night the choppers would be back in the morning. Cavaiani took advantage of a lull in the fighting to rig booby traps throughout the camp. Then he pulled back to a series of bunkers, conceding half the camp to the enemy.

The NVA came at 7:00 P.M. They attacked every fifteen minutes for the rest of the night. Cavaiani had placed his men strategically about the area, preventing the enemy from gaining any ground. He put himself atop the ammo bunker. "I figured if it went up, I'd go quick."

By 2:00 A.M. he knew the situation was hopeless. He gathered the handful of survivors together. "Take off," he told them. "Get away as best you can. I'll cover you."

They fled into the night. When last seen Cavaiani was kneeling on the bunker, an M-60 machine gun cradled in his arms. Back and forth he swept it, knocking down dozens of NVA.

When survivors of the camp reached American lines they told the story of Cavaiani's heroism. They also reported his death.

But the rugged farm boy wasn't dead.

Cavaiani stayed atop the bunker, his fire driving the enemy to cover. When he stood to make his own escape he was shot in the back. In intense pain he crawled into the dark bunker.

From his hiding place he shot several NVA who came looking for him. Then a grenade bounced in through the sandbagged door. The explosion drove dozens of pieces of shrapnel into his body.

Two NVA entered the bunker so Cavaiani played dead. They inspected the "corpse," then set the bunker on fire.

Cavaiani stayed as long as he could. "Soon my hands were blistering and my pant legs were on fire," he remembers. "I crawled out."

Somehow Cavaiani made it to a nearby bunker unnoticed. He killed one NVA who came snooping around then played dead again when two more arrived. They ignored his bloody body to loot abandoned field packs.

When they left Cavaiani crept out of the bunker and into the jungle. For the next week he struggled through the dense forest. He covered forty-two kilometers before he got to Camp Fuller, the nearest FSB.

Since it was before dawn Cavaiani chose to wait outside the wire. He didn't want some nervous sentry to shoot before he could identify himself.

As the sun rose on the horizon, Cavaiani prepared to get the attention of the guard. "I happened to look on the ground. I was quite startled to see two shadows."

Within hailing distance of safety Cavaiani was captured. "It was an old man armed with a rifle even older than him. But it worked," he recalls.

Taken back to Station Hickory, Cavaiani learned that half a dozen of his comrades, including his ARVN interpreter, had also been captured. All, including Cavaiani, were sadistically tortured. Six of his vertebrae and as many ribs were broken during the beatings. Two of his 'Yards were executed in front of him as an example of his fate, but Cavaiani never broke.

After several weeks Cavaiani and the remaining 'Yards and ARVN were sent north. Barely able to walk due to his severe injuries, Cavaiani received no mercy from his guards. Even when the pain caused him to falter, the NVA just beat him some more.

The ragged group finally reached Vinh, where a train waited to carry them to Hanoi. After they boarded, Cavaiani's ARVN interpreter suddenly left. Just as suddenly he returned. This time, though, he wore the uniform of an NVA sub-lieutenant.

"I was never more shocked in my life. So many things became clear after he revealed his treason. If I could have gotten my hands on him I'd have killed him. The NVA were smart enough to keep him away."

Twenty months of imprisonment passed before Cavaiani was released in March 1973. The well-deserved Medal of Honor for his gallant stand at Hickory was presented by President Ford in White House ceremonies on December 12, 1974.

A few months later Cavaiani decided to make the Army his career. "If my experiences could help keep one kid alive it would be worth it," he explained.

Cavaiani has since served as Operations Sergeant Major for several Special Forces Groups. He also devotes much of his free time to Outreach Programs for delinquent youths and helps counsel troubled Vietnam veterans.

LOREN D. HAGEN

Loren D. Hagen enlisted in the Army in June of 1968, two months after graduating from North Dakota State University in his hometown of Fargo. He believed so sincerely in the U.S. war effort that he volunteered for the Special Forces. Two-and-one-half years of training preceded his transfer to Vietnam in December 1970.

Like all new members of the Vietnam Training Advisory Group, 1st Lieutenant Hagen was assigned to a seasoned team before getting his own command. Hagen's training team was led by Staff Sgt. Jon Cavaiani.

"I remember Lieutenant Hagen very well," Cavaiani says. "On our very first patrol I knew he had what it takes to be a good team leader. In fact, I recommended he be given his own team sooner than normal. He was that good."

At dawn on August 7, 1971, two months after and just a few miles away from where Cavaiani had been captured in Quang Tri Province, Hagen's small recon team was hit by a fierce enemy attack. Though subjected to a hail of small-arms and rocket fire, Hagen led his men in repulsing the onslaught. Repeatedly exposing himself to enemy bullets, Hagen rallied his men through a second assault, directing their fire, redistributing ammo, and firing his own weapon into the enemy's ranks.

After an RPG destroyed one of his bunkers, wounding a number of his men, Hagen never hesitated in going to the casualties' rescue. He ignored exploding grenades to crawl toward the position, all the while firing his pistol at the wildly charging NVA. He had almost reached his objective when the enemy shot him dead.

When he accepted his son's Medal of Honor from President Ford on August 8, 1974, Loren H. Hagen said, "While I regret losing my son I have the satisfaction of knowing he died doing exactly what he wanted to."

Lieutenant Hagen was the last member of the U.S. Army to earn a Medal of Honor in Vietnam.

By the end of 1971 only a handful of American combat troops remained in Vietnam. Elements of the 101st Airborne and 1st Cavalry Divisions formed the bulk of American maneuver units. These were assigned primarily to the defense of critical areas near major cities. They witnessed little combat; most experienced only brief skirmishes with enemy forces.

North Vietnam took full advantage of the U.S. withdrawal to press its war in the south. In what became known as the "Easter Offensive," six NVA divisions poured into South Vietnam in late March of 1972. Without American support and strength, one ARVN unit after another collapsed in front of the enemy.

Within six short weeks Quang Tri Province, most of the Central Highlands region, and the area northwest of Saigon were in NVA hands. The end loomed clearly in sight.

Although a separate U.S. infantry brigade was sent north to reinforce American bases at Hué and Da Nang, MACV prohibited it from participating in combat. Those Americans who did see action were either advisors to ARVN units or members of SOG's successor, the Strategic Technical Directorate.

When SOG was deactivated—along with the rest of the Special Forces—its functions had simply been given to a new department with a new title. Nothing else changed. The members of STD still conducted cross-border operations, ambushes, kidnappings, training of indigenous personnel, and the gathering of information on POWs.

The Easter Offensive provided an opportunity for members of STD to continue to demonstrate the courage and resourcefulness that characterized their Vietnam service.

THOMAS R. NORRIS

Thomas R. Norris enlisted in the Navy in September 1967 to be a pilot. The twenty-three-year-old from Silver Spring, Maryland, had a degree in Criminology but—wanted to fly. He spent a year in training at Pensacola, Florida, before faulty depth perception washed him out of the program.

While waiting for reassignment Norris happened to read a magazine article about the Navy's counterintelligence teams, the SEALS. The training, potential for excitement, and the physical challenge all appealed to Norris. His application to the Underwater Demolition School was accepted.

Nearly a year of rugged training followed. In addition to Diving School and parachute training, Norris also attended the Army's Ranger School, Special Forces Officer School, and the Special Forces' Demolition School.

Norris' schedule called for him to begin language training in January 1970. Instead, he went to Vietnam. Another SEAL team had been badly chewed up. Replacements were needed desperately.

After an eight month tour Norris came back to the States to attend language school. Then, in March 1971, he returned to Vietnam.

Norris spent most of his second tour in the Mekong River delta conducting clandestine operations designed to rupture the enemy's supply lines. Then came the 1972 NVA Easter Offensive. Norris's team moved north to help the beleauguered ARVN units.

They were operating with Provisional Recon Units gathering intelligence on advancing NVA when they learned of two U.S. pilots downed deep behind enemy lines in northwest Quang Tri Province. Norris volunteered to bring them out.

Much of what occurred during the rescue mission still remains classified. Only the details needed to write the Medal of Honor citation were ever released.

On the night of April 10, 1972, Norris and five South Vietnamese worked their way through two thousand meters of enemy-infested territory. At dawn they located one of the pilots and returned him to their Forward Operating Base. The next day Norris made two attempts to reach the other pilot. Enemy resistance proved too strong; both tries failed.

Determined to rescue his fellow American, Norris gave it one more try on April 12. He dressed in fisherman's clothing, took one Vietnamese and a sampan, and paddled up an NVA-infested river to where the pilot was held. Under the cover of darkness Norris managed to elude the enemy.

He snatched the injured pilot from the NVA at dawn, then started the hazardous journey back to the FOB. By covering the pilot with bamboo and vegetation Norris spirited his prize past a North Vietnamese patrol vigorously searching for them.

Norris's unprecedented rescue of the two pilots so impressed his superiors that they initiated a Medal of Honor recommendation. Norris startled them by refusing to cooperate. He did not think his actions warranted the country's highest decoration.

Instead, Norris returned to his Vietnamese teammates and more clandestine missions. He remained in Vietnam until the end of October.

By the end of August 1972 all U.S. ground forces had departed Vietnam. The last unit to withdraw was the 7th Cavalry Regiment's 1st Battalion. It had served just under seven years in Vietnam.

During September of 1972 ARVN airborne and marine units recaptured Quang Tri City after weeks of bitter fighting. Most of the province, though, still remained in the enemy's hands. In order to learn more about the NVA's strength there the Strategic Technical Directorate routinely sent its Green Berets and SEALS behind enemy lines.

One such mission was planned for Halloween night. Intelligence headquarters wanted information on a former South Vietnamese naval base located a few kilometers south of the DMZ on the coast of Quang Tri Province. The capture of a prisoner or two would greatly aid the Americans. A five man joint American-South Vietnamese SEAL team prepared for the mission.

MICHAEL E. THORNTON

The assistant U.S. Navy advisor to the three Vietnamese SEALs was twenty-three-year-old Engineman 2nd Class *Michael E. Thornton*. He enlisted in the Navy in the fall of 1967, following his graduation from high school in his hometown of Spartanburg, South Carolina.

After one-and-one-half years of service aboard destroyers as a gunner's mate apprentice, the ruggedly built Thornton volunteered for SEAL training. Almost immediately upon graduation from the rigorous training Thornton shipped overseas to Vietnam, where he served from January 1970 through January 1973.

At dusk on October 31, 1972, Thornton, a Navy lieutenant serving as senior advisor, and the three Vietnamese set out in a junk for their target. After they arrived at the naval base they silently paddled ashore in a rubber raft.

Using pre-arranged hand signals, the five men hid their raft and then stealthily proceeded by foot through the jungle toward the base. A distinct metallic click forced the raiders to halt. Before they could take any action the waiting enemy opened fire.

The men scattered in the darkness, their guns blazing. The

NVA seemed all around. From every direction weapons fired. The lieutenant radioed for naval gunfire from offshore vessels. Within seconds the heavy shells exploded right on target.

Under cover of the fire, Thornton and the Vietnamese moved back to the beach. Only then did Thornton learn the lieutenant wasn't with them.

One of the Vietnamese told Thornton the officer had been hit.

"Was he dead?" Thornton demanded.

The Vietnamese wasn't sure. He thought so.

Either way Thornton knew he couldn't leave the man behind. He turned and plunged back into the jungle.

Through the vicious gunfire Thornton fought his way to the ambush site. He searched frantically in the high swamp grass until he found the lieutenant's unconscious body. Suddenly, a pair of NVA burst out of the night. Two quick shots from Thornton dropped the intruders. He turned back to the inert form.

The lieutenant's face was shattered; a mass of blood, torn tissue, and broken bone glistened in the moonlight. But he still breathed, and Thornton could detect a faint pulse.

Back through the gauntlet of enemy fire Thornton raced, the lieutenant's limp body draped across his shoulder. Several times he stopped to shoot it out with the pursuing NVA. Miraculously, he made it to the water's edge. There, he discovered that the South Vietnamese SEALS had left without them. He paused long enough to inflate the lieutenant's life jacket, then swam out to sea dragging the wounded officer along after him.

For two hours Thornton supported the unconscious officer in the cold water. At last a Navy craft located the two men and pulled them aboard.

Thornton's Medal of Honor was presented by President Nixon on October 15, 1973. Thornton remained in the Navy, serving with SEAL Team Six, the Navy's Delta Force, before receiving a commission as an ensign in 1983.

And what of the Navy lieutenant Thornton had rescued? In a remarkable twist of fate, unique in Medal of Honor history, the man Thornton saved was Lieutenant Tom Norris, the SEAL who had rescued two downed American pilots from behind enemy lines five months earlier.

The gruesome injuries from that night cost Norris his left eye. He spent the following two years in hospitals before taking a medical discharge in 1975. He later joined the FBI as a special agent.

When he learned that his commanding officer had submitted a Medal of Honor recommendation despite his protests, Norris at last relented. His well-earned Medal of Honor for the rescue of the two pilots was presented by President Ford on March 4, 1976.

Thornton's decoration, the last one ever given for saving another Medal of Honor hero's life, is also the last one earned by a member of the U.S. Navy—and the last one earned overall—in Vietnam.

On January 27, 1973, the Paris Peace Agreement was signed, ending the war in Vietnam. Two years later a North Vietnamese offensive quickly overwhelmed the South. The Republic of Vietnam disappeared as a separate nation on April 30, 1975.

CHAPTER
ELEVEN

Troubled
Heroes

O n the dark, drizzly evening of April 30, 1971, a Detroit, Michigan, liquor store clerk shot and killed a would-be robber. The incident would have been unremarkable except the dead man was an active duty Army sergeant—and a recipient of the Medal of Honor.

It was a tragic story that shocked America, rocked the Pentagon, and proved how difficult it can be to be a hero of an unpopular war.

DWIGHT H. JOHNSON

When he came home from the Army in July of 1968, *Dwight H. Johnson* started his search for work. He visited one employment office after another, but it proved to be a futile search. No companies were interested in hiring a black Vietnam vet from Detroit's worst ghetto.

Until November 19, 1968.

On that day President Lyndon Johnson presented the twenty-one-year-old with the Medal of Honor for a remarkable display of gallantry in Vietnam eleven months earlier.

As a tank driver, Johnson had served with the same crew since his arrival in Vietnam in February of 1967. On the night of January 14, 1968, Johnson's platoon commander assigned him to a different M-48. A sick driver prompted the move. Johnson took the change in stride. He already had his orders back to the States. In less than a week he'd be back in the "World."

The next morning the four tanks of Company B, 1st Battalion, 69th Armor, 4th Infantry Division raced down a road toward Dak To in Kontum province. Without warning enemy rockets flashed through the air. Two tanks spun out of control; waves of enemy soldiers poured out of the jungle.

Johnson watched in horror as his old tank burst into flames.

Stan Enders, the gunner in Johnson's tank, and a close friend, remembers: "He was really close to those guys in that tank. He just couldn't sit still and watch it burn with them inside."

Johnson started out of the tank. Enders grabbed him. "Don't go out there," he told Johnson. "There must be 500 of them. You're okay if you stay inside. Don't be crazy . . ."

But there was no stopping Johnson. Out of the hatch he went, through the deadly crossfire to his buddies' aid.

He got the first man out, burned but still alive. Johnson had the man on the ground when the tank's artillery shells blew up, killing those left inside.

"When the tank blew and Dwight saw the bodies all burned and black, he sort of cracked up," Enders recalls.

For the next thirty minutes, first with a .45-caliber pistol and later with a submachine gun, Johnson vented his rage on the North Vietnamese. He charged right into the midst of the ambush, guns blazing. When he ran out of ammo he beat one enemy soldier to death with the stock of his empty machine gun.

At one point in the fight an NVA rushed up to Johnson, pointed his rifle in his face and pulled the trigger. The weapon misfired. Johnson killed the man with one shot.

Nobody knew for sure how many NVA Johnson killed. Some said five, others said twenty. What they did know for sure was that Johnson had done rather well for his first time in combat.

"When it was all over," Enders recalls, "it took three men and three shots of morphine to hold Dwight down. He was raving. He tried to kill the prisoners we had rounded up. They took him to the hospital in Pleiku in a straightjacket."

Johnson lay unconscious for ten hours. Enders saw him in camp the next day. He had been released from the hospital; he was going home. He'd only come back to the tent to pick up his gear and say good-bye to his buddies.

After finishing his two years active duty at Fort Carson, Colorado, Johnson returned to the Detroit tenement where he'd been born out of wedlock. Johnson had a stepfather, but ten years before the Jamaican had been deported as an illegal alien.

Raised by a strict mother in the dreary projects, Johnson had been a good kid. An altar boy and Explorer Scout, he avoided the street gangs, didn't hang out on the corner, didn't do drugs, and didn't get into trouble. He graduated from high school in June of 1965, and was drafted the following year.

When he returned home from Vietnam his friends noticed very little difference in him. Some thought he "was a little quiet," others said he seemed "jumpy and nervous," but to most he was the same Dwight Johnson they'd known before.

Then began the seemingly endless search for employment. A friend remembers, "We went lots of places looking for work, but it was no use."

At the time, Detroit's unemployment rate stood at thirteen percent. Among young blacks it was at least twice that.

Johnson almost secured a job with the post office, but it never came through. He made the rounds of dozens of small factories, but the answer was always the same: No work.

Johnson's friend recalls, "Dwight took the test to be a lineman for the phone company. They told him he passed but they never called him. He later found out three white guys had been hired ahead of him."

Then came the medal.

Companies that could find no work for Dwight Johnson, unemployed black Vietnam veteran, suddenly found plenty of room for Dwight Johnson, Medal of Honor hero.

The irony did not escape Johnson.

Among those who wanted Johnson on their payroll was the U.S. Army. The Army's motives were just as obvious. Having a black war hero serving as a recruiter in a largely black city had its advantages.

Johnson elected to return to the Army. The camaraderie and fellowship he had enjoyed during his two years of service remained as fond memories.

As soon as he put back on his uniform, Johnson became a hot property. He spent very little time as a recruiter. Most of his time was spent in a public relations role. He attended dozens of lunches and dinners for civic organizations. Johnson lived a frantic schedule.

A friend who knew Johnson observes, "He didn't know how to handle all the attention he got. Events half a world away had propelled him into an alien culture. He was forced to play a role for which he had no training."

To add to Johnson's worries he found that his Army paycheck barely covered his expenses. He and his wife, Katrina, who had married in January of 1969, had trouble making the payments on their modest house.

In the spring of 1970 Johnson wrote a bad check for less than fifty dollars. One of Detroit's black leaders made it good. The man did not want any adverse publicity for Detroit's black hero. Unfortunately, it wouldn't be the last bad check.

Guilt over the events in Vietnam—over his survival—also bothered Johnson. He could not understand why he had been ordered to switch tanks. Why had fate spared him? This question-with-no-answer haunted him.

He began staying away from his job as a recruiter, missing appointments, not showing up for speaking engagements. He complained of stomach pains. In the summer of 1970 the Army sent him to the hospital at Selfridge Air Force Base near Detroit for treatment. From there he went to Valley Forge Hospital in Pennsylvania.

At Valley Forge the doctors found no physical basis for his ailment. Johnson agreed to psychiatric evaluation. In the meantime he received a thirty-day convalescent leave—until October 16, 1970. Johnson didn't return on time. He stayed AWOL until January 21, 1971, when he voluntarily returned to Valley Forge.

While AWOL, Johnson spent time with his wife, pregnant with their second child, and with the kids at his old grade school. To the youngsters, Johnson was something special. He had made it. They were proud of him and his medal.

To Johnson, the youngsters posed no threat. They made no promises that could not be kept. They placed no demands on him as a war hero. To them, he was just Dwight Johnson.

Back at Valley Forge Johnson began his psychiatric analysis. For the first time he revealed his anxieties. He talked of how inadequate he felt; how guilty he was over his survival; he expressed doubts about his decision to reenter the Army. He felt the military had lied to him about the role they had for him.

Johnson felt exploited by the Army. He told of how upset he had been when one of his talks at a Detroit black high school had been picketed by protesters who called him an "electronic nigger," a machine that the Army used to enlist blacks to fight in Vietnam. His whole role in the Army confused him.

On March 28, 1971, the hospital gave Johnson a three-day pass. He never returned.

By April Johnson's mortgage payments were nine months in arrears, and foreclosure proceedings began. His car needed seventy dollars in repairs; Johnson could not afford them. On April 28, Katrina entered the hospital for minor surgery. Johnson promised the admitting clerk he'd pay the twenty-five dollar processing fee the next day.

On April 30, Johnson took his eighteen-month-old son to see Katrina in the hospital. She told Dwight that the hospital was pressuring her for the twenty-five dollars. He left, promising to be back with the money that evening.

At nine that night Johnson telephoned a friend. He needed a ride to pick up some money from another friend. Could he drive Johnson to meet the man?

Just after 11:00 P.M., the friend and two others picked Johnson up. He directed them to an unfamiliar white neighborhood.

"Stop here," Johnson told them. "This guy lives down the street and I don't want him to see me coming."

Twenty minutes later Johnson lay dying on the floor of the liquor store.

According to the clerk, Johnson entered the store and asked for a pack of cigarettes. When he opened the register for change Johnson pushed him aside, a gun in his hand.

The two men fought. Johnson fired. A bullet lodged in the clerk's shoulder. The clerk grabbed his own revolver. He shot Johnson twice.

"But he just stood there," the clerk later told reporters, "with the gun in his hand and said, 'I'm going to kill you!' I kept pulling the trigger until my gun was empty."

At the funeral at Arlington National Cemetery, Katrina Johnson said, "They kept pushing him to be some kind of a monument. And they never let up. They never came near him to help. They just wanted a hero to sit at the head table."

One of the real tragedies of the U.S. involvement in Vietnam was its effect on the men who fought the war. Tens of thousands returned home mentally scarred forever by their experiences. Drug addiction, alcohol abuse, and a wide array of psychological disorders plagued the veterans for years to come.

In 1977 the Veterans Administration reported that Vietnam veterans accounted for one-third of the alcoholics under treatment in the VA hospital system. A 1978 presidential commission reported over four hundred thousand Vietnam-era vets had either been convicted of crimes or were awaiting trial. Though Vietnam veterans accounted for less than fifteen percent of VA patients, they committed thirty percent of the in-patient suicides.

DAVID C. DOLBY

Medal of Honor recipients were not exempt from post-war problems. One of the war's earliest heroes, *David C. Dolby* of Oaks, Pennsylvania, was found guilty in 1974 of passing over twelve hundred dollars in bad checks in Hawaii. Dolby had earned his medal with the 1st Cavalry Division in 1966. He was cited for killing three VC machine gunners, carrying a seriously wounded soldier to safety, and crawling under heavy fire to within fifty meters of a VC bunker to set off smoke bombs to aid an air attack.

Dolby was discharged in February of 1968, then worked at a variety of construction jobs around Philadelphia and in Florida. But he was not truly happy. In March 1969 he reenlisted, requesting service in Vietnam. He spent a total of four years in Vietnam. On his last tour he was arrested for brawling at Cam Ranh Bay and received a demotion after marijuana was found in his possession. He took his final discharge in December 1971. Nine months later he was charged with forging checks.

While drugs would prove to be a serious problem in Vietnam, far more men turned to alcohol to block the moral and political dilemmas of the war. The military had always had a lax attitude toward liquor. Vietnam was no different. Clubs for enlisted men, NCOs, and officers could be found on every base in Vietnam. Escape from the war was never more than a quick walk from one's quarters.

RAYMOND M. CLAUSEN

When he returned to Vietnam for a second tour in November 1969, *Raymond M. Clausen* no longer entertained any illusions about the U.S. war effort. When he first went to Vietnam in late 1967, Clausen believed in his country's committment to aid the South Vietnamese in their struggle against Communism. Eighteen months in-country changed his mind.

In spite of his misgivings, though, Clausen volunteered to return to Vietnam. No patriotic motivations stood behind his decision. "There was a whole lot less BS in Vietnam than there was in the States," he says.

Raised in Hammond, Louisiana, Clausen left Southeastern Louisiana University in March 1966 to enlist in the Marine Corps to "help win the war."

Training as a helicopter mechanic came first. It wasn't until December of 1967 that Clausen finally was posted to Vietnam. He spent eighteen months with Marine Air Group 16 before returning to the States in August 1969.

His disillusionment began late in his first tour—after Vietnamization began. Clausen was torn by ambivalent feelings. He couldn't see any purpose to America's involvement if they weren't going to put forth an all-out effort to win. At the same time, he felt that his role as a helicopter crew chief was important.

After he became a senior crew chief Clausen could handpick his missions. Invariably, he chose medevac missions; if there were wounded involved Clausen wanted to help. He didn't want to hurt anyone, only help them.

Clausen battled his inner turmoil with alcohol. He drank heavily, earning several Article 15s and a summary court-martial as a result. He spent more time as a buck private than any other rank.

Even after he rotated back to the States the first time, he continued drinking. He quickly found the stateside Marine Corps much less tolerant of his behavior. The "spit-and-polish" Marine Corps was not for him. After three months stateside he returned to Vietnam.

Fortune placed Clausen back in the same squadron he had served with on his first tour. He was back in familiar territory at the Marine air facility at Marble Mountain, south of Da Nang.

Clausen still drank to mask his frustrations, but at least he felt he could help people.

That's why he volunteered on January 31, 1970, to rescue a platoon of marines trapped in a minefield outside of Da Nang. While pursuing a small NVA force the twenty marines stumbled into an abandoned American minefield. One was dead, eleven wounded, and the others too scared to move. Only a chopper could save them.

Clausen jumped aboard a CH-47 twin-rotor helicopter piloted by Lieutenant Colonel Walter Leadbetter. A few minutes later they hovered above the trapped men.

By leaning out of the craft's open door Clausen could spot areas where mines had already detonated in the tall grass. Assuming that area was safe, Clausen directed Leadbetter to a landing. "Put her down there," Clausen told the colonel. A miscalculation of a few inches could spell disaster. The chopper landed safely.

Once on the ground Clausen disregarded Leadbetter's command to remain on the chopper. He leaped overboard, intent on rescuing the wounded. Ignoring the danger from the hidden mines, he walked carefully to a casualty, picked him up, then carried him back to the chopper. Nearby marines followed Clausen's footprints to the helicopter.

After he got all the marines in that area safely aboard, Clausen directed the CH-47 to another site. Again he calmly walked into the minefield to retrieve wounded men. Even when a mine exploded nearby, killing one and wounding three others, Clausen never hesitated on his mission of mercy. He simply guided Leadbetter to the site of the explosion, loaded up the three wounded, then pulled aboard the dead man.

In all, Clausen made six trips into the hazardous minefield, saving eighteen lives. Colonel Leadbetter recognized Clausen's courage by recommending him for the Medal of Honor.

Clausen still had eight months to serve in Vietnam after his daring rescue. They were not easy ones. The heavy drinking continued, bringing clashes with his superiors.

Shortly after Colonel Leadbetter left the unit, Clausen's new CO ordered him to fly a particular mission. Clausen refused. It wasn't a rescue mission—so he didn't want to go. The CO prepared court-martial charges against Clausen, but Colonel Leadbetter intervened. An Article 15, non-judicial punishment, was prepared instead. Clausen was busted back to private. He stayed a private through his discharge in August 1970, and was the only buck private to earn the Medal of Honor in Vietnam.

Problems continued to plague Clausen as a civilian. Still unable to reconcile his confusion over his role in the war, Clausen kept up his heavy drinking. As a result, he found it hard to hold a job. A severe automobile accident nearly cost him his life; he lay unconscious for two months. The recuperation period delayed the Medal of Honor presentation ceremony until June 15, 1971.

Holding the Medal of Honor did not make life any easier for Clausen. If anything, the mental turmoil increased. Now he not only had to deal with problems related to Vietnam, but he also had to try to live up to other people's expectations. It was almost more than he could handle.

"I couldn't find a reason for my existence," he explains. "I was confused about my role in life."

Then, in 1984, Clausen's life changed. "I was watching TV late one night, drunk as usual," he recalls. "Because there wasn't anything else on, I tuned in a religious program. What I heard made me sit up. For the first time in years things made sense."

Clausen bought a Bible the next day. He read it thoroughly. A few weeks later he joined a church. The Bible had given Clausen a complete new perspective on his life.

"Studying the Bible helped me understand myself," he says. "I've found answers to a lot of questions that had been bothering me. My life is now devoted to God."

Morale and discipline problems abounded in the latter years of America's involvement in Vietnam. Not only had anti-war sentiments spread to Vietnam, but the advent of Vietnamization made it difficult to motivate the troops. In several well-publicized cases combat troops refused to carry out their leader's orders.

Some soldiers expressed their dissatisfaction with gung-ho superiors by "fragging" them. With this technique, an anonymous grenade would be tossed into a hated officer's or NCO's quarters. If the explosion didn't kill or wound the target, at least the message was clear.

Besides the more violent, overt actions against the war, instances of racial violence, black market activities, and crime soared. The lower levels of combat resulted in considerable free time for frontline troops. To combat the boredom, more and more men turned to drugs.

In 1965 less than fifty cases of drug abuses were reported by the Army. In 1970 over eleven thousand soldiers were apprehended on drug charges. By 1971 drug use had reached epidemic proportions. MACV implemented a "Drug Abuse Counteroffensive" to fight the problem.

President Nixon announced in early June 1971 that his new anti-drug campaign would include the identification of heroin users in Vietnam. Henceforth, troops departing the war zone would be required to submit to urinalysis. Those identified as drug users would be placed in drug treatment centers before rotating home.

On June 15, 1971, Nixon presented Medals of Honor to several Vietnam veterans; among them were Peter C. Lemon of Tawas City, Michigan, and Richard A. Penry of Petaluma, California. Nixon's remarks at the ceremony heralded the young men as "champions of democracy" who saw their duty and did it "above and beyond the call of duty." He made a not-too-subtle distinction between these heroes and the malcontents, dissenters, and deserters who worked against his patriotic policies.

Irony was at work, however, for both Richard Nixon and these heroes, at that point standing high on a national pedestal, soon fell with a resounding thud. America erred in believing its leaders and heroes existed without human frailties.

On June 21, 1971, newspapers across the country reported Peter Lemon had been "stoned on pot" the night he earned his medal.

PETER C. LEMON

Born in Canada on June 5, 1950, *Peter Lemon* became a U.S. citizen at age twelve. Like many naturalized citizens, Lemon felt strong ties to his new country. When the United States decided to support South Vietnam in its struggle against Communism, Lemon didn't hesitate to get involved. He enlisted in February 1969, when he was eighteen.

To fully prepare himself for combat Lemon volunteered for Recondo (reconnaisance/commando) training after he arrived in Vietnam in July 1969. When he completed the grueling course he joined the 1st Infantry Division's Ranger Company.

He went to the 1st Cavalry Division's Recon Company in March 1970 after the 1st Infantry Division rotated home. Over the next few weeks Lemon got acquainted with the other eighteen men of his platoon on recon patrols conducted deep within enemy territory. The teams crossed into Cambodia several times in their search for the enemy.

Early on the morning of April 1, Lemon returned from patrol to his base camp at Fire Support Base Illingsworth. This FSB was one of five ringing the city of Tay Ninh, fifty miles northwest of Saigon. During the past few weeks several of the other FSBs had been attacked by the NVA.

"We knew our turn was coming," Lemon says. "Our recon patrols had seen too many signs of the NVA around the base. Everybody was on alert."

The NVA came that night. Between three hundred and four hundred hardcore enemy soldiers hit FSB Illingsworth. Lemon fired back at the enemy hordes from his defensive position on the perimeter. In the midst of the battle Lemon's CO, Lieutenant Greg Peters, ordered him and another soldier to man an abandoned .50-caliber machine gun.

"We couldn't get the darn machine gun to work," Lemon recalls. "We tried desperately for at least five or ten minutes to open fire on the enemy. Then a mortar shell went off by us, wounding me and totally destroying my buddy."

Badly shaken, Lemon went back to his bunker. From an open container he scooped up grenades, throwing them as rapidly as he could into the ranks of the swarming NVA. When another buddy went down, Lemon carried him through the fire to the aid station. He was wounded again while returning to his bunker.

Undeterred, Lemon ignored the pain to continue battling the attackers. When an NVA RPG gunner continued sending accurate rounds into the perimeter, Lemon crawled atop his exposed bunker to spot the weapon. He knocked it out with a well-aimed burst from his machine gun.

After an hour of heavy fighting the enemy attack abated. Lemon, bleeding from shrapnel wounds in the head, neck, leg, and arm, moved to a fortified bunker where he discovered a wounded ARVN soldier he knew. For some reason the man's wounds were untended. Lemon comforted the man, and then, when medics arrived, refused aid for his own serious wounds until his friend was treated.

"I didn't think I was hit that badly and here was this ARVN bleeding to death. I told the medics to take care of him first," Lemon says.

Lemon himself was evacuated later that night. He spent a month in the hospital before being reassigned to a support unit. On December 4, 1970, he was honorably discharged.

Lemon returned to his parents' home, where he spent long hours wandering the nearby woods, deep in thought about his Vietnam service, trying to overcome his feelings of survivor's guilt. He'd lost many friends in the war, including three good buddies that night at Illingsworth. His grief was nearly overwhelming.

When word of the Medal of Honor came he thought about refusing it. "I didn't think what I'd done was out of the ordinary. But I guess you can't split the medal up among twelve guys. That's who it really belongs to."

A week after the presentation ceremony reporters from the *Detroit Free Press* interviewed the new hero.

"It was the only time I ever went into combat stoned," they quoted Lemon as saying. "We were all partying the night before. We weren't expecting any action because we were in a support group.

"All the guys were heads. We'd sit around smoking grass and getting stoned and talking about when we'd get to go home."

The newspaper articles shocked America.

Lemon says that the reporters took his comments out of context. According to him, they misquoted him.

"I was a young kid, just back from Washington where I'd met the President," Lemon says. "I was a little cocky, a little over-confident when these two hot-shot reporters from the *Free Press,* long-haired, hippie-types, interviewed me. We talked about drug use in Vietnam, but I never said I used drugs in combat, because I didn't."

Even though the story received national exposure, vilifying Lemon, he never bothered to dispute it. He didn't think his protests would be heard. "What would they do," he asks rhetorically, "put a retraction on page thirty?"

The newfound notoriety coupled with his anxieties over his role in Vietnam were more than Lemon could handle. He left his family in Michigan and set out for Colorado. In the tranquility of the Rockies he hoped to reconcile his tortured emotions about the war.

"I had deep guilt feelings over the loss of my friends. I wasn't sure if I had done enough to keep them alive."

Lemon dropped out of society for the next five years. He found anonymity working as a carpenter on construction projects throughout Colorado, an anonymity that allowed him to deal with his confused feelings. Eventually he came to terms with his guilt. He became determined to get on with his life.

In 1976 Lemon used his GI Bill benefits to enroll in college. In the next four years he earned not only his Bachelor degree, but a Master of Science in business as well. He then started a successful specialized insurance brokerage firm which he headed for four years before selling out.

Today, as a senior executive of another prosperous insurance agency, Lemon enjoys a level of success that eludes most men. The fight at Illingsworth, though, continues to bother him.

"There isn't a day goes by," he says, "that I don't think about that night and getting the Medal of Honor."

The Medal reminds him of a past he'd like to forget.

"I'd trade the Medal in an instant if it would bring back my three buddies killed in that fight," he says.

RICHARD A. PENRY

When twenty-one-year-old "Butch" Penry came home from Vietnam in August 1970 he told his mother, "I'm not running anymore, Mom. From now on, all I'm going to do is walk."

It was years before Mrs. Penry understood what her son meant.

Born and raised in Petaluma, California, *Richard A. Penry*

went to work as a dishwasher in a local restaurant after graduating from high school in 1966. He'd worked his way up to chef when he was drafted in March of 1969. Six months later he went to Vietnam as an infantry replacement for Company C, 4th Battalion, 12th Regiment, 199th Light Infantry Brigade.

In Binh Tuy Providence, sixty miles northeast of Saigon, on the night of January 31, 1970, Penry's platoon worked silently to set up a night ambush. In the waning daylight the NVA launched their own ambush. The opening fusillade of mortars, rockets, and automatic weapons fire seriously wounded the company commander and dozens of others. Small pockets of wounded men lay isolated throughout the site, vulnerable to the enemy.

Reacting with incredible courage to the dire situation, Penry gave first aid to the wounded CO, then moved the command post to a more secure area. After that he made three trips outside the perimeter to retrieve radios. All proved defective.

When thirty NVA charged into a group of wounded men, Penry single-handedly drove them off with machine gun fire and grenades. That threat over, he went after a fourth radio. At last he found one that worked. With it he called for medevac choppers.

Word reached Penry of five wounded men isolated close to an enemy bunker. Ignoring the threat of death, Penry crawled through the gunfire to their aid. He administered first aid, then led them all back to safety.

In the inky blackness Penry had to use a strobe light to guide the choppers into the LZ. As one of the few left unwounded, he personally carried eighteen casualties to the LZ. After all the wounded were evacuated Penry joined another platoon and led them in pursuit of the enemy.

It was quite a night for the husky soldier.

After receiving his Medal of Honor Penry talked about the war and what he had seen. "In Vietnam," he told one reporter, "you have no way of knowing who the enemy is. A fellow will sell you a soft drink in the daytime and while doing so be your friend. The same fellow will try to kill you the same night."

On the matter of drugs in Vietnam Penry spoke candidly. "Marijuana grows there like trees grow in the United States. When one runs out of tobacco, he can pick a twig and smoke it, and if he has to pay for it the price is really cheap. Many American soldiers were smoking marijuana. When caught, these soldiers were either restricted or lost some of their pay. The Army used more drastic methods against those caught with any hard stuff."

So did the civilian police in the U.S., as Penry learned.

Late on the morning of October 4, 1973, Richard Penry was arrested by Petaluma police and the Sonoma County Sheriff's office on charges of selling cocaine to an undercover officer. The crimes occurred on September 21 and 24, 1973, when Penry allegedly sold a total of 950 dollars worth of cocaine to the narcotics agent.

"With that amount," said one official, "a guy has to be considered a distributor—in effect, one who sells the stuff to 'retailers,' who in turn sell to users."

Penry's mother disagreed. "If he didn't have the Medal of Honor they wouldn't have arrested him," she said. "They just want to get their names in the paper for arresting a war hero."

Penry's attorney agreed. Robert Mackey stated in a motion seeking dismissal of the case that Penry had been "entrapped into commiting an offense."

In the end Mackey's argument made no difference. Penry pleaded guilty. He was sentenced to a term of probation. He would avoid jail.

After sentencing Penry, too, dropped out. He felt his status as a war hero had brought undue attention to his personal life. He wanted nothing further to do with the press.

Mrs. Penry was happy with her son's decision. Perhaps more clearly than others she recognized the frailties of human behavior.

"Heroes are just ordinary people," she said.

For many young men who wished to avoid military service during the Vietnam years Canada loomed as a safe haven. Because Canadian-American treaties didn't allow for the extradition of war protestors, escape to Canada offered an easy alternative to those who did not want to serve their country.

Thousands of draftable men fled to Canada, particularly during the later years of the war. Most draft evaders remained in Canada, enjoying their new life, until President Carter offered them a general pardon in 1976.

A handful of those who evaded the draft later regretted their decision. They returned to the United States willing to face the consequences of their actions. Most ended up serving in the military. Some went to Vietnam. At least one found the decision to return to be the start of a personal hell.

KENNETH M. KAYS

When his draft notice arrived at his parents' home in Fairfield, Illinois, nineteen-year-old *Kenneth M. Kays* took off for Canada. His application for status as a conscientious objector had recently been turned down, leading to the induction notice. He seemed content to sit the war out, to let others do the fighting.

After thirty days he had a change of heart.

"I decided to come home and go into the Army," Kays recalls. "I thought I could become a medic and help people."

He arranged a deal with the authorities: He would report for induction if guaranteed service as a medic. The Army agreed. Kays reported for induction on September 24, 1969. After basic training he went to Fort Sam Houston, Texas, for specialized training as a medic. In the last week of April 1970 he arrived in Vietnam, where he joined the 101st Airborne Division's 1st Battalion, 506th Infantry.

Two weeks later, as a patient at Fitzsimmons General Hospital in Denver, Colorado, minus the lower half of his left leg, Kays was a candidate for the Medal of Honor.

Fire Support Base Maureen was one of several similar outposts manned by elements of the 101st Airborne in Thua Thien Province. Beginning in early April the NVA had been attacking different FSBs in an attempt to break the pressure on their movements in the A Shau Valley. They hit Maureen on May 7, 1970.

Kays was assigned to Company D that night. He was still getting accustomed to the routines of duty in Vietnam when the 803rd NVA Regiment struck the FSB. Assault rifle fire, RPGs, and satchel charges killed and wounded a number of infantrymen in the opening moments of the attack.

Disregarding the heavy fire and the NVA sappers stealing through the night, Kays left the safety of his bunker to help his wounded buddies. In the darkness he heard something fall alongside him. To his horror he realized it was a satchel charge. Before he could react the device exploded. The blast blew off the lower portion of his left leg.

With a veritable hell raging around him, Kays calmly and expertly affixed a tourniquet to his bloody stump. With that in place, Kays continued crawling to the wounded. He found one man, patched him up, then dragged him to the aid station.

Rather than have his own wound treated, Kays went back into the carnage looking for more wounded. Ignoring the intense pain from his wound, Kays moved about the perimeter, treating his buddies, using his own body to shield them. At one point he actually crawled outside the perimeter to treat one wounded American and pull him to safety.

After several hours of savage fighting the NVA were beaten back. The company commander found Kays crawling to another casualty. Kays refused treatment until all the other wounded men had been evacuated. He finally collapsed from loss of blood.

The Army discharged Kays on December 28, 1970. He returned to Fairfield.

"When he got back from the service," his father said, "he seemed normal enough, but I guess the thought that he had lost part of his leg hadn't hit him. Like, he'd go to dances and run around just as if nothing had happened.

"Then all of a sudden, about the time he got that medal, he stopped talking to me and his mother. He started raising hell and smoking grass."

Kays was one of nine Vietnam veterans who received the

medal from President Nixon on October 15, 1973. He was non-chalant about the ceremony, according to his father. "He acted like the whole thing was a joke," Mr. Kays said.

Kays refused to cut his long hair and beard for the presentation ceremony. As a result, the Army refused to let him wear a uniform.

The reason Kays even went to the White House, he later said, was to "look Nixon in the eye." When the President entered the room Kays alone remained seated. Everyone thought it was because of his leg. But when the President approached him to hang the medal around his neck, he stood up. "No one caught on," he said.

Right from the start Kays had trouble handling being a hero. He refused a parade in his hometown. He ran away from the press, hiding for three weeks in a cabin in the woods.

"I can't handle being a hero," he said then. "I just don't think I've been that brave. Besides, being a Medal of Honor man doesn't make me any better than anyone else."

On April 4, 1974, the local police arrested Kays for growing mairjuana in his parents' greenhouse. On April 23, the court fined him and gave him one year probation.

Two weeks later the Fairfield police arrested him again on the same charge.

In an interview given at the time Kays said, "I believe a man must be true to himself, must do what he thinks is right. But first, he must be free to find himself so that he'll know what is right. Marijuana is a tool in that quest."

Kays refused to participate in a system that obstructed his search.

"They [the authorities] see my adherence to responsibility as irresponsibility," Kays further stated. "All they are is what they've been told. What purpose is served by restricting freedom?"

On May 31, 1974, Kays was arrested on charges of reckless driving after he made half-a-dozen loops through town at sixty miles per hour, honking his horn. "I was trying to wake the dead," he explained.

One week later Kays' father committed him to the Chester Mental Health Center in Chester, Illinois. According to the petition, Kays was "yelling and screaming and was irrational" when the elder Kays visited his son's trailer that morning.

"I'm just concerned about my son's welfare," Mr. Kays told reporters.

On June 10, 1974, Kays voluntarily committed himself to the state mental institution in Anna, Illinois.

Kays could not be held in any of the institutions unless so committed by a court of law. After a few weeks care he was released. For the next five years Kays wrestled with what experts called "survivor's guilt," an inability to cope with his own survival while his friends had died.

His mother found notes Kays had written to dead buddies— apologizing for not having reached them quickly enough on the battlefield to save them.

"Listen," Kays said, "that survivor's guilt was worse than any pain I felt from my leg."

In August 1979 the police arrested Kays on charges that he had terrorized two of his neighbors. He yelled at them, chased them to another neighbor's house, then threw a flower pot through a glass door. He then took the couple's car for a wild ride through his hometown.

Like most people in Fairfield, Kays' parents were extremely concerned about his mental health. That's why his father refused to bail him out of jail.

"Why should I?" he asked. "If Kenny gets out, he'll just do the same thing over."

On August 14, 1979, a Circuit Court judge sent Kays to the Chester Mental Health Center "until such time as he is able to understand the charges brought against him."

For the next six years Kays remained in treatment. In 1985 he was released to his father's care.

Those who knew him were glad to see Kays return home. "No one ever wished him ill," said one resident. "We just wanted to see him helped."

CHAPTER
TWELVE

Final
Heroes

P resident Ronald Reagan ____ stepped to the podium in front of several hundred people gathered in the Pentagon's inner courtyard. It was February 21, 1981, just one month past his inauguration. Speaking solemnly, he said, "Several years ago we brought home a group of Americans who obeyed their country's call and fought as bravely and well as any Americans in history.

"They came home without a victory not because they had been defeated but because they had been denied permission to win."

President Reagan then called forward a forty-five-year-old retired Green Beret. In the terse words of the official citation, President Reagan told of the nearly overlooked heroism of the stocky Texan—thirteen years earlier.

ROY P. BENAVIDEZ

As he passed the command shack on his way back from Mass at the Special Forces encampment at Loc Ninh seventy-five miles north of Saigon on the Cambodian border on May 2, 1968, Staff Sgt. *Roy P. Benavidez* heard yelling over the radio. In the background was noise he described as "a popcorn machine gone wild."

Three Green Berets—Sgt. First Class Leroy Wright, Staff Sgt. Floyd Mousseau, and Specialist Four Brian T. O'Connor— and nine Montagnards were on a secret mission about twenty-five miles west of Loc Ninh, ten miles inside Cambodia. They walked into a clearing and suddenly found themselves facing an NVA patrol. Although the Americans and Montagnards were dressed in North Vietnamese Army uniforms the disguises didn't work. The NVA opened up. The rifle fire was soon followed by enemy mortars and grenades.

Wright, who carried secret documents, died in the initial

exchange of fire. All the others fell wounded. Still, they sent out a blistering hail of their own fire, momentarily stopping the NVA. Benavidez had overheard O'Connor's frantic calls for help.

Benavidez knew immediate action had to be taken. Quickly, he ran to the airfield. There he encountered Warrant Officer Larry McKibben, a chopper pilot. He explained the situation. "Let's go," McKibben said.

"McKibben was in a unit nicknamed 'Greyhounds'," Benavidez recalls. "All of their pilots had vowed never to leave a Special Forces member behind. They knew what we were up against."

They took off. First, they rescued the crew of a gunship shot down near the isolated patrol. McKibben's Huey took a number of hits during the rescue mission.

They flew back to Loc Ninh, dropped off the wounded crew, made some quick repairs, then headed back into Cambodia.

The enemy fire was so heavy McKibben could get no closer than fifty yards from the stranded team. He hovered inches above the ground; Benavidez leaped.

"I made the sign of the cross, then jumped out," Benavidez remembers. "I was running like hell. The men were about one hundred feet away when suddenly something blew up behind me. It knocked me down. My right leg was stinging and bleeding, and blood was running down my face.

"I was scared. I shouted, 'Hail Mary, full of grace, help me' and kept on running."

He made it to O'Connor. The Specialist Four was still fighting. Benavidez looked around for a radio—his had been smashed when he was knocked to the ground. O'Connor gave him his. Benavidez instructed McKibben to make strafing runs on the NVA. After three passes McKibben brought the Huey in for a landing.

Lifting Wright's body to his shoulder, Benavidez ran through the fusillade of fire. He put the body with its secret documents aboard, then helped two wounded 'Yards aboard. Determined to rescue the others, Benavidez guided McKibben by holding the front of the chopper's strut and giving hand signals.

Rounds slammed into the chopper's aluminum skin. Suddenly an AK-47 round hit Benavidez in the back. He dropped to the ground. An instant later the chopper exploded.

McKibben was dead. The co-pilot sat stunned, a piece of wood imbedded in his head.

"Hell was in session," Benavidez says. "Sergeant Mousseau's head was half blown off, from his left ear to his left eye. I started dragging the wounded to cover."

Benavidez called for air support. Soon helicopters and jets crisscrossed the sky, their fire keeping the enemy at bay.

On the ground, Benavidez organized the survivors into a tight defense. He passed out ammo, distributed water, and inspired the men to hold on.

After three hours and three unsuccessful rescue attempts another chopper finally landed. Benavidez got the wounded aboard. He was on his way to get Wright's body from the wrecked chopper when an NVA soldier charged him, bayonet gleaming on the end of his rifle. The blade slid into Benavidez's back and right arm.

"He gave me a rifle butt to the jaw and knocked me down. I was yelling at O'Connor to shoot, but I had my back to the slick. He got me again in the left arm."

The thick-set Green Beret sergeant threw the enemy to the ground. He pulled his own knife and buried it into the man's chest.

Covered with blood from over a dozen wounds, Benavidez started pulling Wright's body to the Huey. He had to hold his intestines in with one hand while pulling Wright with the other. Once at the chopper eager hands pulled the corpse aboard.

As Benavidez threw his leg up to board the chopper, thirty North Vietnamese burst from the treeline. Benavidez grabbed a machine gun from the floor of the chopper and fired. He killed two NVA trying to crawl under the Huey and two more charging the cockpit.

So much blood ran down Benavidez's face he had to shake his head back and forth to keep his eyes clear. The helicopter crew throught he was signaling he didn't want to go. Two of them grabbed Benavidez and forcibly pulled him aboard.

"Me and Mousseau were holding hands on the flight to the hospital. He died on me. I cried like a baby."

When the chopper landed a doctor took one look at Benavidez, said he wouldn't make it, and ordered him placed with the dead. With a mouth so badly injured he couldn't talk, Benavidez communicated the only way he could—he spit in the doctor's face. The medics took him into surgery.

The surgeons cut Benavidez open from the middle of his back to the front of his left lung. Almost all of his major organs required repair. Half his left lung was removed; two pieces of shrapnel were left in his heart. From Saigon Benavidez went to a hospital in Japan. A few weeks later he was transferred to Fort Sam Houston Hospital. It was like old home week. Benavidez had been sent there previously to recover from wounds received during his first tour in Vietnam.

Born August 5, 1935 in Cuero, Texas, Benavidez had been orphaned at age eight. He and his brother went to live with an uncle in El Campo, Texas.

Life was hard. For six months each year the youngster picked crops with the rest of his new family. He had to leave school after the seventh grade to work full time. At seventeen he enlisted in the Texas National Guard.

A few years later Benavidez realized the Army could be an avenue for improving his life. Through the Army he could earn a high school diploma. He enlisted. He served in Korea and Germany before being accepted to airborne training.

He went to Vietnam in 1964 as an advisor. He had nearly completed his tour when he had a disastrous encounter with a land mine.

"I was paralyzed from the waist down. The doctors told me I'd never walk again."

Benavidez proved them wrong. He started exercising by crawling out of bed, pulling himself up the wall, and then just standing there, building up his weakened muscles. He eventually took a few cautious steps. Gradually, he rebuilt his shattered limbs. He walked, slowly and painfully, but he walked. That goal reached, he started running.

Less than a year after being told he would never walk again, the Special Forces accepted Benavidez for training. In April 1968 he went back to Vietnam.

For his incredible display of raw courage that bloody day in May of 1968, Benavidez's commanding officer, Lieutenant Colonel Ralph Drake, recommended him for the Distinguished Service Cross. It was awarded in September 1968.

Six years later Colonel Drake developed more information on the sustained nature of Benavidez's heroism and the fact that his presence at the battle site was completely voluntary. He recommended the DSC be upgraded to the Medal of Honor. Unfortunately, the legal time limit for submitting the recommendation had expired. The award could not be processed.

Late in 1974 Congress passed a law extending the time limit for Vietnam awards. Colonel Drake resubmitted the paperwork.

The Decorations Board acknowledged Benavidez's bravery but could not find the necessary second witness. Without him, they had no choice but to disapprove the award.

Twice more the recommendation was submitted. Twice more the Board rejected it. The regulations were clear; there had to be two corroborating witnesses.

Then, in 1980, the Army found the missing eyewitness.

Benavidez had thought Brian O'Connor was dead. Brian O'Connor thought Benavidez was dead.

"Last time I saw him, he was floating in his own blood," O'Connor said when he was found living in the Fiji Islands.

In testimony before the Decorations Board, O'Connor said, "I was ready to die, and I'm sure the other team members realized the futility of continuing on against such odds. It was Benavidez's indomitable spirit and courage that made us hold on for that extra five or ten minutes that dragged into hours."

With O'Connor's statements the Board unanimously approved Benavidez's Medal of Honor.

In 1973 Congress authorized the burial of an Unknown Soldier from the Vietnam War in Arlington National Cemetery alongside the Unknown Soldiers from World Wars I and II, and the Korean War. Just as the Vietnam War did not offer the kind of inspirational symbols found in previous wars, the search for the remains of an unidentified American serviceman proved difficult and controversial.

THE UNKNOWN SOLDIER

The nature of the war in Vietnam and the advances made in forensic medicine nearly thwarted the efforts to designate a Vietnam Unknown.

Unlike earlier wars, where the deceased might remain unattended for weeks at a time, medical evacuation teams in Vietnam were often on the battlefield while the fighting still raged. In addition, because most firefights were limited to units of company-size or smaller and were contained in small geographical areas, identification of the dead was relatively easier than before.

In World War II, seventy-five percent of the casualties were caused by the more destructive forces of artillery shells and mortars; only ten percent were wounded by gunfire. Gunshot wounds, by comparison, accounted for forty percent of the casualties in Vietnam with enemy mortars or artillery responsible for only twenty-one percent. That also helped in identifying casualties.

Technical advances, along with detailed military and medical records, enabled the medical scientists to identify nearly all the remains, including those returned after hostilities ceased. The Army's Central Identification Laboratory in Honolulu, Hawaii, even used a technique known as photo superimposition to identify remains. Computers would reconstruct facial features so they could be compared with photographs of servicemen listed as missing.

The emotional stress on those whose loved ones were still unaccounted for in Southeast Asia also played a role in delaying the designation of a Vietnam Unknown. The National League of POW-MIA Families opposed the entombment of an Unknown. A spokesperson for that organization told reporters, "The major problem is that they could be interring somebody who might eventually be identified."

But in the late 1970s Vietnam veterans began pressing their Congressmen to expedite the designation of an Unknown. They saw the delay as further evidence of the country's rejection of their service and sacrifices. Support for their cause came even from the American Legion, who began pushing the issue.

But the government would not be hurried. Responding to critics, the White House issued a statement: "We have resisted congressional and veterans groups' pressure to rush the process, thus ensuring integrity for the families. The burial will be an act of national unity that will spark greater public awareness that the Vietnam War is not behind us . . ."

By 1982 only four sets of unidentified remains were held at the Army's laboratory. While this was an obvious relief for the families of the missing, it also posed a further dilemma for those campaigning for an Unknown. There was a strong possibility that the remains would eventually be identified.

That's exactly what happened to two of them.

Then, the third set was thought to "possibly not be American," according to the Army. Chances were good the body was that of a Southeast Asian.

That left one set of remains. An Army spokesman said, "Information we have on this individual does not match anything we've got." All they knew was that the casualty died after 1973, but was not one of the remains returned to U.S. control by the Vietnamese after 1975.

Though it happened by default, an Unknown from Vietnam finally existed.

To preserve the casualty's anonymity, the Army ordered all records pertaining to the case destroyed. Personnel at the Army's identification laboratory were told not to discuss any aspect of the investigation. An Army spokesman said, "He's an American. We know he died in the conflict, but we just don't know who it is. We used every trick, but we cannot match him to any known missing soldier. We think we can say this is a true Unknown from the Vietnam War."

Official designation of the remains took place on May 17, 1984. In a dockside ceremony at the Pearl Harbor Naval Base Marine Corps Sgt. Major Allan J. Kellogg placed a wreath at the foot of the casket. Kellogg had earned a Medal of Honor in Vietnam in 1970 by throwing himself on an enemy hand grenade.

Pallbearers then placed the casket aboard the USS *Brewton* to start the long voyage to Washington, DC. Once there the casket lay in state in the Capitol Building's Rotunda. Thousands filed past the casket to pay their respects.

At noon on Memorial Day, May 28, a military funeral procession carried the casket to Arlington National cemetery.

In the cemetery's amphitheater hundreds of invited guests, including over one hundred Medal of Honor recipients from all wars, joined tens of thousands of spectators viewing the ceremonies on national television. The honorary pallbearers were Vietnam Medal of Honor heroes from each military branch: Walter J. Marm and Jon R. Cavaiani, Army; Jay Vargas and Allan J. Kellogg, Marine Corps; James E. Williams and Michael E. Thornton, Navy; and George E. Day and James P. Fleming, Air Force. President Reagan gave an emotionally-charged speech during the somber funeral services.

"Today we pause to embrace him and all who served so well in a war whose end offered no parades, no flags, and so little thanks. About him we may well wonder as others have: As a child, did he play on some street in a great American city? Did he work beside his father on a farm in America's heartland? Did he marry? Did he have children? Did he look expectantly to return to a bride?

"We will never know the answers to those questions about his life. We do know, though, why he died. He saw the horrors of war but bravely faced them, certain his own cause and his country's cause was a noble one, that he was fighting for free men everywhere."

President Reagan then assured the families of MIAs the quest for their loved ones was not over. "We write no last chapters," he said. "We close no books. We put away no final memories."

The President then presented the Medal of Honor by stating we should "debate the lessons learned at some other time: Today we simply say with pride, 'Thank you, dear son. May God cradle you in His loving arms.' We present to you our nation's highest award, the Medal of Honor, for service above and beyond the call of duty in action with the enemy during the Vietnam Era."

The Vietnam War was unlike any other war fought by the United States. With unclear political goals, no military objectives, and no victory, our involvement in Vietnam produced only frustration and bitterness for the participants.

Yet despite all the problems associated with the war in Vietnam, there still existed a common thread with America's earlier conflicts—the role of the individual fighting man.

Whether they manned a picket line outside Gettysburg in 1863 or stood guard at Khe Sanh in 1968, the men had much in common. The loneliness, the hardships, the dangers, and the fears of war never changed. And, though they existed one hundred years apart, both soldiers offered their lives in defense of their country's principles.

Many men went to Vietnam with the hope of fulfilling the promise they made to defend their country. The adversities and discouragement awaiting them there made it difficult to keep that promise. Staying true to their committment made them all heroes.

A handful of warriors went far above and beyond that committment. Their heroic actions so impressed their comrades they were selected to receive their country's highest honor. These gallant men must never be forgotten. For to forget them would mean their sacrifices were made in vain.

Appendix:

Register of Vietnam Medal of Honor Heroes

APPENDIX

NAME AND RANK	UNIT	DATE OF ACTION	PLACE OF ACTION	HOMETOWN
*Adams, William E. MAJ, USA	1st Aviation Brigade	May 25, 1971	Kontum Province	Craig, CO
*Albanese, Lewis PFC, USA	1st Cavalry Division	Dec. 1, 1966	Phu Huu	Seattle, WA
*Anderson, James, Jr. PFC, USMC	3rd Marine Division	Feb. 28, 1967	Cam Lo	Compton, CA
*Anderson, Richard A. LCPL, USMC	3rd Marine Division	Aug. 24, 1969	Quang Tri Province	Houston, TX
Anderson, Webster SFC, USA	101st Airborne Division	Oct. 15, 1967	Tam Ky	Winnsboro, SC
*Ashley, Eugene, Jr. SFC, USA	5th Special Forces Group	Feb. 6–7, 1968	near Lang Vei	New York, NY
*Austin, Oscar P. PFC, USMC	1st Marine Division	Feb. 23, 1969	near Da Nang	Phoenix, AZ
Baca, John P. SP4, USA	1st Cavalry Division	Feb. 10, 1970	Phuoc Long Province	San Diego, CA
Bacon, Nicky D. SSG, USA	Americal Division	Aug. 26, 1968	near Tam Ky	Phoenix, AZ
Baker, John F., Jr. PFC, USA	25th Infantry Division	Nov. 5, 1966	near Quan Dau Tieng	Moline, IL
Ballard, Donald E. Corpsman, USN	3rd Marine Division	May 16, 1968	Quang Tri Province	Kansas City, MO
*Barker, Jedh C. LCPL, USMC	3rd Marine Division	Sep. 21, 1967	near Con Thien	Park Ridge, NJ
*Barnes, John A., III PFC, USA	173rd Airborne Brigade	Nov. 12, 1967	Dak To	Dedham, MA
Barnum, Harvey C., Jr. 1LT, USMC	3rd Marine Division	Dec. 18, 1965	Ky Phu	Cheshire, CT
Beikirch, Gary B. SGT, USA	5th Special Forces Group	Apr. 1, 1970	Kontum Province	Greece, NY
*Belcher, Ted SGT, USA	25th Infantry Division	Nov. 19, 1966	Plei Djerang	Zanesville, OH
*Bellrichard, Leslie A. PFC, USA	4th Infanty Division	May 20, 1967	Kontum Province	San Jose, CA
Benavidez, Roy P. SSG, USA	5th Special Forces Group	May 2, 1968	Cambodia	El Campo, TX

APPENDIX

NAME AND RANK	UNIT	DATE OF ACTION	PLACE OF ACTION	HOMETOWN
*Bennett, Steven L. CPT, USAF	20th Tactical Air Spt Sqdrn	June 29, 1972	near Quang Tri	Lafayette, LA
*Bennett, Thomas W. CPL, USA	4th Infantry Division	Feb. 9–11, 1969	Pleiku Province	Morgantown, WV
*Blanchfield, Michael R. SP4, USA	173rd Airborne Brigade	July 3, 1969	Binh Dinh Province	Wheeling, IL
*Bobo, John P. 2LT, USMC	3rd Marine Division	Mar. 30, 1967	Quang Tri Province	Niagara Falls, NY
'Bondsteel, James L. SSG, USA	1st Infantry Division	May 24, 1969	Binh Long Province	Allen, MI
*Bowen, Hammett L., Jr. SSG, USA	25th Infantry Division	June 27, 1969	Binh Duong Province	Ocala, FL
Brady, Patrick H. MAJ, USA	44th Medical Brigade	Jan. 6, 1968	near Chu Lai	Seattle, WA
*Bruce, Daniel D. PFC, USMC	1st Marine Division	Mar. 1, 1969	Quang Nam Province	Michigan City, IN
*Bryant, William M. SFC, USA	5th Special Forces Group	Mar. 24, 1969	Long Khanh Province	Newark, NJ
Bucha, Paul W. CPT, USA	101st Airborne Division	Mar. 16–19, 1968	Binh Duong Province	St. Louis, MO
*Buker, Brian L. SGT, USA	5th Special Forces Group	Apr. 5, 1970	Chau Doc Province	Albion, ME
*Burke, Robert C. PFC, USMC	1st Marine Division	May 17, 1968	Quang Nam Province	Monticello, IL
*Capodanno, Vincent R. LT (Chap), USN	1st Marine Division	Sep. 4, 1967	Quang Tin Province	Staten Island, NY
*Caron, Wayne M. Corpsman, USN	1st Marine Division	July 28, 1968	Quang Nam Province	Middleboro, MA
*Carter, Bruce W. PFC, USMC	3rd Marine Division	Aug. 7, 1969	Quang Tri Province	Hialea, FL
Cavaiani, Jon R. SSG, USA	Vietnam Trng Advisory Grp	June 4–5, 1971	Quang Tri Province	Ballico, CA
Clausen, Raymond M. PFC, USMC	1st Marine Air Wing	Jan. 31, 1970	Thua Thien Province	Hammond, LA
*Coker, Ronald L. PFC, USMC	3rd Marine Division	Mar. 24, 1969	Quang Tri Province	Alliance, NB

268

APPENDIX

NAME AND RANK	UNIT	DATE OF ACTION	PLACE OF ACTION	HOMETOWN
*Connor, Peter S. SSG, USMC	1st Marine Division	Feb. 25, 1966	Quang Ngai Province	South Orange, NJ
*Cook, Donald G. CPT, USMC	POW	Dec. 30, 1964– Dec. 7, 1967	South Vietnam	Burlington, VT
*Creek, Thomas E. LCPL, USMC	3rd Marine Division	Feb. 13, 1969	near Cam Lo	Amarillo, TX
*Crescenz, Michael J. CPL, USA	Americal Division	Nov. 20, 1968	Hiep Duc Valley	Philadelphia, PA
*Cutinha, Nicholas J. SP4, USA	25th Infantry Division	Mar. 2, 1968	near Gia Dinh	Yulee, FL
*Dahl, Larry G. SP4, USA	27th Trans Battalion	Feb. 23, 1971	near An Khe	Seattle, WA
*Davis, Rodney M. SGT, USMC	1st Marine Division	Sep. 6, 1967	Quang Nam Province	Macon, GA
Davis, Sammy L. PFC, USA	9th Infantry Division	Nov. 18, 1967	near Cai Lay	Martinsville, IN
Day, George E. MAJ, USAF	POW	Aug. 26, 1967– Mar. 14, 1973	North Vietnam	Sioux City, IA
*De La Garza, Emilio A. LCPL, USMC	1st Marine Division	Apr. 11, 1970	near Da Nang	East Chicago, IN
Dethlefsen, Merlyn H. CPT, USAF	354th Tactical Fighter Sqdrn	Mar. 10, 1967	over North Vietnam	Royal, IA
*Devore, Edward A., Jr. SP4, USA	9th Infantry Division	Mar. 17, 1968	near Saigon	Harbor City, CA
*Dias, Ralph E. PFC, USMC	1st Marine Division	Nov. 12, 1969	Que Son Mountains	Shelocta, PA
*Dickey, Douglas E. PFC, USMC	3rd Marine Division	Mar. 26, 1967	Quang Tri Province	Rossburg, OH
Dix, Drew D. SSG, USA	IV Corps-MACV	Jan. 31– Feb. 1, 1968	Chau Phu	Pueblo, CO
*Doane, Stephen H. 1LT, USA	25th Infantry Division	Mar. 25, 1969	Hau Nghia Province	Walton, NY

269

APPENDIX

NAME AND RANK	UNIT	DATE OF ACTION	PLACE OF ACTION	HOMETOWN
Dolby, David C. SP4, USA	1st Cavalry Division	May 21, 1966	Binh Dinh Province	Oaks, PA
Donlon, Roger H.C. CPT, USA	7th Special Forces Group	July 6, 1964	near Nam Dong	Saugerties, NY
Dunagan, Kern W. CPT, USA	Americal Division	May 13–14, 1969	Quang Tin Province	Bishop, CA
*Durham, Harold B., Jr. 2LT, USA	1st Infantry Division	Oct. 17, 1967	Hau Nghai Province	Tifton, GA
*English, Glenn H., Jr. SSG, USA	173rd Airborne Brigade	Sep. 7, 1970	Phu My	Altoona, PA
*Estocin, Michael J. Lt CDR, USN	Attack Squadron 192	Apr. 20 & 26, 1967	Haiphong, N. Vietnam	Turtle Creek, PA
*Evans, Donald W., Jr. SP4, USA	4th Infantry Division	Jan. 27, 1967	Tri Tam	Covina, CA
*Evans, Rodney J. SGT, USA	1st Cavalry Division	July 18, 1969	Tay Ninh Province	Florala, AL
Ferguson, Frederick E. CWO, USA	1st Cavalry Division	Jan. 31, 1968	Hué	Phoenix, AZ
*Fernandez, Daniel SP4, USA	25th Infantry Division	Feb. 18, 1966	Cu Chi	Albuquerque, NM
Fisher, Bernard F. MAJ, USAF	1st Air Commando Sqdrn	Mar. 10, 1966	Thua Thien Province	Kuna, ID
Fitzmaurice, Michael J. SP4, USA	101st Airborne Division	Mar. 23, 1971	Khe Sanh	Cavour, SD
*Fleek, Charles C. SGT, USA	25th Infantry Division	May 27, 1969	Binh Duong Province	Petersburg, KY
Fleming, James P. CPT, USAF	20th Special Ops Sqdrn	Nov. 26, 1968	near Duc Co	Sedalia, MO
Foley, Robert F. CPT, USA	25th Infantry Division	Nov. 5, 1966	near Quan Dau Tieng	Newton, MA
*Folland, Michael F. CPL, USA	199th Infantry Brigade	July 3, 1969	Long Khanh Province	Richmond, VA
*Foster, Paul H. SGT, USMC	3rd Marine Division	Oct. 14, 1967	near Con Thien	San Mateo, CA

APPENDIX

NAME AND RANK	UNIT	DATE OF ACTION	PLACE OF ACTION	HOMETOWN
*Fournet, Douglas B. 1LT, USA	1st Cavalry Division	May 4, 1968	A Shau Valley	Lake Charles, LA
*Fous, James W. PFC, USA	9th Infantry Division	May 14, 1968	Kien Hoa Province	Omaha, NB
Fox, Wesley L. 1LT, USMC	3rd Marine Division	Feb. 22, 1969	Quang Tri Province	Front Royal, VA
*Fratellenico, Frank R. CPL, USA	101st Airborne Division	Aug. 19, 1970	Quang Tri Province	Chatham, NY
Fritz, Harold A. 1LT, USA	11th Armored Cavalry Rgmt	Jan. 11, 1969	Binh Long Province	Lake Geneva, WI
*Gardner, James A. 1LT, USA	101st Airborne Division	Feb. 7, 1966	My Canh	Dyersburg, TN
*Gertsh, John G. SSG, USA	101st Airborne Division	July 15–19, 1969	A Shau Valley	Sheffield, PA
*Gonzalez, Alfredo SGT, USMC	1st Marine Division	Jan. 31– Feb. 4, 1968	Hué	Edinburg, TX
*Graham, James A. CPT, USMC	1st Marine Division	June 2, 1967	Quang Tin Province	Brandywine, MD
*Grandstaff, Bruce A. PSG, USA	4th Infantry Division	May 18, 1967	Pleiku Province	Spokane, WA
*Grant, Joseph X. 1LT, USA	25th Infantry Division	Nov. 13, 1966	Tay Ninh Province	Boston, MA
*Graves, Terrence C. 2LT, USMC	3rd Marine Division	Feb. 16, 1968	Quang Tri Province	New York, NY
*Guenette, Peter M. SP4, USA	101st Airborne Division	May 18, 1968	Quan Tan Uyen	Troy, NY
Hagemeister, Charles C. SP4, USA	1st Cavalry Division	Mar. 20, 1967	Binh Dinh Province	Lincoln, NB
*Hagen, Loren D. 1LT, USA	Vietnam Trng Advisory Grp	Aug. 7, 1971	Quang Tri Province	Fargo, ND
*Hartsock, Robert W. SSG, USA	25th Infantry Division	Feb. 23, 1969	Hau Nghia Province	Cumberland, MD
*Harvey, Carmel B. SP4, USA	1st Cavalry Division	June 21, 1967	Binh Dinh Province	Chicago, IL

271

APPENDIX

NAME AND RANK	UNIT	DATE OF ACTION	PLACE OF ACTION	HOMETOWN
Herda, Frank A. SP4, USA	101st Airborne Division	June 29, 1968	near Dak To	Parma, OH
*Hibbs, Robert J. 2LT, USA	1st Infantry Division	Mar. 5, 1966	Don Dien Lo Ke	Cedar Falls, IA
*Holcomb, John N. SGT, USA	1st Cavalry Division	Dec. 3, 1968	near Quan Lo	Richland, OR
²Hooper, Joe R. SSG, USA	101st Airborne Division	Feb. 21, 1968	near Hué	Moses Lake, WA
*Hosking, Charles E. MSG, USA	5th Special Forces Group	Mar. 21, 1967	Phuoc Long Province	Ramsey, NJ
Howard, Jimmie E. SSG, USMC	1st Marine Division	June 16–18, 1966	Quang Ngai Province	Burlington, IA
Howard, Robert L. SFC, USA	MACV-SOG	Dec. 30, 1968	Laos	Opelika, AL
*Howe, James D. LCPL, USMC	1st Marine Division	May 6, 1970	Quang Nam Province	Liberty, SC
*Ingalls, George A. SP4, USA	1st Cavalry Division	Apr. 16, 1967	near Duc Pho	Corona, CA
Jackson, Joe M. LTC, USAF	311th Air Commando Sqdrn	May 12, 1968	Kham Duc	Newnan, GA
Jacobs, Jack H. CPT, USA	MACV (9th ARVN Inf Div)	Mar. 9, 1968	Kien Phong Province	Ford, NJ
Jenkins, Don J. PFC, USA	9th Infantry Division	Jan. 6, 1969	Kien Phong Province	Quality, KY
*Jenkins, Robert H., Jr. PFC, USMC	3rd Marine Division	Mar. 5, 1969	FSB Argonne	Interlachen, FL
Jennings, Delbert O. SSG, USA	1st Cavalry Division	Dec. 27, 1966	Kim Song Valley	Stockton, CA
*Jimenez, José F. LCPL, USMC	1st Marine Division	Aug. 28, 1969	Quang Nam Province	Eloy, AZ
³Joel, Lawrence SP6, USA	173rd Airborne Brigade	Nov. 8, 1965	Bien Hoa Province	Winston-Salem, NC
⁴Johnson, Dwight H. SP5, USA	4th Infantry Division	Jan. 15, 1968	near Dak To	Detroit, MI
*Johnson, Ralph H. PFC, USMC	1st Marine Division	Mar. 5, 1968	near Quan Duc Valley	Charleston, SC

272

APPENDIX

NAME AND RANK	UNIT	DATE OF ACTION	PLACE OF ACTION	HOMETOWN
*Johnston, Donald R. SP4, USA	1st Cavalry Division	Mar. 21, 1969	Tay Ninh Province	Columbus, GA
[5]Jones, William A. COL, USAF	602nd Special Ops Sqdrn	Sep. 1, 1968	Dong Hoi, N. Vietnam	Charlottesville, VA
*Karopczyc, Stephen E. 1LT, USA	25th Infantry Division	Mar. 12, 1967	Kontum Province	Bethpage, NY
*Kawamura, Terry T. CPL, USA	173rd Airborne Brigade	Mar. 20, 1969	Camp Radcliff	Oahu, HI
Kays, Kenneth M. PFC, USA	101st Airborne Division	May 7, 1970	Thua Thien Province	Fairfield, IL
*Kedenburg, John J. SP5, USA	MACV-SOG	June 13, 1968	Laos	Brooklyn, NY
*Keith, Miguel LCPL, USMC	III Marine Amphib Force	May 8, 1970	Quang Ngai Province	Omaha, NB
Keller, Leonard B. SGT, USA	9th Infantry Division	May 2, 1967	Ap Bac Zone	Rockford, IL
Kelley, Thomas G. LT, USN	River Assault Division 152	June 15, 1969	Kien Hoa Province	Boston, MA
Kellogg, Allan J., Jr. GSGT, USMC	1st Marine Division	Mar. 11, 1970	Quang Nam Province	Bethel, CT
Kerrey, Joseph R. LT, USN	SEAL Team One	Mar. 14, 1969	Nha Trang Bay	Lincoln, NB
Kinsman, Thomas J. SP4, USA	9th Infantry Division	Feb. 6, 1968	near Vinh Long	Onalaska, WA
[6]Lambers, Paul R. SSG, USA	25th Infantry Division	Aug. 20, 1968	Tay Ninh Province	Holland, MI
Lang, George C. SP4, USA	9th Infantry Division	Feb. 22, 1969	Kien Hoa Province	Hicksville, NY
*Langhorn, Garfield M. PFC, USA	1st Aviation Brigade	Jan. 15, 1969	near Plei Djereng	Riverhead, NY
*Lapointe, Joseph G., Jr. SP4, USA	101st Airborne Division	June 2, 1969	Quang Tin Province	Dayton, OH
Lassen, Clyde E. LT, USN	Helicopter Spt Squadron 7	June 19, 1968	North Vietnam	Venice, FL
*Lauffer, Billy L. PFC, USA	1st Cavalry Division	Sep. 21, 1966	near Bong Son	Tucson, AZ

NAME AND RANK	UNIT	DATE OF ACTION	PLACE OF ACTION	HOMETOWN
*Law, Robert D. SP4, USA	1st Infantry Division	Feb. 22, 1969	Binh Long Province	Ft. Worth, TX
Lee, Howard V. CPT, USMC	3rd Marine Division	Aug. 8–9, 1966	near Cam Lo	Bronx, NY
*Lee, Milton A. PFC, USA	101st Airborne Division	Apr. 26, 1968	near Phu Bai	San Antonio, TX
*Leisy, Robert R. 2LT, USA	1st Cavalry Division	Dec. 2, 1969	Phouc Long Province	Seattle, WA
Lemon, Peter C. SP4, USA	1st Cavalry Division	Apr. 1, 1970	Tay Ninh Province	Tawas City, MI
*Leonard, Matthew PSG, USA	1st Infantry Division	Feb. 28, 1967	near Suoi Da	Birmingham, AL
Levitow, John L. Airman, USAF	3rd Special Ops Sqdrn	Feb. 24, 1969	over Long Binh	Glastonbury, CT
Liteky, Angelo J. CPT (Chap), USA	199th Infantry Brigade	Dec. 6, 1967	near Phuoc Lac	Jacksonville, FL
Littrell, Gary L. SFC, USA	MACV (2nd ARVN Ranger Group)	Apr. 4–8, 1970	Kontum Province	Henderson, KY
Livingston, James E. CPT, USMC	3rd Marine Division	May 2, 1968	Dai Do	McRae, GA
*Long, Donald R. SGT, USA	1st Infantry Division	June 30, 1966	near Srok Dong	Blackfork, OH
*Lozada, Carlos J. PFC, USA	173rd Airborne Brigade	Nov. 20, 1967	Dak To	Brooklyn, NY
*Lucas, Andre C. LTC, USA	101st Airborne Division	July 1–23, 1970	FSB Ripcord	Seattle, WA
Lynch, Allen J. SP4, USA	1st Cavalry Division	Dec. 15, 1967	near My An–2	Dolton, IL
Marm, Walter J. 2LT, USA	1st Cavalry Division	Nov. 14, 1965	Ia Drang Valley	Washington, PA
*Martini, Gary W. PFC, USMC	1st Marine Division	Apr. 21, 1967	Binh Son	Charleston, WV
*Maxam, Larry L. CPL, USMC	3rd Marine Division	Feb. 2, 1968	Cam Lo	Burbank, CA

APPENDIX

NAME AND RANK	UNIT	DATE OF ACTION	PLACE OF ACTION	HOMETOWN
McCleery, Finnis D. PSG, USA	Americal Division	May 14, 1968	near Tam Ky	San Angelo, TX
*McDonald, Phill G. PFC, USA	4th Infantry Division	June 7, 1968	near Kontum City	Greensboro, NC
McGinty, John J. SSG, USMC	3rd Marine Division	July 18, 1966	Song Ngan Valley	Louisville, KY
*McKibben, Ray SGT, USA	1st Aviation Brigade	Dec. 8, 1968	near Song Mao	Felton, GA
*McMahon, Thomas J. SP4, USA	Americal Division	Mar. 19, 1969	Quang Tin Province	Lewiston, ME
McNerney, David H. 1SG, USA	4th Infantry Division	Mar. 22, 1967	Polei Doc	Houston, TX
*McWethy, Edgar L., Jr. SP5, USA	1st Cavalry Division	June 21, 1967	Binh Dinh Province	Leadville, CO
*Michael, Don L. SP4, USA	173rd Airborne Brigade	Apr. 8, 1967	Tay Ninh Province	Lexington, AL
Miller, Franklin D. SSG, USA	MACV-SOG	Jan. 5, 1970	Laos	Sante Fe, NM
*Miller, Gary L. 1LT, USA	1st Infantry Division	Feb. 16, 1969	Binh Duong Province	Covington, VA
Modrzejewski, Robert J. CPT, USMC	3rd Marine Division	July 15–18, 1966	Song Ngan Valley	Milwaukee, WI
*Molnar, Frankie Z. SSG, USA	4th Infantry Division	May 20, 1967	Kontum Province	Logan, WV
*Monroe, James H. PFC, USA	1st Cavalry Division	Feb. 16, 1967	Bong Son	Wheaton, IL
*Morgan, William D. CPL, USMC	3rd Marine Division	Feb. 25, 1969	Laos	Pittsburgh, PA
Morris, Charles B. SGT, USA	173rd Airborne Brigade	June 29, 1966	Long An Province	Galax, VA
*Murray, Robert C. SSG, USA	Americal Division	June 7, 1970	near Hiep Duc	Tuckahoe, NY
*Nash, David P. PFC, USA	9th Infantry Division	Dec. 29, 1968	Dinh Tuong Province	Whitesville, KY
*Newlin, Melvin E. PFC, USMC	1st Marine Division	July 4, 1967	Quang Nam Province	Wellsville, OH

275

APPENDIX

NAME AND RANK	UNIT	DATE OF ACTION	PLACE OF ACTION	HOMETOWN
*Noonan, Thomas P., Jr. LCPL, USMC	3rd Marine Division	Feb. 5, 1969	A Shau Valley	Woodside, NY
Norris, Thomas R. LT, USN	MACV-STD	Apr. 10–13, 1972	Quang Tri Province	Silver Spring, MD
Novosel, Michael J. CWO, USA	68th Medical Group	Oct. 2, 1969	Kien Tuong Province	Etna, PA
*Olive, Milton L. PFC, USA	173rd Airborne Brigade	Oct. 22, 1965	Phu Cong	Chicago, IL
*Olson, Kenneth L. SP4, USA	199th Infantry Brigade	May 13, 1968	Bien Hoa Province	Paynesville, MN
O'Malley, Robert E. CPL, USMC	3rd Marine Division	Aug. 18, 1965	near An Cu'ong–2	New York, NY
*Ouellet, David G. Seaman, USN	River Squadron Five	Mar. 6, 1967	Mekong River	Wellesley, MA
Patterson, Robert M. SP4, USA	101st Airborne Division	May 6, 1968	near La Chu	Fayetteville, NC
*Paul, Joe C. LCPL, USMC	3rd Marine Division	Aug. 18, 1965	near Chu Lai	Vandalia, OH
Penry, Richard A. SGT, USA	199th Infantry Brigade	Jan. 31, 1970	Binh Tuy Province	Petaluma, CA
*Perkins, William T., Jr. CPL, USMC	1st Marine Division	Oct. 12, 1967	Quang Tri Province	Sepulveda, CA
*Peters, Lawrence D. SGT, USMC	1st Marine Division	Sep. 4, 1967	Quang Tin Province	Binghamton, NY
*Petersen, Danny J. SP4, USA	25th Infantry Division	Jan. 9, 1970	Tay Ninh Province	Horton, KS
*Phipps, Jimmy W. PFC, USMC	1st Marine Division	May 27, 1969	near An Hoa	Santa Monica, CA
*Pierce, Larry S. SGT, USA	173rd Airborne Brigade	Sep. 20, 1965	near Ben Cat	Taft, CA
Pittman, Richard A. LCPL, USMC	1st Marine Division	July 24, 1966	Quang Tri Province	Stockton, CA
*Pitts, Reily L. CPT, USA	25th Infantry Division	Oct. 31, 1967	Ap Dong	Oklahoma City, OK
7Pless, Stephen W. CPT, USMC	1st Marine Air Wing	Aug. 19, 1967	near Quang Nai	Newnan, GA

276

APPENDIX

NAME AND RANK	UNIT	DATE OF ACTION	PLACE OF ACTION	HOMETOWN
⁸Port, William D. PFC, USA	1st Cavalry Division	Jan. 12, 1968	Quang Tin Province	Petersburg, PA
*Poxon, Robert L. 1LT, USA	1st Cavalry Division	June 2, 1969	Tay Ninh Province	Detroit, MI
*Prom, William R. LCPL, USMC	3rd Marine Division	Feb. 9, 1969	near An Hoa	Pittsburgh, PA
*Pruden, Robert J. SSG, USA	Americal Division	Nov. 29, 1969	Quang Ngai Province	St. Paul, MN
*Rabel, Laszlo SSG, USA	173rd Airborne Brigade	Nov. 13, 1968	Binh Dinh Province	Minneapolis, MN
*Ray, David R. Corpsman, USN	1st Marine Division	Mar. 19, 1969	Phu Loc 6	McMinnville, TN
Ray, Ronald E. 1LT, USA	25th Infantry Division	June 19, 1966	Ia Drang Valley	Auburndale, FL
*Reasoner, Frank S. 1LT, USMC	3rd Marine Division	July 12, 1965	near Da Nang	Kellogg, ID
*Roark, Anund C. SGT, USA	4th Infantry Division	May 16, 1968	Kontum Province	San Diego, CA
Roberts, Gordon R. SP4, USA	101st Airborne Division	July 11, 1969	Thua Thien Province	Lebanon, OH
*Robinson, James W., Jr. SGT, USA	1st Infantry Division	Apr. 11, 1966	Phuoc Tuy Province	Cicero, IL
Rocco, Louis R. SFC, USA	Advisory Team 162-MACV	May 24, 1970	near Katum	Albuquerque, NM
Rogers, Charles C. LTC, USA	1st Infantry Division	Nov. 1, 1968	FSB Rita	Mt. Hope, WV
*Rubio, Euripedes CPT, USA	1st Infantry Division	Nov. 8, 1966	Tay Ninh Province	Ponce, PR
*Santiago-Colon, Hector SP4, USA	1st Cavalry Division	June 28, 1968	Quang Tri Province	Salinas, PR
*Sargent, Ruppert L. 1LT, USA	25th Infantry Division	Mar. 15, 1967	Hau Nghia Province	Hampton, VA
Sasser, Clarence E. PFC, USA	9th Infantry Division	Jan. 10, 1968	Dinh Tuong Province	Angleton, TX
*Seay, William W. SGT, USA	48th Trans Group	Aug. 25, 1968	near Ap Nhi	Brewton, AL

APPENDIX

NAME AND RANK	UNIT	DATE OF ACTION	PLACE OF ACTION	HOMETOWN
*Shea, Daniel J. PFC, USA	Americal Division	May 14, 1969	Quang Tri Province	Norwalk, CT
*Shields, Marvin G. CM3, USN	Seabee Team 1104	June 10, 1965	Dong Xoai	Port Townsend, WA
*Sijan, Lance P. CPT, USAF	POW	Nov. 9, 1967–Jan. 21, 1968	North Vietnam	Milwaukee, WI
*Sims, Clifford C. SSG, USA	101st Airborne Division	Feb. 21, 1968	near Hué	Port St. Joe, FL
*Singleton, Walter K. SGT, USMC	3rd Marine Division	Mar. 24, 1967	Quang Tri Province	Memphis, TN
*Sisler, George K. 1LT, USA	MACV-SOG	Feb. 7, 1967	Laos	Dexter, MO
*Skidgel, Donald S. SGT, USA	1st Cavalry Division	Sep. 14, 1969	Binh Long Province	Plymouth, ME
*Smedley, Larry E. CPL, USMC	1st Marine Division	Dec. 21, 1967	Quang Nam Province	Union Park, FL
*Smith, Elmelindo R. SSG, USA	4th Infantry Division	Feb. 16, 1967	Kontum Province	Honolulu, HI
Sprayberry, James M. 1LT, USA	1st Cavalry Division	Apr. 25, 1968	Thua Thien Province	Sylacauga, AL
*Steindam, Russell A. 1LT, USA	25th Infantry Division	Feb. 1, 1970	Tay Ninh Province	Plano, TX
*Stewart, Jimmy G. SSG, USA	1st Cavalry Division	May 18, 1966	near An Khe	Middleport, OH
Stockdale, James B. CPT, USN	POW	Sep. 4, 1969	North Vietnam	Abingdon, IL
*Stone, Lester, R., Jr. SGT, USA	Americal Division	Mar. 3, 1969	LZ Liz	Harpursville, NY
*Stout, Mitchell W. SGT, USA	44th Artillery	Mar. 12, 1970	Khe Gio Bridge	Lenoir City, TN
*Stryker, Robert F. SP4, USA	1st Infantry Division	Nov. 7, 1967	near Loc Ninh	Throop, NY
Stumpf, Kenneth E. SP4, USA	25th Infantry Division	Apr. 25, 1967	near Duc Pho	Menasha, WI

APPENDIX

NAME AND RANK	UNIT	DATE OF ACTION	PLACE OF ACTION	HOMETOWN
Taylor, James A. 1LT, USA	Americal Division	Nov. 9, 1967	west of Que Son	Arcata, CA
*Taylor, Karl G., Sr. SSG, USMC	3rd Marine Division	Dec. 8, 1968	Quang Tri Province	Laurel, MD
Thacker, Brian M. 1LT, USA	92nd Artillery	Mar. 31, 1971	Kontum Province	Columbus, OH
Thornton, Michael E. PO, USN	MACV-STD	Oct. 31, 1972	Quang Tri Province	Spartanburg, SC
Thorsness, Leo K. MAJ, USAF	357th Tactical Fighter Sqdrn	Apr. 19, 1967	over North Vietnam	Walnut Grove, MN
Vargas, Jay CPT, USMC	3rd Marine Division	Apr. 30–May 2, 1968	Dai Do	Winslow, AZ
*Warren, John E., Jr. 1LT, USA	25th Infantry Division	Jan. 14, 1969	Tay Ninh Province	Brooklyn, NY
*Watters, Charles J. MAJ (Chap), USA	173rd Airborne Brigade	Nov. 19, 1967	near Dak To	Jersey City, NJ
*Wayrynen, Dale E. SP4, USA	101st Airborne Division	May 18, 1967	Quang Ngai Province	McGregor, MN
*Weber, Lester W. LCPL, USMC	1st Marine Division	Feb. 23, 1969	Quang Nam Province	Hinsdale, IL
Wetzel, Gary G. PFC, USA	1st Aviation Battalion	Jan. 8, 1968	near Ap Dong An	Oak Creek, WI
*Wheat, Roy M. LCPL, USMC	1st Marine Division	Aug. 11, 1967	Quang Nam Province	Moselle, MS
*Wickam, Jerry W. CPL, USA	11th Armored Cavalry Rgmt	Jan. 6, 1968	near Loc Ninh	Leaf River, IL
*Wilbanks, Hilliard A. CPT, USAF	21st Tactical Air Spt Sqdrn	Feb. 24, 1967	near Dalat	Cornelia, GA
*Willett, Louis E. PFC, USA	4th Infantry Division	Feb. 15, 1967	Kontum Province	Brooklyn, NY
⁸Williams, Charles Q. 2LT, USA	5th Special Forces Group	June 9–10, 1965	Dong Xoai	Vance, SC
*Williams, Dewayne T. PFC, USMC	1st Marine Division	Sep. 18, 1968	Quang Nam Province	St. Clair, MI
Williams, James E. BM1C, USN	River Section 531	Oct. 31, 1966	Mekong River	Charleston, SC

279

APPENDIX

NAME AND RANK	UNIT	DATE OF ACTION	PLACE OF ACTION	HOMETOWN
*Wilson, Alfred M. PFC, USMC	3rd Marine Division	Mar. 3, 1969	Quang Tri Province	Odessa, TX
*Winder, David F. PFC, USA	Americal Division	May 13, 1970	Quang Ngai Province	Mansfield, OH
*Worley, Kenneth L. LCPL, USMC	1st Marine Division	Aug. 13, 1968	Bo Ban	Farmington, NM
Wright, Raymond R. SP4, USA	9th Infantry Division	May 2, 1967	Ap Bac Zone	Mineville, NY
*Yabes, Maximo 1SG, USA	25th Infantry Division	Feb. 26, 1967	near Phu Hoa Dong	Oak Ridge, OR
*Yano, Rodney, J.T. SPC, USA	11th Armored Cavalry Rgmt	Jan. 1, 1969	over Bien Hoa	Kealakekua, HI
*Yntema, Gordon D. SGT, USA	5th Special Forces Group	Jan. 16–18 1968	near Thong Binh	Holland, MI
Young, Gerald O. CPT, USAF	37th Air Rescue Sqdrn	Nov. 9, 1967	near Khe Sanh	Colorado Springs, CO
*Young, Marvin R. SSG, USA	25th Infantry Division	Aug. 21, 1968	near Ben Cui	Odessa, TX
Zabitosky, Fred W. SSG, USA	MACV-SOG	Feb. 19, 1968	Laos	Trenton, NJ

* Posthumous award
[1] Bondstell died April 9, 1987.
[2] Hooper died May 6, 1979.
[3] Joel died Feb. 4, 1984.
[4] Johnson died Apr. 30, 1971.
[5] Jones died Nov. 15, 1969.
[6] Lambers died Dec. 1, 1970.
[7] Pless died July 20, 1969.
[8] Port died Nov. 27, 1968.
[9] Williams died Oct. 15, 1982.

INDEX

INDEX

INDEX

INDEX

ABOUT THE AUTHOR

Edward F. Murphy, an Army veteran of the Vietnam War, is the president of the Medal of Honor Historical Society, a nonprofit research organization. He lives with his wife in Mesa, Arizona.